Philosophy of Biology

D0713892

Is life a purely physical process? Does the theory of natural selection conflict with theism and, if so, how can we rationally choose between them? What is human nature? Which of our traits are essential to us?

Biology is the branch of science most immediately relevant to many distinctively human concerns, so it is natural that it should be the site of great controversy and debate. The philosophy of biology addresses not only those questions that biology cannot yet (or perhaps ever) answer but also the further questions about why biology may be unable to answer those questions.

In this volume, Daniel McShea and Alex Rosenberg—a biologist and a philosopher, respectively—join forces to create a new gateway to the philosophy of biology, making the major issues accessible and relevant to biologists and philosophers alike.

Exploring concepts such as supervenience, the controversies about geno-centrism and genetic determinism, and the debate about major transitions central to contemporary thinking about macroevolution, the authors lay out the broad terms in which we should assess the impact of biology on human capacities, social institutions, and ethical values.

Alex Rosenberg is R. Taylor Cole Professor of Philosophy at Duke University. He is the author of *Philosophy of Science: A Contemporary Introduction* (2nd edition, 2005) and co-editor with Yuri Balashov of *Philosophy of Science: Contemporary Readings* (2002).

Daniel W. McShea is Associate Professor of Biology at Duke University.

Routledge Contemporary Introductions to Philosophy

Series editor:
Paul K. Moser
Loyola University of Chicago

This innovative, well-structured series is for students who have already done an introductory course in philosophy. Each book introduces a core general subject in contemporary philosophy and offers students an accessible but substantial transition from introductory to higher level college work in that subject. The series is accessible to nonspecialists and each book clearly motivates and expounds the problems and positions introduced. An orientating chapter briefly introduces its topic and reminds readers of any crucial material they need to have retained from a typical introductory course. Considerable attention is given to explaining the central philosophical problems of a subject and the main competing solutions and arguments for those solutions. The primary aim is to educate students in the main problems, positions, and arguments of contemporary philosophy rather than to convince students of a single position.

Classical Philosophy
Christopher Shields

Epistemology, 2nd edition
Robert Audi

Ethics
Harry Gensler

Metaphysics, 2nd edition
Michael J. Loux

Philosophy of Art
Noël Carroll

Philosophy of Language
William G. Lycan

Philosophy of Mind, 2nd edition
John Heil

Philosophy of Religion
Keith E. Yandell

Philosophy of Science, 2nd edition
Alex Rosenberg

Social and Political Philosophy
John Christman

Philosophy of Psychology
José Bermudez

Classical Modern Philosophy
Jeffrey Tlumak

Philosophy of Biology

A Contemporary Introduction

Alex Rosenberg and Daniel W. McShea

Routledge
Taylor & Francis Group

NEW YORK AND LONDON

First published 2008
by Routledge
270 Madison Ave, New York, NY 10016

Simultaneously published in the UK
by Routledge
2 Park Square, Milton Park, Abingdon, Oxon OX14 4RN

*Routledge is an imprint of the Taylor & Francis Group, an informa
business*

© 2008 Alex Rosenberg and Daniel W. McShea
Typeset in Garamond by Prepress Projects Ltd, Perth, Scotland.

Printed and bound in the United States of America on acid-free
paper by Sheridan Books, Inc.

Library of Congress Cataloging in Publication Data
Library of Congress Cataloging-in-Publication Data
Rosenberg, Alexander, 1946-
Philosophy of biology : a contemporary introduction / Alex
Rosenberg and Daniel W. McShea.
     p. cm. – (Routledge contemporary introductions to philosophy)
Includes bibliographical references and index.
ISBN 0–415–31592–1 (hardback : alk. paper) – ISBN
0–415–31593–X (pbk. : alk. paper) – ISBN 0-203-92699-4 (ebook)
1. Biology—Philosophy. I. McShea, Daniel W. II. Title.
QH331.R667 2008
570.1—dc22
2007040181

British Library Cataloguing in Publication Data
A catalogue record for this book is available from the British
Library.

ISBN 10 0–415–31592–1 (hbk)
ISBN 10 0–415–31593–X (pbk)
ISBN 10: 0–203–92699–4 (ebk)

ISBN 13: 978–0–415–31592–0 (hbk)
ISBN 13: 978–0–415–31593–7 (pbk)
ISBN 13: 978–0–203–92699–4 (ebk)

For three friends and colleagues from whom
we have learned much biology and not a little
philosophy: Robert Brandon, Fred Nijhout, and
Louise Roth

Contents

Acknowledgements

AR I would like to acknowledge the encouragement, guidance, and support of David Hull in my earliest explorations of the philosophy of biology and the stimulation and influence of Elliott Sober's, Philip Kitcher's, and Kim Sterelny's work in many of my own contributions to the subject. Along with the work of Robert Brandon, these philosophers have set out a budget of problems and an agenda of solutions that I still wrestle with after 30 years of work in the philosophy of biology. To Robert Brandon I especially owe a debt of gratitude for the day-to-day collaboration that has made the last half-dozen years of my work in the field the most rewarding period since I began to explore the philosophy of biology. During this time I shared with him and other faculty the stimulation of postdoctoral fellows and students such as Marshall Abrams, Fred Bouchard, Tamler Sommers, Stefan Linquist, Marion Hourdequin, Grant Ramsey, Russell Powell, Bill Wojtack, Sahar Akhtar, Leonore Fleming, and David Kaplan, all of whom have read and commented on earlier drafts of this book in one form or another. Finally, I wish to record how great a pleasure and how instructive a process it has been to teach the philosophy of biology and to write about it with someone who combines an understanding of biology and its philosophy as completely as Dan McShea.

DWM I would like to acknowledge my philosophy mentors, Robert Brandon, Robert McShea, Dave Raup, and Leigh Van Valen (not all of whom will approve of being cast in that role and none of whom bears any responsibility for the more absurd of my philosophical views). Let me also acknowledge my graduate student and postdoctoral collaborators, Gabe Byars, Airlie Sattler, Chuck Ciampaglio, Phil Novack-Gottshall, Ed Venit, Kriti Sharma, Dave McCandlish, Carl Anderson, Jon Marcot, and Carl Simpson, as well as my students in independent studies and courses on evolution and the philosophy of biology. Their enthusiasm has been inspirational, and they have also been my best critics, challenging me to devise better arguments and clearer ways of presenting ideas. If anything in this book is unclear or wrong, it is because I did not pay enough attention to their questions and counter-arguments. I also thank the Biology Department at Duke University for uncommon support and collegiality and for tolerating so amiably a crypto-philosopher-wanna-be in their midst. Special thanks are due to the people who were kind and patient enough to review all of, or portions of, the manuscript, specifically Jeff Ihara,

Carl Simpson, Tony Dajer, Leigh Van Valen, and two anonymous reviewers. Finally, I am grateful to Alex Rosenberg. I have benefited enormously from his energy (for projects such as this book) and from arguing philosophy with him over the years, and even more from his largeness of heart and generosity. He has been an extraordinary colleague, collaborator, and friend.

Both AR and DWM wish to thank David Crawford for help in correcting the final version.

AR also needs to thank the National Humanities Center for the fellowship and the infrastructural support that enabled him to complete and revise this work.

Introduction

What is the philosophy of biology?

Philosophy asks two kinds of questions

Philosophy, Aristotle wrote, begins with wonder. And, for a long time, philosophy meant the same thing as science. Indeed, in some universities, physics is still called "natural philosophy," and philosophy is taught in the department of "moral science." The reason is not hard to see. The history of Western philosophy is the history of a discipline that has been "spinning off" sciences since about 300 BC when Euclid wrote the *Elements* and established the separate discipline of mathematics. It was only much later, in the seventeenth century, that physics finally established itself as a discipline distinct from philosophy, followed in the late eighteenth century by chemistry, and, as we will argue in the next chapter, by biology as late as 1859, when Darwin published *On the Origin of Species*. This process continues, for there are other disciplines, still in the process of spinning themselves off from philosophy. As the sciences establish their separate existences, two questions arise: Do the sciences leave anything to philosophy when they "spin off," and, if so, why do they leave unfinished business to philosophy? The answer to the first question is obvious. Each of the sciences leaves to philosophy issues that they might be expected to answer but have not. Consider the question of what a number is. A number is not after all a numeral, which is just the symbol we use to name a number. For "2," "II," "two," "dos," and "dho" all name the very same number, in Arabic, Roman, English, Spanish, and Hindi notation. We may hold, as many followers of Plato still do, that numbers are "abstract objects," or that there are no such things and that numbers are mental constructs. But it will be in vain to look to mathematics for an answer to the question of what a number is. That question has remained one for philosophical inquiry since Plato. Or consider the question of what time is. Time is a variable in many of the most important physical laws. Newton's second law, for example, tells us that force equals mass×acceleration, $F = ma$, where acceleration is defined as the rate of change of velocity with respect to time, $a = dv/dt$. But the question of what is time, t in the equation, has remained unanswered in physics and left to philosophers.

Biology too has left questions that philosophy addresses. In fact, the questions biology leaves to philosophy are hard to avoid and of great interest beyond biology (and beyond philosophy for that matter). This is part of the reason that the philosophy of biology has become one of the liveliest and most publicly visible of philosophy's subdisciplines. Another is that the questions biology leaves to philosophy are the most immediately relevant to many distinctively human concerns. For example, it is to biology that many look for insight into "human nature." It is biology that appears to address the question of what is "life" and whether things have a meaning or purpose beyond the merely physical and chemical processes that constitute them. Now, biological science itself does not tell us whether it has the power to answer these questions. And for that reason there are lively debates about biology's scope and limits, its authority to answer such perennial questions of deep human concern. These questions about biology's scope and limits are clearly philosophical ones.

Like the other natural sciences, biology is an experimental discipline, and, as such, it is a fallible one. For experiments, observation, and collecting data can never establish the truth of a theory with perfect certainty. Like other scientists, however, biologists have the confidence that though their findings are always subject to revision and improvement, their method—the scientific method—is the right one, indeed, the only way to assure the increasing reliability of their results. But there are disputes within biology, and between biologists and other scientists, both about what the "scientific method" is and about whether various research programs and their results honor that method. Then there are disputes about whether and why the application of the scientific method in biology differs from that in the physical sciences. And, finally, there are disputes about whether there is any such thing as *the* scientific method, with the emphasis on the uniqueness suggested by the definite article. All of these issues are well and truly part of the agenda of the philosophy of biology and, of course, the philosophy of science generally. For the sciences cannot themselves answer questions about the warrant of their own methods, the justification of their modes of research, and the adequacy of each discipline's distinctive approaches to its own and other disciplines' domains. A physicist's argument that biology should be more like physics, or a chemist's claim that biological facts need to be explained by chemistry, cannot be settled by experiment and observation, if they can be settled at all. These questions are the purview of the philosophy of these sciences and the philosophy of science in general. This does not mean that scientists have no right to express views about these matters or that only philosophers of science are qualified to do so. It means merely that when informed participants debate these issues, they are engaged in a philosophical dispute.

Recall now our second question. If there are questions that the sciences cannot answer, why do such questions exist? This can be construed as a question about the limits of science. It is well known that many people reject the findings and theories of natural science in favor of other beliefs, often religious ones, and often with the accompanying claim that some facts of the world are forever beyond the reach of science. No science is more often met with claims of this sort than biology. Questions about the meaning of life are often said to lie in this unreachable domain. Some go even further, arguing that questions about the origin of life, or of the human species, lie there also. Further, there are social and behavioral scientists, and scholars in the humanities too, who deny the relevance of biology to their research questions, for example questions having to do with the causes of human behavior or the foundation of ethics. Now it would seem that those who hold that biology, or other natural sciences, cannot answer certain questions owe an account of why not, as of course do those who argue that science *can* answer them. And these accounts of the limits of science, or of the absence of limits, will be philosophical arguments, as traditionally understood.

Like biology, philosophy is divided into subdisciplines: metaphysics studies the basic kinds of things, processes, and properties in the universe, and addresses questions about them such as: What are numbers? Does God exist? Are all events governed by physical law, and, if so, is there such a thing as human freedom? Epistemology, or the theory of knowledge, treats the nature, extent, and grounds of knowledge: What distinguishes knowledge from mere opinion? Why are mathematical truths more certain than scientific theory? Can we reliably infer the future from the past? The philosophy of science, of course, overlaps these two subdisciplines considerably. It also intersects with logic, the subdivision that seeks to identify the principles of valid reasoning, and that therefore is of the greatest importance in science and mathematics. Beyond these three subdivisions of philosophy, there are those of ethics, aesthetics, and political philosophy. These last subdivisions might seem most clearly to be addressing questions beyond the limits of scientific inquiry, questions about what ought to be the case, and not just what, as a matter of fact, is the case. But it is a more than curious fact about biology that it is the only scientific discipline that anyone has ever supposed might be able to answer the questions of moral and political philosophy. Evolutionary biology in particular has often, at least since Darwin's day, inspired a hope of putting ethics on a "scientific" footing. We will address this hope in the last chapter of this book. Meanwhile, let us draw a working definition of philosophy from this section: it is the discipline that addresses those questions that the sciences cannot (yet, or perhaps ever) answer and the questions about why the sciences cannot answer these questions. Thus, the philosophy of biology addresses those questions that arise from biology but that biology cannot answer, at least not yet, and the further questions about why biology may be unable to answer these questions.

Philosophy and language

So, what are these questions biology raises but cannot address? Here are some candidates:

1 Is life a purely physical process? Are biological processes "nothing but" complex physical and chemical ones? If so, what does this mean for the science of biology as an independent discipline?

2   Does evolution have any goal or purpose, perhaps one that might give our existence meaning or intelligibility?

3   Is there any such a thing as evolutionary progress? Is complexity increasing in evolution? If so, is that increase inevitable? And what, if anything, does increasing complexity say about values? Are more complex organisms somehow better than, or higher forms of life than, less complex ones?

4   Does the theory of natural selection conflict with theism, and, if so, how can we rationally choose between them?

5   What is human nature? Which of our traits are essential to us? Are some traits innate? Do any determine our characters more than others? Are they fixed or not? Are socially important human traits more the result of heredity, nature, and our genetic programs than the result of learning, nurture, and our environments?

6   To what extent are humans adapted in the biological sense? To what environmental conditions are we adapted, and at what level does this adaptation occur—the individual human, the family or the lineage, the whole population, or perhaps the species?

If we ask any one of these questions, almost inevitably the right initial response turns out to be: "It depends." And what it depends on is the meaning of key words in each of the questions. How we eventually answer these questions will turn on what meaning we agree to confer on terms such as "life," "purpose," "progress," "complexity," "theism," "genetic program," "adaptation," and so on. For this reason a great deal of the philosophy of science, and analytical philosophy generally, is given over to the clarification of the meaning of the concepts in which questions are framed. Philosophy is not itself an experimental, observational discipline. It does not have its own domain of data about the world. Rather, philosophy addresses the questions raised by the sciences—at least in part—by clarifying the concepts on which these questions hinge.

Sometimes, the result of such a philosophical analysis is to show that a question is ambiguous and that the difficulty or debate about its answer reflects the failure to see the ambiguity. It might reveal that a crucial concept such as "life," "program," or "adaptation" has two or more alternative meanings. Armed with this insight, we can then decide which alternative meaning is relevant and appropriate. This may not settle the matter. The focal question may remain unanswered. But at least we will have a clearer idea of what the question means. And we will also have a clearer idea of what would count as a satisfactory answer.

How do we go about deciding on the meaning of a crucial concept? Only rarely will looking up the word in a dictionary help, for dictionaries usually provide many alternative meanings and our problem is to decide which among the alternative meanings is the one relevant to our inquiry. Just try to answer the question whether life is wholly a matter of physical and chemical processes by looking up the word "life" in a dictionary. Moreover, many of the concepts with which the philosophy of science is concerned are discussed in technical terms, neologisms, the meaning of which are given in large part by the scientific theories in which they figure. Consider the term "positive charge" in physics. Suppose someone asked what it is that positively charged protons have and that negatively charged electrons lack (the word positive implying that something is present or added and negative implying an absence or loss). This silly question simply reflects ignorance of the relevant theory and a reliance on the dictionary meanings of "positive" or "negative." To be clear on the meaning of the concepts with which the philosophy of biology deals, we need to understand the scientific theories in which these concepts figure. This of course makes the biologist who understands these theories at least as much of an expert on questions in the philosophy of biology as the philosopher!

So deciding on the meaning of a scientific concept requires that we understand the theory in which it figures. Further, understanding a scientific theory requires that we be able to identify the domains in which it explains and predicts phenomena, and the experimental techniques and instruments that can be employed to test the theory. And, indeed, many of the questions the philosophy of biology considers are questions about the domain of a theory and the domain's appropriate methods of investigation. Consider, for example, question 6 above, about whether biological theory can explain human social phenomena. Does the domain of the notion of adaptation by natural selection include human behavior? In other words, is human behavior the sort of phenomenon that the theory could in principle explain? Does the theory's domain extend to human societies? Just what is the range of entities to which the notion is applicable?

What all this means is that the process of identifying the meanings of the scientific terms we need to make our philosophical questions unambiguous is not really separable from the development of scientific theory itself. It also means that the difference between philosophy and theoretical science is not a matter of kind but of degree. Of course there will be differences between laboratory and field science on the one hand and theory and the more abstract inquiries of the philosopher on the other, but these differences lie on a continuum. Because philosophers' interests are abstract, they do not require laboratories. Instead, they often proceed by undertaking "thought experiments." Philosophers will often have to create "science fiction" scenarios, to explore scientifically impossible scenarios, in order to extract the logical relations of implication, exclusion, and compatibility between scientific theories and data—and among theories themselves. Scientists are advised not to lose patience with such explorations. For one important aspect of scientific progress is—beyond the increasing precision of tests that confirm or falsify scientific theories—the broadening of the domain of those theories. And such advancement requires the same kind of thought experiment, albeit more tightly constrained by immediately available data than the philosopher needs to worry about.

Once the key terms in a question have been made clear, we can turn to considering how it may be answered. Of course, it may be that, once made clear, a question no longer troubles us. Perhaps the answer to the question is obvious, or perhaps the question rests on a false presupposition, or is otherwise "defective" in a way that is obvious. Not every interrogative sentence expresses a bona fide question. Some are what philosophers call "pseudo-questions." Some obvious examples include the following: "Do green ideas sleep furiously?" "What time is it on the sun when it is noon at Greenwich, England?" or "Did you phone your wife?" asked of a 10-year old girl. The first of these "questions" looks grammatically like one, but once we know the meanings of the terms that express it, we see that it is a pseudo-question, one that has the right syntax but really has no coherent content. The second question can be disposed of once we recognize that local time at a point on the Earth depends on the Earth's position with respect to the sun, and it makes no sense to ask what the sun's position is with respect to itself. The last question makes syntactic and semantic sense but is based on several false presuppositions: that the pronoun "you" refers to a married person, and a married male person to boot. None of these questions can be answered, but they can be disposed of as not needing answers. Some philosophers have held that many or all philosophical questions are like these pseudo-questions. On their view philosophical problems are dissolved, not solved. They are disposed of, not answered.

Suppose that one held, as some scientists who have no patience with philosophy do, that there are no real philosophical questions, no questions in the philosophy of science. One might hold, for example, that all real questions can, at least ultimately, be answered by science, given enough genius, enough time, and enough money, leaving nothing to philosophy. On this view, questions such as "What is time?" or "Is abortion morally wrong?" will turn out to be either questions to which empirical inquiry broadly considered can give definitive answers or pseudo-questions expressing pseudo-problems that need dissolution, not solution. If all real questions can be answered by science, then there is no such subject as philosophy, defined as the discipline addressing questions not answered by science and questions about why science cannot answer these questions.

The view that science will ultimately answer all real questions and that the remainder will turn out to be pseudo-questions, faces a serious problem, however. For it must be granted that there are many questions raised by science that it cannot *yet* answer. And in that case, why be so confident that all these questions are either answerable by science or pseudo-questions? There are only two ways to respond. The first is quite tedious. It is to take on each and every apparently unanswerable question and show what is the matter with it, show why we need not take it seriously, or else show that it is in principle answerable. The second is to show that in principle there can be no real questions beyond the reach of science. But notice that either of these two endeavors is properly and recognizably a philosophical project! We have a right to conclude, therefore, that even those who assert that science alone will eventually answer every real question owe us an argument for this claim, and that any such an argument will be a philosophical one. That makes philosophy pretty much unavoidable, even for those who deny that there are any real questions for philosophy to address.

In any case, in the absence of such an argument, we can safely assume that the sciences really do raise questions that they cannot answer and that once we have identified these questions, the philosophy of science should address them.

The agenda of the philosophy of biology

Darwinian theory is central to the philosophy of biology. One reason is its relevance to the questions listed at the beginning of the previous section, questions that interest almost all thinking people. Another is the very large amount of evidence that the theory is correct, a claim that cannot be made by other theories—coming mainly from the social and behavioral sciences—relevant to those same issues. In the physical sciences, there are other theories that are more strongly confirmed by scientific experiment. For example, quantum electrodynamic theory makes predictions that have been confirmed to 12 decimal places. That is an accuracy roughly equivalent to measuring the distance from the tip of the spire of the Empire State Building in New York City to the point of the Space Needle in Seattle to within the breadth of a single hair. But, for all its accuracy, the theory appears to have little explanatory relevance to human life. The atomic theory that stands behind the Periodic Table of the Elements is also a very well-established theory with ever-increasing application in technology and engineering. But its account of the chemical relations among the atoms that compose our bodies, for all its completeness, will not answer questions about human nature, human behavior, human institutions, and human history. Darwin's theory does not attain the standards of accurate prediction and detailed explanation that theories in physics and chemistry do, but it is potentially far more relevant to questions about ourselves.

On the other hand, there are theories in the social and behavioral sciences that, unlike Darwinian theory, were developed explicitly to explain and (more recently) to predict human behavior, human action, and the large-scale social processes, i.e. culture and history. Indeed, social and behavioral scientists have been offering such theories at least since the late nineteenth century. Most of them should be familiar: Freud's psychodynamic theory, Skinner's behavioral learning theory, the competing theories of social structure and function attributed to Durkheim and Weber, Marxist economic theory, classical, Keynesian, and neoclassical economic theory, and their successors. One reason that there are so many such theories, and that we could go on listing others, is that none has secured anything like the scientific confirmation required for general acceptance in science, social or natural, and therefore we continue to seek more such theories. Were any of these theories well enough confirmed, we might be able to rely on them to explain human affairs, or at least to do so to a greater extent than a theory such as Darwin's, which may have significant implications for the human sciences but secures its considerable scientific support in other domains. Alas, none of these theories has secured general acceptance in its discipline to match the well-established role of Darwinian theory in biology.

Darwin's theory of natural selection and its subsequent scientific elaboration more fully combines explanatory relevance to human affairs with independent scientific confirmation than any other theory in science. And this is what makes the theory a potential lightning rod for public controversy. Exploring its implications for humans, some see in it the gravest threat to religion generally or theism in particular. Others find in it the rationalizations for the worst excesses of capitalism. Some treat it as destructive of the very essence of our humanity, on which our values and the very meaning of life depend. Still others see Darwinian theory and the biological understanding it inspires as finally providing the basis for an enduring moral concern for all living things and the planet on which we and other living things find ourselves.

Whether or not Darwinian theory has any such implications is a question that biology certainly cannot yet answer. It may turn out to be a question that biology can never answer. And that of course is what makes the question a philosophical one. And it explains why the philosophy of biology has become so consequential a subject, so consequential that among all the technical subdisciplines of philosophy it is about the only one to find itself represented on bestseller lists, to be expounded in courts of law examining constitutional issues of church and state, and to be the subject of debate in popular culture generally.

The aim of this book is to shed light on at least some of these human questions, but to do so we will need to guide the reader through the narrower scientific and philosophical issues on which answers to the big questions may turn. Thus, a great deal of our concern will be with matters the relevance of which for the lively public debates—the nature–nurture debate, the intelligent design debate, and so on—may not be obvious until understood. To get to the big questions, we will need to travel through issues that may look technical, complicated, and even out of touch with the target questions. We think, we hope, that the pay-off is worth the journey, and also that the journey itself will prove valuable in its own right.

Decades ago, the famous evolutionary biologist Theodosius Dobzhansky wrote, "Nothing in biology makes sense except in the light of evolution." This statement needs some explanation and qualification. First, evolution is descent with modification, the notion that all organisms are modified descendants of a common ancestor. It is broader than Darwin's theory of natural selection, which is a mechanism of change, an explanation for how modification occurs. (And as will be seen, selection is not the whole story.) Second, the statement overreaches somewhat. Biological questions can be posed the answers to which involve evolution only very indirectly (for example, questions relating to the physical properties—the biomechanics—of biological materials). Nevertheless, understood as a claim about shared ancestry, as well as natural selection, we think it is close to true. And that is why, as will be seen, evolution emerges as central in every chapter and virtually every section of this book. Biology is inescapably historical.

We begin in the first chapter by discussing the theory of natural selection, its structure, the scientific problems it raises, common misunderstandings of the theory, and its major metaphysical consequence, the extension of the mechanistic worldview of the physical sciences to the life sciences. This extension raises an epistemological problem about the kind of knowledge that biological theory provides. For Darwin's theory does not look much like the sorts of theories familiar in physics and chemistry, the explanatory and predictive powers of which have vindicated mechanism as a metaphysical worldview for these disciplines. Differences between biology and the physical sciences, and indeed between it and the human sciences, must be reflected in the epistemology of biological science, in the kinds of knowledge it provides. For this reason, philosophers of biology have been as interested in the grounds of the theory of natural selection as in its structure. In Chapter 2 we consider how and why scientific theory should turn out to look so different in biology from the way it looks in physics. We do so by examining the question of why there seem to be no scientific laws in biology, or none to rival those of physical science in scope, simplicity, and power. Answering this question will reveal a great deal about the nature of biological theory and also shed light on the human sciences too, as we shall see in the last chapter.

Chapter 3 continues the examination of epistemic issues raised by Darwinian theory, in particular three "technical issues" about evolution that vex biology but that are often invisible to nonspecialists. One is the nature and extent of biological adaptation and the role of constraints of various kinds in shaping organismal design. It will turn out that adaptation and constraint—often considered to be alternatives in evolutionary explanation—are for certain kinds of questions jointly essential to explanation. The second is the role of statistics and probability in biology. It will be seen that the notion of objective chance—so essential to Darwinian thinking—is only imperfectly understood and remains problematic. The third is the foundation of functional explanation and description. We will show that two very different conceptions of function survive in biology, and that the imperfect overlap between them has consequences for how questions about function are posed and answered, both in biology and in the social sciences. In general, we try to show how these apparently abstract matters bear on the larger questions that drive interest in the philosophy of biology. For example, we show in this chapter how the problem of reconciling the theism of the Abrahamic religions with biology's commitment to natural selection turns in part on how we are to understand "probability" and "drift."

Chapter 4 examines the relationship between molecular biology and the other subdisciplines of biology, from cell biology to paleontology. It raises the question of whether all biological processes can or must eventually be explained by theories about their macromolecular constituent processes. The issue is reductionism. Biologists and philosophers have argued mainly against reductionism, yet it persists both among many physical scientists and even a few prominent biologists. It is clear that answers to the reductionism question will drive a good deal of future scientific research in the discipline. Further, the reductionism question is relevant to a number of important philosophical issues such as the mind–body problem and determinism versus free will. All of this makes reductionism a threat or a promise that few philosophers or biologists will be neutral about. Reductionism is a very old issue in biology. But in addressing it we cover some new territory, issues that have arisen or become especially problematic only in recent decades on account of new discoveries. One is the problem of what is a gene. The modern understanding of genetic mechanisms makes the concept of a gene problematic, varying as it does from one research context to another. The gene of molecular biology seems not to refer to the same concept as the gene in population genetics. If population biology is reducible to genetics, in what sense of the word "gene" is it so reducible? Another issue has to do with the dynamics of complex systems of interacting components, such as the gene networks in an organism are said to be. Such networks seem, from an antireductionist standpoint, to have higher-level properties and to be affected by higher-level controls, that raise new challenges to the reductionist view. Finally, the principle of natural selection seems to present a barrier to the reduction of biology to physical science. In particular, it seems to create an unbridgeable gap between explanation at the level of chemistry and physics and that at the level of macromolecules. If so, then the scope of reduction will be limited, necessarily coming to an end at the level of molecular biology.

In the last three chapters of the book, we turn to some more specific issues. The question of whether evolution is progressive—raised briefly in Chapter 1—is addressed at length in Chapter 5, along with the further issue of the evolution of complexity. Progress has an evaluative component, which raises the question of whether it is even a proper subject for putatively value-neutral science. If it is, if progress can be understood in a way that makes it suitable for scientific study, what does evolutionary theory predict about progress? Is it an expectation or merely a possibility? And then, what is the relationship between progress and complexity? If they are related, what does the history of life tell us about complexity and how it changes? The discussion reveals how advances in empirical science sometimes can hinge critically on advances in conceptual clarification.

In Chapter 6, we return to the connected questions of metaphysics and epistemology that biology raises. The metaphysical ones are those about whether, along with genes, cells, and organisms, biology must recognize "higher levels" of organization—for example groups or societies of organisms—and questions about whether there is something causally unique about genes and the genome that should accord them a special explanatory role in biology. Finally, in Chapter 7, we consider the relationship between biology and the social sciences and, more narrowly, between biology and human nature. Humans are members of a biological species, and therefore arguably human adaptations are not exempt from the operation of natural selection. But the degree to which human psychology and behavior is molded by selection, and the mechanism by which it is molded—for example by selection at the level of the individual versus the level of the group—are open questions. And then there is a pressing further question: if biology *is* relevant to human affairs, what are the implications for distinctively human concerns such as ethics?

Our outline of the agenda of the philosophy of biology is not aimed at settling any of its debates. Indeed, the authors of this book have divergent views about almost all of the unavoidable questions biology raises and cannot (yet) answer. Our aim is to provide the reader with the resources to see how serious the questions are and what would count as good answers to them.

1 Darwin makes a science

Overview

There is an important sense in which biology as a science began only when Darwin hit upon the theory of natural selection in the late 1830s, although he did not publish the theory until 1859 (after A.R. Wallace hit upon it too, and threatened to scoop him). Of course there had been scientists making important discoveries about the biological world at least since Aristotle in the third century BC. In the 200 years prior to Darwin's birth, Harvey and van Leeuwenhoek stand out for their discoveries that, respectively, the heart beats to circulate the blood and all living things are composed of cells. And there was Linnaeus' system of classification of living things and his naming system for genus and species, the binomial nomenclature. But it can be argued that until Darwin's achievement, none of these findings, explanations, or classifications could be organized into anything with a right to call itself a science. Darwin's evolutionary theory explains more than just common descent, the shared ancestry of all organisms on Earth. It identifies a causal process that produces the adaptations we see everywhere in nature, one that replaces other accounts of the adaptation, other accounts that could not be causal or even in principle scientifically testable.

In this chapter we consider this argument that biology did not really exist as a science at all until Darwin's discovery of the mechanism of natural selection. We also discuss some controversies. Natural selection has been controversial from the very first time the idea was publicly expounded. Some of these controversies are based on misunderstandings, but some are real. In this chapter we separate common misunderstandings about Darwin's theory from the real issues that any defender of the theory must come to grips with.

Teleology and theology

Before Darwin, philosophers such as Immanuel Kant had despaired of our ever creating a science of biology on a par with sciences such as physics and chemistry. "There will never be," Kant (1790) wrote, "a Newton for the blade of grass." What Kant meant by this claim was that biological processes could not be understood or explained by the operation of the sort of mindless causal properties of mass and velocity, position and momentum, force and acceleration that promised to suffice in Newton's mechanics to explain everything physical. By the end of the nineteenth century, electric charge and electromagnetic fields were added to the list of causes, enabling science to explain almost all physical processes, including heat, flight, electricity, and magnetism. And, soon after, most of chemistry could similarly be explained on the basis of atomic theory.

But until Darwin the biological seemed permanently, and logically, conceptually, necessarily, out of the explanatory reach of merely physical causes. Take a cotton plant: it moves its leaves throughout the day to track the sun, and it does so *in order to* maximize the amount of sunlight that falls on its petals. Even more impressively purposeful or goal directed is the cowpea plant. When well-watered plants of this species move in a way that maximizes the amount of sunlight to fall on their leaves, they do so apparently *in order to* produce starch from water and CO_2 through a chemical reaction catalyzed by chlorophyll. And the plant produces starch *in order to* grow. But when the surrounding soil is dry, these same plants move their leaves *in order to minimize* their exposure to sunlight so that they retain water that would otherwise evaporate. It looks like explanation in biology connects events, states, processes, and things with their *future* goals, ends, and purposes, not with the *prior* causes that bring them about. It was Aristotle who distinguished the prior physical causes we are familiar with in physical explanations, from the purposes, goals, or ends with which biological processes are explained. The former he called "efficient causes" and the latter "final causes." The Greek word for "end" or "goal" is *telos* from which comes the English word "teleological." A teleological explanation shows why something happened by identifying the end, purpose, or goal that it brought about. Why does the heart pump? Kant would have answered that it does so in order to circulate the blood. Circulating the blood is an effect of the heart pumping, and this effect explains it, even though circulation happens afterward as a result of the pumping. Things have not changed much in three centuries. Ask a molecular biologist why the DNA molecule contains thymine whereas the RNA molecule transcribed from the same DNA molecule contains uracil (even though both would appear to perform nearly the same function). The answer is teleological: Although the two molecules are otherwise the same in nucleotide composition, DNA is made of thymine *in order to* minimize mutation (in particular, what are called point mutations arising from deamination), whereas RNA contains uracil *in order to* minimize the costs of protein synthesis.

And of course it is not just biological explanations that are "teleological," i.e. that cite future ends, goals, or purposes to explain past structures, processes, and events. The whole vocabulary of biology is teleological. Consider some of the most basic nouns in biology: codon, gene, promoter, repressor, organelle, cell, tissue, organ, fin, wing, eye, coat, stem, chloroplast, membrane. Almost all of these terms are defined—at least conventionally—by what the thing *does*, or what it does when working normally. And not just anything it does, for each of these does many things. Take a shark's fin, for example: it provides stability while swimming, but it also reflects light, makes turbulence behind it in the water, adds weight and surface area to the body, signals to humans the presence of a predator near the surface, attracts the interest of connoisseurs of shark fin soup, and so on. But only one (or maybe a couple) of these things a fin does is its *function*. The function of a fin is the only one among these effects that define what is to be a fin: a fin is an appendage of a fish or whale, one of whose functions is to provide stability. In other words, it is something the animal has "in order to" provide stability while swimming. Well, if fish have fins in order to swim stably, one may ask, who arranged this neat trick for them? And the same question arises for practically every other feature of organisms that has biological interest. For almost everything biological is ordinarily described in terms of its function. So almost everything biological raises a teleology problem. In contrast, a question such as "What is the function of the electron?" is not one physicists ordinarily consider.

Teleological explanations, which explain by citing goals, ends, or purposes, are troublesome. For they explain events, states, and processes, not by showing how they came about from prior causes but by identifying the future effects they will lead to. The trouble is we know that future events cannot bring about past ones. For one thing, it is hard to see how something that does not yet exist (because it is in the future) could bring about something that does already exist and may have existed for some time in the past. For another, we seem to be allowing the behavior of something seeking a goal to be explained by the goal even when it fails to achieve the goal. A sperm cell moves up the uterus "in order to" fertilize the ovum, even when, as in almost every case, it fails to do so.

Aristotle may in fact have recognized the first of these problems, the impossibility of future causation. For he argued that final causes had to be "immanent," meaning somehow embodied or represented in the prior states of the organism's life, directing its course towards some goal.

Of course some immanent teleological explanations seem unproblematic. These are the "in order to" explanations we employ to explain our own behavior. "Why are you taking organic chemistry?" "In order to get into medical school." Or "Why do you want to go to medical school?" "In order to please my parents." In these cases, the "in order to" relation reflects our desires, and our beliefs about the means to bring them about. So, we can "unpack" the explanation of why I am taking organic chemistry into: (i) the desire to get into medical school; and (ii) the belief that taking organic chemistry is necessary for getting into medical school. The beliefs and desires that underwrite the "in order to" explanations of our actions are almost never made explicit. But making them explicit turns the apparent teleological explanation of why I am taking organic chemistry into a nonteleological explanation in terms of prior causes for later effects. I am taking organic chemistry (now), because at sometime in the past I came to desire to go to medical school, and I came to believe that taking organic chemistry is necessary for going to medical school.

But in biology there does not seem to be a similar strategy available for turning statements about purposes, goals, ends, and the means to achieve them into causal relations between earlier events and later ones they bring about. Because, to a first approximation, science seeks to explain by uncovering prior causes, biology before Darwin was arguably not a science. Of course, before Darwin, one could explain all the "in order to" explanations in biology on the model of explanations of human action, simply by appealing to the "desires" and "beliefs" of God. Why does the heart beat? The explanation that it does so in order to circulate the blood turns out to be shorthand for something like: it was God's will (i.e. God wanted) that blood circulate through vertebrate bodies, and he knew (i.e. believed correctly) that making a heart that beats would be a good way to do so. Of course, as God is omnipotent (all powerful), he can cause the object with the desired future effect to exist. For each "in order to," there is a set of statements about God's knowledge and his will (God's infallible and always benevolent versions of our beliefs and desires) that show the underlying causal basis of the teleological explanation.

Now there are several problems about this way of saving teleological explanation. To begin with, invoking God to explain natural phenomena is, in the view of many, simply to change the subject from science to theology. Now the acceptability of teleological explanations will hinge on the soundness of arguments for and against God's existence. Second, invoking God's will and his omnipotence to explain biological events and processes seems to be too easy. As far back as the eighteenth century, Voltaire was ridiculing "in order to" explanations for this reason. In his book *Candide*, Voltaire has Dr. Pangloss explain why the nose has a bridge by pointing out that noses bear bridges in order to support eye glasses. We detect adaptations everywhere in nature—the exoskeleton of insects adapted to prevent dehydration; the intricate complexity of the mammalian eye so perfectly suited to the available sources of light, reflectance, luminosity, etc.; even perhaps morning sickness in early pregnancy, seemingly exquisitely arranged to protect the fetus from foods the mother might eat that are even slightly harmful. In each of these cases, the explanation turns out to be exactly the same. God's good will, her complete knowledge, and her omnipotence, together account for the arrangement.

But surely an omniscient, omnipotent God could have chosen some different arrangement of things to attain the very same outcome. God could have made water less evaporative so that insects would not dehydrate so quickly, or arranged the digestive systems of pregnant females to digest all poisons instead of becoming more sensitive to them. Why didn't God do so? Notice that an attempt to answer this question by identifying the constraints imposed by the physical and chemical laws and the local conditions in which

God operated to realize her will immediately raises questions about why God should be constrained in any way. She can create, arrange, suspend any chemical or physical law, or local conditions she chooses. There is, of course, no answer to the question, why did God choose the course she did, and not some other one, at least none that is open to testing by data, experiment, observation, etc. This question is pretty clearly a matter of theology, not science.

Making teleology safe for science

So appeals to God will not bail out teleological explanations for science, will not turn them into causal ones. This of course is where Darwin's theory of adaptation by natural selection comes in. According to the most widely known contemporary statement of Darwin's theory (Lewontin 1978), adaptation results if three facts obtain:

1 There is reproduction with some inheritance of traits in the next generation.
2 In each generation, among the inherited traits there is always some variation.
3 The inherited variants differ in their fitness, in their adaptedness to the environment.

The simplicity of these statements hides their tremendous explanatory power, and also leaves unspoken some important implications and fosters several potentially serious misunderstandings. Before discussing these implications, and forestalling these misunderstandings, it is as well to give a simple illustration of the explanatory power. Why do giraffes have long necks? The short answer could be "in order to reach the tasty leaves at the tops of the trees that other animals can't reach." A slightly more scientific way of expressing the same explanatory facts is to say, "Having a long neck is an adaptation for the giraffe" (or "The function of the giraffe's neck is to reach leaves that other savannah mammals cannot"). But the fuller version of the explanation goes something like this: The length of a giraffe's neck is a somewhat inherited trait. Long-necked giraffes have long-necked offspring, not invariably so and not always as long, but usually and sometimes longer. Never mind for the moment the details of why such traits are inherited in this pattern. Observation and measurement are sufficient to convince us that they are. Observation also reveals that, as with all inherited traits, there is always variation in the length of necks in each generation of giraffes. This variation is never in just one direction, say only toward longer necks; some long-necked giraffes have offspring with shorter necks, and vice versa. This will be true no matter whether trees get taller or shorter or other animals, say some insect species, come along who can compete with giraffes for the highest leaves in the trees. This point about variation in heritable traits is sometimes expressed by calling them "blind," though this expression is plainly metaphorical. More often the independence of variation from features of the environment that might make a variation useful or not is expressed by calling it "random" (and this is the source of a possible misunderstanding that we will forestall later). Now, let us say that at some time in the distant past, a long-necked variant appeared among a small number of giraffes, just as average and short necks appeared as well. And it appeared not because a long neck would be advantageous but just because variation is the rule. Further, let us say that this longer-necked giraffe did better at feeding off the high leaves than shorter-necked ones and did better than other mammals competing with giraffes for resources in the same environment. That is to say the hereditary trait of having a longer neck was "fitter" in the giraffe's environment. So giraffes with the long necks survived longer and had more longer-necked offspring. As the total giraffe population that could be supported by their environment was limited, the proportion of longer-necked giraffes in the whole population increased from generation to generation. This was because in each generation they out-competed the shorter-necked giraffes for limited resources (leaves high enough up on trees that only giraffes could reach them) and, therefore—owing to their longer life, greater strength, etc.—had more offspring. After a sufficiently large number of generations, the population of giraffes came to consist only of long-necked ones. Thus, Darwin's theory explains why giraffes have long necks by identifying a causal process that in the long run would produce long necks without any person or force acting "in order to" provide for the nourishment of giraffes. Having a long neck is an adaptation for giraffes. That is to say they have it because in the past there was hereditary variation in neck length and the longer variants just happened to be fitter in the environment where giraffes found themselves. (We feel constrained to note that the point of this story is only to illustrate how adaptation arises in principle, using a well-worn example that many find easy to grasp. In fact, however, giraffes may have evolved long necks for very different reasons. They could have been an adaptation for intimidation of predators or of other giraffes, perhaps in male–male competition. Or it could be that in giraffes, neck length, and body size are connected in growth in such a way that animals with larger bodies grow disproportionately longer necks. If so, then selection for large body size might have produced a long neck as a side effect. The treetop leaves possibility is an example of an evolutionary "just so" story. We will discuss such stories, and alternative nonadaptive modes of evolutionary explanation in Chapter 3.)

Darwin called this process natural selection and the name has stuck. The theory of natural selection explains the traits of extant flora and fauna by tracing their evolution back through successive rounds of natural selection by the environment operating on the variation in hereditary traits each generation presents. "Natural selection" is not an entirely apt name for the process, as it misleadingly suggests the notions of choice, desire, and belief built into the theological account of adaptations. It evokes an agent doing the choosing, if not God then perhaps Mother Nature, actively picking the best of the litter. But the selection process is more passive than that. Perhaps "environmental filtration" is a better label than "natural selection." The environment does not "select," but rather it filters, preventing the less fit from passing through. Moreover, it is particularly important to recognize that environments change over time, and that what is adaptive in one environment can be maladaptive in another. For instance, as global warming accelerates, the grizzly bear's thick warm coat may become maladaptive. This fact has important implications for the notion that natural selection generates continued improvement in absolute terms, that later organisms are better, in some important sense, than earlier ones. In fact, arguably, Darwinian theory demands no such thing. The theory implies only that there will be adaptation to local environments. But as environments change, and improvement tracks only local environments, there is no commitment in the theory to long-term "progress." Indeed, extinction is a fate not restricted to the dinosaurs. We shall discuss progress further in Chapter 5.

Another potential source of misunderstanding has already been mentioned. The theory requires that in every generation heritable traits vary to some degree, and that this variation is "random." The theory requires inheritance of traits and it requires variation in these traits across generations. It is entirely silent on the mechanism of inheritance and the source of variation. Darwin had theories about both inheritance and variation but they were mistaken. The later independent discovery of the right theory of heredity and the source of variation greatly strengthened biology's confidence in Darwin's theory of natural selection. But the theory would have worked with many different hereditary mechanisms and sources of variation, and it did not imply or require any particular one. At most it required that there is one or more mechanisms of heredity and one or more sources of variation in heritable traits for each generation in every evolving lineage. The theory of natural selection does however rule out one cause of variation in heritable traits, namely a future cause in which new variation is guided by the needs of the individual who bears it. Indeed that is the major thrust of the word "random" in the phrase "random variation" in Darwin's theory. It is not that the appearance of a new trait is undetermined, that it is not fixed by prior causes. It is rather that the causes that fix it are independent of, unconnected with, the factors that determine its adaptedness. We say that variation is random "with respect to" adaptation. To put it another way, the usefulness of a trait in the environment in which it appears—its goal, purpose, or end—is not among the causes responsible for its appearance. Philosophers, theologians, and others noticed almost immediately after the appearance of *On the Origin of Species* that Darwin's theory made goals, purposes, ends, and future causes of any sort completely superfluous to biology.

Nowadays a great deal is known about the mechanism of heredity and the source of variation. Hereditary transmission proceeds mainly via genes composed of nucleic acids, and variation results from recombination of genes and mutation. As some of this mutation is caused by quantum processes (such as radioactive decay), at least some of the variation that the environment filters many would call random in the sense of lacking a deterministic cause. But nothing in the mechanism of natural selection requires indeterminism. Indeed, the term "blind" may be more apt, less misleading, than "random" for the sort of variation required by natural selection. Variation can be said to be blind with respect to need, or to the environment. In that case, the process of natural selection as a whole could be described—in the sociologist Donald Campbell's apt phrasing—as "blind variation and selective retention" (Campbell 1974). The phrasing is especially apt in that it emphasizes that, according to Darwin's theory, nature has no foresight.

Notice that the three requirements listed above for the operation of natural selection—reproduction, heredity, and differential fitness or adaptedness—do not mention organisms. They do not mention actual animals and plants and their traits, which are assumed to be the subjects or the "domain" of the theory of natural selection. One reason is that the theory is supposed to explain not just the origin of adaptation in these organisms but also the evolution of higher units—colonies or societies of multicellular units—and of lower ones—single-celled organisms. Also, the theory is intended to apply more broadly to explain the evolution of genes and other molecules within organisms, units that are not living at all. And finally, many believe it is supposed to apply to the origin of life, that is to the evolution of single cells from large macromolecules, which again are not organisms at all. Thus, formally the theory cannot be expressed solely as a claim about giraffes, or about mammals generally, or even about animals generally, or, for that matter, about organisms. Rather, it must be expressed as a general claim about the evolution of reproducing things with heritable variation and differential fitness or adaptedness.

To express the generality of natural selection as a mechanism, David Hull (and, independently, Richard Dawkins) introduced the terms "replicator" and "interactor" (or, for Dawkins, "vehicle"). In Hull's definition, a replicator is anything that passes on its structure largely intact through successive replications. An interactor or a vehicle is anything that acts as a cohesive unit in its environment in such a way as to make a difference for the replicators that generate it. These terms have taken on a life of their own in evolutionary theory and other biologists and philosophers have modified them in various ways. Nevertheless, it is easy to see how the two concepts provide the theory with the generality it requires. And here is one way in which such generality is useful. We can begin to paint a picture of how life originated on Earth, even without knowing the details of the process. Perhaps the first evolving entities were simple macromolecules that functioned simultaneously as replicators and interactors. Then variation arising in these macromolecules could in some cases have produced associations of them, which if better adapted than their predecessors would have preferentially survived. Further random variation and filtration of the better adapted might have eventually produced a separation of the replication and interaction functions, as well as further buildup, eventually generating larger and more complex entities of a sort that we are willing to call living. Long continued, this process could in principle produce the entire range of adaptation we know today, in other words, the entire explanatory domain of Darwinian theory. The point is that the generality of the replicator–interactor concepts enables us to tell this story—to develop hypotheses about the origin and diversification of life on Earth—without knowing any of the actual details of the actual process: which macromolecules, combining in what way, under what environmental conditions. Indeed, as we will discuss later, the theory is sufficiently general that we can use it to speculate about the origin and evolution of life not just on Earth but anywhere in the universe.

Misunderstandings about natural selection

Skeptics, detractors, and students learning Darwin's theory of natural selection for the first time are often incredulous. How could a theory based on such a simple mechanism as blind variation and selective retention actually explain all of the adaptation we see in biology? Most of the hereditary variations we see in nature are either slight differences that appear and reappear irregularly, or they are larger but extremely maladaptive hereditary defects. How could the environment selecting on extremely slight differences from generation to generation produce a structure such as, for example, the eye, a structure that—whether in an insect, octopus, or human—consists of many intricate parts, all of them highly adapted to the particular environments of insects, octopi, and humans. Darwin recognized this problem for his theory in one of the most famous passages of *On the Origin of Species*:

> To suppose that the eye, with all its inimitable contrivances for adjusting the focus to different distances, for admitting different amounts of light, and for the correction of spherical and chromatic aberration, could have been formed by natural selection, seems, I freely confess, absurd in the highest possible degree.
>
> (Darwin 1859: 186)

The skeptic allows that Darwin's mechanism can bring about slight changes, for instance in a laboratory where the experimenter can manipulate the environment of some rapidly reproducing organism such as a bacterium or a fruit fly. And the skeptic can easily see how animal breeders can modify their stocks in ways advantageous to farmers or fanciers over thousands of years. But the changes produced in both cases are quite small, compared with the change from, say, single-celled protist to mammal, from an amoeba-like ancestor to a modern goat. What is more, the experimenter or the breeder begins with a highly adapted creature and is able to carefully control the environment—the probabilities of reproduction for each organism—to bring about the desired effect. What the skeptic really wants, one suspects, to confirm Darwin's theory, is an experiment that begins with a random collection of early-Earth molecules and produces complex, intelligent species like us over a period of about 3.5 billion years of unmanipulated evolution by natural selection. The biologist must admit that no such experiment, or even one close to it, is in the offing. So, why are biologists so strongly convinced that Darwinian natural selection underlies evolution? The reason is that natural selection—random variation and environmental filtration—is the only mechanism known in nature that can produce adaptation, that can produce the "in order to" that characterizes so many of the features of organisms. In fact, as we explain in the next section, it is hard even to think of an alternative mechanism.

For some, Darwin's theory presents puzzles having to do with complexity, randomness, and directionality. They ask how complex functional designs can arise by a random process such as natural selection. For example, the evolution of a complex structure like a wing capable of sustained flight (as in a bird) from a fin (as in a primitive fish) might seem to be impossible, given the randomness of the process of natural selection and the enormous number of modifications necessary. The first part of the answer is that natural selection is not random. It is a process that requires some randomness in its "input." Variations arising are not targeted toward solving problems posed by the environment. But the "output" of natural selection is decidedly nonrandom, the differential survival and reproduction of the variants that are better adapted. The second part of the answer is that natural selection can act cumulatively, and that is what makes complex adaptations possible. Selection first transformed a fin into a walking limb, strong enough to support a large animal on land, and then later transformed a walking limb into a wing, capable of producing sustained powered flight. Complexity is possible because later adaptations build on earlier adaptations. In other words, complex adaptations are not produced in big leaps but in smaller steps, each one of which is adaptive, and function can change from one step to the next. A wing is not a better fin or even a better leg. It is something entirely different, serving a different function. Looking only at the endpoints, the gap covered might seem impossibly large, and the reason is that natural selection to some extent covers its tracks. Looking at a fin or wing, the intermediate walking limb stage is not evident, at least not superficially evident. Though natural selection covers its tracks, a great deal of biology has been devoted to uncovering them. One of Darwin's earliest arguments for natural selection was based on the close similarity in parts, their numbers, and spatial relations to one another (their "homology") of the bones in fins, legs, and wings. Two hundred years later, molecular biologists can trace the genealogy of the bird's wing back through the reptile's leg to the fish's fin in the similarities and differences of the gene sequences that control the development of each. They can show how the DNA sequence differences and similarities between the genes involved in limb development in birds, reptiles, and fish enable us to date their common ancestors and say something about how the homologies and the differences among the bones of their different limbs are due to differences in DNA sequences. In the fruit fly *Drosophila*, it is known that a small mutation in the right gene is all it takes to turn its antennae into a pair of legs. Increasingly, molecular biology is able to uncover the tracks evolution has hidden, so that adaptations begin to look expectable instead of miraculous.

What about directionality? The notion of cumulative change might seem to suggest a kind of directedness to the process of adaptation, a drive toward greater complexity. In fact, however, it is an open question whether there is in evolution any preferred tendency for complexity to build up. What is clear, however, is that nothing in the current understanding of natural selection predicts a drive toward greater complexity. Increases occur, but in our fascination with them we tend to forget the frequent decreases. Winged animals become flightless, as in the evolution of penguins. Animals with walking limbs lose them when they return to the water, as in the evolution of whales (from a common ancestor with hippopotamuses!). Complexity is reversible, and selection is expected to favor decreases whenever opportunities for adaptive simplicity arise . . . which could be often!

Thus, the randomness of variation is not a problem for selection theory. Nor is the buildup that seems to underlie complex adaptation. Given random variation and environmental filtration, plus at least occasional accumulation, the evolution of structures such as wings and eyes is not surprising. (As we shall see, the big problem for the theory of natural selection is not an adaptation like the eye but an adaptation like sex. What is it about the environment of living things that makes sex adaptive?) That said, it must also be pointed out that, as a cause of adaptation, natural selection has its limitations.

Evolutionary biologists sometimes describe the challenges that the environment presents to organisms as "design problems," though they recognize that the expression is even more misleading than "natural selection." (If Darwin is right, there is no designer who sets the "design problems" or solves them. So, the expression is a metaphorical way of identifying a dimension of the organism's environment that poses a challenge to its survival and reproduction.) Being fittest is a matter of a line of descent solving these "design problems" better than its competing lineages. But the best among competing solutions to a design problem does not have to be, and rarely is, a complete, or elegant, or even a very good solution. Variations that arise will often be "quick and dirty" solutions to design problems, advantageous for the moment but perhaps not in the long run—and perhaps not as advantageous as other possible variants that have not arisen yet but that might "solve" the design problem better. A "better but slower to emerge" solution may yet appear, but if it does, it will have to compete with the quick and dirty one. Often too the quick and dirty solution just makes the better one unreachable.

Examples of such satisfactory but imperfect solutions to design problems are not hard to find. The giraffe's long neck is adapted to browsing at treetop levels, but it makes drinking difficult; it would be easy to dream up an anatomical structure that would solve both problems at once. Or consider the relatively poor design reflected in the frequency with which we choke on food or drink. Did the alimentary canal have to intersect the respiratory system?

The classic example of an imperfection is the "blind spot" in the human eye. A simple experiment reveals it: hold a piece of paper with a black dot on it in front of one eye and cover the other; move it until the dot disappears from your visual field. Near the center of one's visual field, where one would suppose vision is and needs to be most acute, there is no vision at all. This is owing to the fact that the optic nerve is connected to the retina, not from the back but from the front, and then bends around 180 degrees to connect up to the brain behind, passing right through the visual field. This strikingly bad piece of "design" is presumably a vestige of a much earlier quick and dirty solution to the problem of vision in vertebrates. It is certainly not essential to high-resolution vision as it did not arise in the largely independent evolution of eyes in molluscs—squids, octopi, and their relatives. Why was the attachment of the optic nerve not later reversed in vertebrate evolution? Perhaps the necessary variation did not arise. Alternatively, it could be that the many parts of the vertebrate eye have been selected for compatibility with one another, and their mutual dependencies are now too deeply entrenched to permit major rearrangements, even when big rearrangements would offer significant improvements. The quick and dirty solution excluded the slow and elegant one. The lesson is that while natural selection explains adaptations, apparent perfections of design, it also explains some of the imperfections of design we see in organisms.

Is Darwinism the only game in town?

So natural selection explains the appearance of purposiveness of adaptation. And this is not a process involving an active, literal process of "selection." Rather it is the passive filtering out of the maladapted and the less well adapted. Also, natural selection operates on random variation, but selection is not itself a random process. It produces adaptation to a local environment or, speaking metaphorically again, solutions to "design problems." In other words, it filters available variations for the best quick and often dirty solution to the organism's present design problems, a solution in which the good, or the merely "good enough," is sometimes the enemy of the best.

The scientific evidence that supports the theory of natural selection is diverse and immense, direct and indirect, from laboratories and from the field. But in addition to all the evidence biologists have amassed in favor of the theory, there is another powerful argument for it. It is one that biologists are reluctant to rely on and philosophers hesitant to articulate. It is, however, important to state this almost a priori argument in favor of the theory of natural selection's explanation of adaptation. Physical science provides an account of the origin and development of the universe, from the Big Bang onward, in which true teleology, purposes, and goals have no role, at least outside of human purposes and goals. And future causation has no role at all. The methods of physical science excluded explanation by future causes long before it was shown to be physically impossible by Einstein's special theory of relativity. The method and the theory place a consistency constraint on the rest of science, including biology. Either biology must honor this prohibition against future causation or it must take a stand against physics and deny the truth of its most well-established theories while rejecting one of its most fundamental methodological rules. Naturally, this is something no biologist is willing to do.

Are there alternatives to natural selection as the cause of adaptation? Two hundred years ago, the French biologist Jean-Baptiste Lamarck (1809) offered a theory based on use and disuse, accepted by some before Darwin (and to some extent by Darwin himself). Consider again the neck of the giraffe. Lamarck's theory was that from an early age, each giraffe was stretching its neck to reach the tasty leaves at the tops of trees, and that a lifetime of stretching not only lengthened the giraffe's neck but the longer neck was inherited by its offspring. Enough generations of stretching and its transmission and, *voila*, long-necked giraffes. This theory has the virtue, like Darwin's, of offering a straightforward account of adaptation based entirely on past causation. The disadvantages are: there is no evidence in its favor and plenty of evidence against it. Obvious evidence against Lamarck is all around us in human history. For example, in China girls' feet were bound for millennia, without any effect on their size at birth or their size if left unbound. Equally important, Lamarck's theory requires that there be a causal chain from the act of neck stretching in some giraffe parent to that parent's hereditary material (in modern terms, its DNA), so that the parent can produce an offspring with a longer neck. But there is no evidence whatever that use or disuse of any part of the body has any effect on the nucleotide sequence in the body's germ cells. Accordingly, in addition to lacking any empirical support whatever, Lamarckism is incompatible with the modern genetic theory of heredity, which is itself strongly confirmed. So, it seems we can rule out any sort of environmental fit as the source of heritable variation, and hence we can rule out Lamarckism.

There are other in-principle alternatives. For example, the adaptedness of organisms to their environment here on Earth could have been engineered by a species of technologically sophisticated aliens. However ludicrous it sounds, we cannot rule such an alternative on purely physical grounds. That is to say this alternative does not contradict any known physical laws. But as these aliens are themselves highly enough adapted to engineer adapted organisms here on Earth, the question immediately arises of how *their* adaptations—including superior intelligence and sophisticated technology— arose on whatever world those aliens inhabit. One possibility is the operation of a Lamarckian mechanism on their world. Suppose it were to turn out that intelligent life emerged elsewhere in the universe owing to Lamarckian mechanisms in which use and disuse of traits to solve "design problems" caused changes in hereditary material that controlled the character of traits in the next generation. Such a mechanism would of course greatly expedite evolution and explain why the aliens were so far advanced as to be able to engineer adaptation on our planet. A Lamarckian genetic mechanism would of course be an extremely elegant adaptation. Instead of quick and dirty temporary or merely satisfactory solutions to design problems, it would swiftly provide extremely efficient ones.

But the existence of so perfect an adaptation as a Lamarckian genetic mechanism would inevitably raise the question of how *it* could have emerged in a world without purposes, goals, ends, or future causes or, of course, a designer to put it in place. Some philosophers and biologists will argue that once we exclude future causation and God, the only causal process that could put such an elegant adaptation in place is the very same one that biologists believe put the quick and dirty adaptations in place in our world: Darwinian natural selection. More generally, it will be argued, once we exclude God and future purposes, the explanation for the existence of any particular adaptation must invoke causal processes operating on prior traits that are less well adapted (or perhaps not adaptive at all) than the one the existence of which is to be explained. Otherwise, our explanation will beg the question of how adaptation is possible at all. The great appeal of Darwinian natural selection is that it honors this requirement on explanations of adaptation. The question is whether any other mechanism could do so.

Suppose we impose this requirement on explanations. Then even if Lamarckian mechanisms actually did operate on Earth or, indeed, even if the Earth's flora and fauna were the result of extraterrestrial aliens' gardening and zoo-keeping, the ultimate source of adaptation would still have to be blind variation and selective retention! For if the extraterrestrials' traits (like the ability to cultivate terrestrial flora and fauna) are adaptive for them, we will still need to explain their traits causally. Further, such a Lamarckian mechanism is itself so wonderfully adaptive that its emergence requires nonadaptive, purely causal explanation as well. What, other than Darwinism, could produce it? It's not hard to imagine a hereditary mechanism arising without natural selection in which use and disuse have some arbitrary effect on the hereditary material. But it is much harder to see how a mechanism could arise in which the effect is *adaptive*, again without natural selection. In sum, Darwinism seems to be "the only game in town," not just the best explanation of adaptation but the only physically possible purely causal explanation, the only one consistent with what we already know about the physical laws (the laws of special and general relativity, quantum mechanics, thermodynamics) that govern the universe. Of course biologists have no need to adopt so strong an argument for Darwinian theory. Indeed, some will want to treat the theory as a much more limited one, one that makes claims only about the Earth over the last 3.5 billion years. As we shall see, this limitation of the theory's domain to Earth has some advantages and also presents some difficulties. If the theory is understood as a specific claim about the natural history of the Earth, then the evidence needed to test it would be finite, and we could, at least in principle, establish its truth (or falsehood). On the other hand, limiting the theory in this way saps it of some of its explanatory power, even for local adaptation on Earth.

Of course, arguing that the only way adaptation could have arisen is by natural selection is not the same thing as claiming that adaptive evolution was inevitable on Earth or anywhere else. Adaptive evolution by natural selection might never have happened, if the environment never stayed constant long enough to give blind variation a chance to generate adaptations that could be "selected for" or, on the other hand, if the environment changed too little or too slowly. Nor would much adaptive evolution have happened if the rate of introduction of new variation was much lower, or much higher, than it is. So in this sense adaptive evolution is not an inevitable feature of any universe that obeys our physical and chemical laws. And of course evolution here on Earth might slow down or even come to a halt if the tempo of variation changed radically. So the claim that adaptive evolution by natural selection is "the only game in town" is not a claim that adaptive evolution was inevitable. Rather it is a claim that *when it occurred*, it happened only through random variation and environmental filtration.

Though it is tempting to hold that natural selection is the only possible way that adaptation could have arisen, there are reasons to be a little wary of this claim. Recall that Kant, the eighteenth century philosopher of science who denied that there would be a Newton for the blade of grass, believed that he could show that Newtonian mechanics was "the only game in town." That is to say Kant sought to explain the universality of Newton's laws by showing that they are a body of necessary truths, that the universe could not behave in accordance with any laws other than the ones Newton discovered. To show this Kant tried to derive Newton's laws about the universe from principles of logic that govern human thought. Kant's derivations are invalid. What is worse (he would have been embarrassed to learn), about 100 years after he thought he had proved their necessity, Newton's laws were shown to be false—good approximations, but strictly speaking false in light of the theory of relativity and quantum mechanics. The lesson of Kant's failure is cautionary. We cannot imagine, and have no evidence for, an Earthly or extra-terrestrial alternative to the process of adaptation Darwin hypothesized, but perhaps we should not assert categorically that there is none.

The reigning confidence in Darwin's mechanism for the explanation of the appearance of purpose has led psychologists, sociologists, anthropologists, economists, and other students of human behavior, action, and institutions to invoke his theory to explain apparently purposive phenomena in all their disciplines. The twentieth century psychologist B.F. Skinner suggested that operant conditioning in animals and humans, which is known to be able to produce highly purposive behavior, is just blind variation and selective retention applied *ontogenetically* instead of *phylogenetically*. That is to say it is a mechanism that builds up learned behavior in an animal's lifetime and especially its early development (ontogeny), not just in the course of its evolution (phylogeny). Similarly, neuroscientists (such as Edelman and Kandel) have proposed that, in development, the neural connections in the brain are a result of random generation of connections and selective retention of functionally appropriate ones, the connections that allow the brain to work properly. And a "blind variation and selective retention" mechanism has also been used in the development of artificial intelligence programs (e.g. genetic algorithms) to write programs to solve problems in computer science in cases in which the computer scientist does not know how to proceed.

Darwinian thinking is not obligatory is these realms. Human behavior has many sources other than conditioning. The connections of the brain might instead have formed in a highly directed way (as a result of selection in the past, of course), rather than by blind variation and selective retention. Computer scientists can apply their own native purposiveness (itself the product of selection in the past, of course) to solve problems directly, without any Darwinian computer intermediate. But Darwinism—while clearly not the only game in town in these fields—has nevertheless generated some fascinating possibilities, such is the power of the principle. Small wonder that Darwin's great defender, Thomas Huxley, when he first read *On the Origin of Species* in 1860 is supposed to have exclaimed, "How stupid of me not to have thought of that!"

Philosophical problems of Darwinism

The extension of the theory of natural selection beyond biology to all of the behavioral and social sciences has been controversial. When added to the controversies that Darwinism has provoked at home in biology, it should not be surprising that the theory has been subjected to close scrutiny, both scientific and philosophical. What are these controversies and why should they concern philosophers?

One is about how much of biology the theory can explain. Biologists all agree that it explains adaptation. But the question remains whether every feature of every plant and animal that has emerged in the natural history of this planet is an adaptation, or even whether most are. Some biologists think that the explanatory power of the theory of natural selection is quite limited. It might explain appendages in animals, but it is not so obvious that it explains bilateral symmetry, the similarity between left and right sides of many animals. Does it explain why some rhinoceros species have two horns and others just one? Does it explain the Cambrian explosion, a geologically short period of time 500 million years ago in which most of the major modern groups of animals arose? Does it explain why there are both sexual and asexual species? Does it explain human behavior and human social organization? The debate about how many of the characteristics of organisms are biological adaptations is implicitly one about the range of the theory's application. Equivalently, it is a debate about the limits of selective explanation.

Further, there is a universally acknowledged chance element in biology, often called "drift." The role of drift has been a vexed question among biologists for almost a century, and one to which philosophers have devoted themselves as well. And yet another group of critics is concerned with the domain of the theory, those who question its application to human beings. In particular, some of those who favor radical social change think that adaptationist explanations of human traits such as gender and sex roles, intelligence, violence, and criminality somehow undermine their preferred social programs. These are all disputes about the domain of the theory's application. To settle them, we first need a statement of the theory itself that everyone will accept. There can be no agreement on a theory's range of application so long as there is no agreement on precisely what the theory says. And here again philosophers can help, disambiguating the theory of natural selection, identifying its logical implications for the various domains to which the theory's application is disputed.

So there are those who deny that the theory explains everything in biology. And then there are those who deny that it explains anything, an eclectic group including mainly religious thinkers but also some respected scientists. Some of these critics have strong motives to undermine the theory, many of the devout because it threatens the view that life was created by God to fulfill a divine plan. For them as we shall see, natural selection has a feature that makes it completely unsuitable as a tool for God to use in creating the Earth's flora and fauna. And some contend that the theory is somehow logically or conceptually defective, and therefore unacceptable.

Perhaps the most famous charge is that the theory is a trivial tautology, vitiated by a circular definition which deprives it of all explanatory force. These opponents claim that the theory has no domain of explanatory application, that it can be refuted and dismissed even before any evidence has been examined, owing to purely logical or methodological defects. The charge focuses on the concept of fitness and a bumper-sticker-length summary phrase for natural selection, coined by the nineteenth century philosopher, Herbert Spencer, "survival of the fittest." The theory explains evolution as the result of the increase in the population of "fitter" variants, whose fitter ancestors survived longer in competition with less fit conspecifics and therefore had more opportunities to reproduce than the less fit. Or, more briefly, the theory says that those who are fitter are the ones that survive and reproduce more. But, the critic says, when evolutionary biologists define fitness, they can do so only in terms of survival and reproduction, and therefore we can substitute "survive and reproduce" for "are fitter." And, in that case, the theory says merely that those who survive and reproduce are the ones that survive and reproduce, a completely untestable claim. And therefore the theory of natural selection can no more explain any actual case of evolution than the statement that all bachelors are unmarried adults can explain why Sir Elton John was unmarried (at the time he was still a bachelor). Presumably the fact that he was then a bachelor simply redescribes this fact about him in fewer words than that he was then an unmarried male, and because it is simply another description of the same fact about Sir Elton, it cannot explain that fact. Explanations must adduce facts that go beyond the facts they explain. Otherwise "self-explanation" would suffice. Why X? Because X. Accordingly, unless evolutionary biologists or philosophers of biology can provide a noncircular definition of fitness, the theory of natural selection explains nothing biological. As we shall see, it is by no means easy to provide such a definition.

Finally, we need to understand the explanatory and evidential relations between the theory of natural selection and other theories in the natural sciences, in particular those of physics and chemistry. To see why, consider the treatment accorded the theory of natural selection by nineteenth century physics. In the 1880s Lord Kelvin argued that Darwin's theory of natural selection and the chronology of life's appearance based on it must be false, because the evolution of modern organisms would have required—by the estimates of that time—at least hundreds of millions of years. Could the Earth be that old? Given the best available account of combustion, Kelvin calculated, the sun—and therefore the Earth—could be no more than 40 million years old. Ergo, evolution by Darwinian mechanisms could be excluded by their incompatibility with the best available physics. Kelvin's argument posed a serious threat to the theory, not removed finally until the late 1940s by Hans Bethe's Nobel Prize-winning account of the thermonuclear reactions that power the sun's combustion, which increased the calculated age of the solar system, and therefore the Earth, by a factor of 100. The point is that Darwinian theory needs to be logically and empirically consistent with theory in the physical sciences. Further, some would argue that if it can be grounded in physical science, explained by or derived from physical theories, then this would provide the strongest possible support for Darwinism. For then all of the evidence for the best current theories in physics and chemistry would count as evidence for the theory of natural selection too.

But establishing whether the theory is consistent with, or derivable from, physical theories again requires that we have an agreed upon, clear, and explicit understanding of exactly what the theory claims. Providing such an account of the exact content of the theory of natural selection is a central concern of the philosophy of biology.

So quite a number of questions hover around the theory of natural selection. There are questions about whether the theory is true and nontautologous. There are questions about scope, about how much of the biology of organisms it explains. And then there are questions about the relationship of the theory to theories in other fields, especially in physics and chemistry. Finally, there are questions about whether the theory, even if well supported by data and theory in the natural sciences, has implications for the social and behavioral sciences. All of these require that we get straight about the meaning and structure of the theory of natural selection. And this is a job for philosophers.

Summary

Organisms show such pervasive adaptation to their environments that in explaining them it is hard to escape the notion of purpose: plants have chlorophyll *in order to* produce starch. But we have seen that a world of physical causes such as Newton described has no room for real ends, goals, or purposes, at least none that cause the events that lead up to their attainment. The future cannot cause the past. Accordingly, biology needs an alternative account of how its "teleology" is possible, or it needs to banish teleology from its descriptions and explanations.

Before Darwin this problem was solved by appeal to the existence of an omnipotent and benevolent designer, God. The weaknesses of this appeal were known: lack of predictive power, absence of independent evidence for God's existence, incoherences in the theist's definition of God. But there was no alternative explanation of the adaptedness of living things.

Darwin's theory provides a far more scientifically attractive theory, one free from the specific weaknesses of theism, and easy to link up with the rest of science. It provides a purely causal, nonteleological explanation of biological processes and structures that exploits what physical science tells us about them. But Darwin's theory has its own conceptual problems, to which must be added the common misunderstandings of the theory. Solving these problems and dissipating these misunderstandings is crucial to understanding the nature of biology.

Among the misunderstandings of Darwin's theory are the ideas that evolution enables us to identify organisms such as humans as "higher" and others such as yeast as "lower," that there has been persistent progress in evolution from more primitive to more sophisticated, that natural selection is powerful enough to provide perfect solutions to "design problems," and that evolution by natural selection is a wholly random process that miraculously and improbably produces order from disorder.

Among the criticisms it faces are the claims that it is no more empirically testable than the theory of God's design that it replaces, that it leaves unexplained various imperfections and defects among biological creatures, and that it is hard to reconcile with other more established parts of science such as physics. These are serious problems but they are ones that biologists typically ignore. We will make it our business to either answer these criticisms or show why they must be taken seriously.

Suggestions for further reading

There is no substitute for reading Darwin's own words. *On the Origin of Species* is, as he put it, "one long argument," and readers always find insights and evidence that no summary or textbook version of the theory can provide. His complete works are available online at http://darwin-online.org. uk/contents.html. The first edition of the *Origin* is "pure" Darwin; later editions added qualifications, and even an invocation of God in the book's last paragraph that was not there in the first edition. Modern "ultra-Darwinist" expositions of the theory of natural selection include Dawkins's *Blind Watchmaker*, and Dennett's *Darwin's Dangerous Idea*. These works may be contrasted with the many scientific and popular works of Stephen J. Gould, in whose view Darwin is far less univocal and more qualified in his commitment to natural selection as the agency shaping evolution. This matter is taken up at length in the next chapter. Gould's magnum opus is *The Structure of Evolutionary Theory*. More popular expositions of his view can be found in *Ever Since Darwin* and *The Panda's Thumb*.

Ernst Mayr, a renowned evolutionary biologist, wrote a number of histories of biology, and especially evolution, and participated in many of the controversies among philosophers and biologists over his 100-year lifetime. *The Growth of Biological Thought* develops many of his views about Darwinism while tracing its prehistory as well as its post-Darwinian fate. Other important works on the reception and interpretation of the theory of natural selection by philosophers of biology include Michael Ghiselin's *The Triumph of the Darwinian Method*, and Michael Ruse's *The Darwinian Revolution*.

Jonathan Hodge and Gregory Radick's *The Cambridge Companion to Darwin* contains a collection of papers by leading contributors to the philosophy of biology identifying the major implications of Darwin's theory for a range of philosophical issues.

William Paley's *Natural Theology: Or Evidences of the Existence and Attributes of the Deity Collected from the Appearances of Nature* represented the best explanation of adaptation prior to Darwin, an inductive argument for the existence of a Designer. Darwin studied these volumes carefully as a university student. Excerpts from this work are widely available in introductory anthologies of philosophy.

Many academic journals publish papers on Darwin, his theory, and its philosophical significance. The ones focusing steadily on these subjects include *Biology and Philosophy* and *Studies in the History and Philosophy of the Biological and Biomedical Sciences*.

2 Biological laws and theories

Overview

Sciences are characterized by their distinctive theories, the phenomena the theories explain and predict, and the central concepts, formulae, models, and research programs that these theories motivate. The revolutions in physical science that take their names from scientists, all the way from Newton to Einstein, began with the discovery of laws of nature, or else close approximations to them. So we might reasonably expect that the core of Darwin's revolution that made biology a science is to be found in the laws that constitute his theory.

But, as we shall see in this chapter, identifying biological laws is not easy. Indeed, it appears to be extremely difficult to locate any such laws in the discipline that have the features that we recognize in chemical and physical laws. This should immediately make us suspicious that biology is "different" from the physical sciences, different in its explanations, in its relation to the evidence that supports its explanatory theories, and in the way in which its development is driven by theory. A few philosophers and more than one physical scientist have concluded that biology's differences from their disciplines are defects to be repaired. On the other hand, far more philosophers, and almost all biologists, have concluded that the difficulty of identifying laws in their discipline shows how much more difficult and different it is from the physical sciences. In any case, what biological science, and especially evolutionary biology, do have are a set of very important mathematical models, with names famous in biology attached to them: Mendel's "laws," Fisher's sex ratio model, the Hardy–Weinberg equilibrium. Whether these models can or do the work that laws do elsewhere in science is a matter we will explore in this chapter.

What about Darwinian theory? If Darwin made a science, as we argued in Chapter 1, then surely his theory embodies one or more laws of natural selection. Much of this chapter is devoted to considering why it is difficult to draw such a conclusion. And—as we will see in later chapters—many other issues in the philosophy of biology have their origins in the difficulty in locating such laws in the theory of natural selection.

Causation, laws, and biological generalizations

The theory of natural selection is now well understood. And the philosophy of science provides at least some account of what a scientific theory should look like, about what form it should take, as well as a philosophical thesis about why theories in science should take this form. We ought, therefore, to be able to render the theory of natural selection into this form, to make it a good scientific theory by the standards of the rest of science. If we cannot, we face a Hobson's choice: give up the notion that natural selection is a theory like others in natural science, or give up this notion of what a theory is that we have drawn from the other natural sciences. To many philosophers, neither alternative is attractive. Either way we invite challenges to the scientific status, evidence, and meaning of natural selection.

The word "theory" of course has a variety of different meanings. Sometimes it is used to mean a speculative hypothesis, as in "that's only a theory." As the term is employed in science, however, a theory need not be in much doubt, witness "the theory of relativity" or "quantum theory," two theories in which scientists generally have enormous confidence. As the term is used in physical science, a theory is a body of scientific laws that work together to explain phenomena in a well-defined domain. For example, Newton's three laws of motion together with the inverse square law of gravitational attraction suffice to explain (and predict) motion—velocity and acceleration—of uncharged bodies in a vacuum. To explain and predict the behavior of charged bodies in a vacuum, in the presence of an electric field, we need to add Coulomb's inverse square law of electrostatic force. As we add other conditions, we can add more laws that govern the operation of these conditions on bodies.

Why are theories in physical science sets of *laws*? The standard answer in the philosophy of science begins with the assumption articulated in Chapter 1 that scientific explanation proceeds by identifying causes. It adds to this assumption that causal relations are matters of lawful regularity: every cause gives rise to its effect through the operation of one or more general laws. These laws may be unknown, as in the case of historical explanation, such as the explanation of why the British entered World War I. Or they may be well known, as in the case of the explanation of an eclipse. Or they may be well known but too numerous or complex to bother mentioning. We could explain the flight of a bird as the result of its flapping its wings, leaving implicit the discussion of the physical laws involved in the wing and air motions that produce flight. Why insist that every cause–effect relation reflect the operation of one or more laws, known or unknown? It was the eighteenth century philosopher David Hume who first gave a compelling argument for this claim.

Hume (1738) argued that when we examine the apparently most familiar causal sequences we know, say the extinguishing of a flame when a match drops into water or, for that matter, the experience of willing your left hand to raise and its rising, all we ever see, hear, smell, feel, or, more generally, *experience*, is the first event followed by the second. It's certainly not the case that the first event, the cause, *had to* bring about the second, the effect, not as a matter of logic anyway. Logic does not require that water extinguish a flame. Indeed, so far as logic is concerned, a flame could just as well cause water to explode the way it might cause gasoline to explode. Think about it this way: to say "That bachelor is married" violates logic. But saying "The flame caused the water to explode" is another matter altogether. There is no logical contradiction, just a violation of physics.

So why does fire cause gasoline to explode and not water? To say it is because gasoline is flammable, and water is not does not help much. For to say that gasoline is flammable and water is not is just to say that vapor from the former burns rapidly when it comes in contact with fire and water vapor doesn't burn at all. These are of course valid generalizations about fire, gasoline, water, and their vapors, but they do not really illuminate the nature of the causal process. Rather, flammability and its opposite are just restatements of our observations.

Take a simple case of causation that we think we understand well, a billiard ball colliding with another and the second moving away. Compare this obviously causal sequence with a purely accidental sequence, such as your taking off your hat immediately before someone asks you what time it is. What is the difference? It seems to be that the former sequence occurs over and over again in our experience, and in that of others, whereas the latter does not. In fact, you have taken your hat off frequently in the past without immediately being asked the time, and you expect that you will do so again in the future. But you never expect the collision of billiard balls to be followed by anything other than at least one of them moving away. We say there is a "constant conjunction" between the two events. The impact of one billiard ball on a second is constantly conjoined with the departure of the second. Now you might think that the difference has something to do with the availability of lower level causes in the billiard ball case and its unavailability in the hat and time case. You might think that the billiard ball case is truly causal because there is something special, some logical necessity, about the microscopic causes acting at the atomic and molecular level. But in fact, there is not. A submicroscopic examination of the atoms or even subatomic particles that constitute the billiard balls at the moment of collision would reveal nothing more than the motion of some atoms or particles followed by the motion of others, in other words, constant conjunction of distinct events at the atomic level.

So we explain the behavior of colliding billiard balls as the result of causes, and causes necessarily refer to constant conjunctions of events. And constant conjunctions are what laws record. So if explanation requires causes, then it would seem to require laws.

What about singular events? Seemingly we can explain the sinking of the RMS *Titanic* without recourse to constant conjunctions, indeed, seemingly, we *must* do so. After all, the striking of an iceberg by the *Titanic* was a singular event, one that prior to April 14, 1912 had never occurred in the history of the universe and will never occur again. And seemingly for such singular events, there can be no law-like regularity, no constant conjunctions. However, a full explanation of the event actually does involve constant conjunctions and laws. The known laws would include the many laws of physics involved in the collision, the breaching of the hull, the movement of water through the breach, and so on. The unknown ones would include the laws governing the brains and minds of the ship's captain and crew who chose the particular course that led to the collision. The point is that explanations of singular events, no matter how bizarrely improbable and unrepeatable, involve lawful regularities, even if only implicitly.

Hume's insight that causation is a law-governed sequence has had a profound effect on the philosophical analysis of scientific methods. For the sciences are all self-consciously causal inquiries, and that includes both theoretical and experimental science. Therefore, they seek laws. We can go further yet. Laws are required for reliable prediction: without lawful regularities, there can be no prediction. And laws allow technology to advance in a systematic way. If we set out to build a better mousetrap, we need to assume and to know the regularities of the materials we use and of their interactions.

Accordingly, if evolutionary biology is a science, then it is also causal inquiry and it needs to uncover and exploit laws. One might suspect ahead of time that the relevant laws will be biological ones. The relevant laws of physics are physical. Those of chemistry are chemical. Surely the laws we use to explain biology will be biological laws. We shall see.

There are many statements about biology that might be considered to be laws with more or less plausibility. Beginning at the lowest level of generality, there are claims about particular species:

- Robins' eggs are blue.
- Humans have 23 pairs of chromosomes.

Few are likely to identify these general claims as laws of nature. But there are certainly more general claims, about particular groups of species, or higher taxa:

- Snakes have scales.
- Mammals have four-chambered hearts.

Then there are apparent regularities that cut across higher taxa:

- Arctic birds and mammels tend to have lower surface-area-to-volume ratios than non-Arctic species (because lower ratios of surface to volume reduce heat loss).

- Evolution is irreversible, also called Dollo's law. (It asserts, for example, that if species A evolves into species B, it will never evolve back into species A.)

And of course there are claims alleged to be true of all biological systems, such as:

All genes are composed of nucleic acids.

And the central dogma of biology, enunciated by Francis Crick (1958):

Genetic information moves from DNA to RNA to proteins but never from proteins backwards to the genetic material.

There are statements that biologists call laws, such as Mendel's laws of segregation and independent assortment, and the Hardy–Weinberg Law:

Mendel's law of segregation In a parent, the two alleles for each character separate in the production of gametes, so that only one is transmitted to each individual in the next generation.

Mendel's law of independent assortment The genes for each character are transmitted independently to the next generation, so that the appearance of one character in an offspring will not affect the appearance of another character.

Hardy-Weinberg law In an infinite, randomly mating population, and in the absence of mutation, immigration, emigration, and natural selection, gene frequencies and the distribution of genotypes remain constant from generation to generation.

Apparently, there are also laws derived from the theory of natural selection, such as the competitive exclusion principle:

In the long run, only one species can occupy a given niche.

And of course there are various versions of the fundamental principles of natural selection itself such as one couched in terms of replicators—things, such as genes, that make highly accurate copies of themselves most of the time, and interactors—things, such as bodies, that the replicators "build" to assure their survival and copying opportunities (Dawkins 1989):

If there are replicators and interactors, then the differential reproduction of interactors causes the differential perpetuation of the replicators.

Or the more well known but controversial principle of natural selection:

> PNS If x is fitter than y in environment E, then, probably, x will have more descendants than y in E, where x, y may be individual genes, genotypes, organisms, groups, species, or perhaps other biological entities.

So, it looks like biology is chock-a-block with generalizations and laws that reflect the operation of causes in some cases and in other cases enable us to identify causes and so to explain (and sometimes predict) biological processes in the same way the laws of chemistry and physics enable us to do so.

But there are serious problems facing the claim that any one of these generalizations is a law, as law has traditionally been understood in the philosophy of science. According to some biologists and philosophers of science, seeing why reveals a great deal about the differences between biology and the physical sciences. According to others, the failure of these examples to satisfy so called "standard" conditions for being a law (that have been drawn from philosophers' reflections on physical laws) forces a reappraisal of the philosopher's theory of what a law is. As noted in the introduction, the direction of influence between biology and philosophy is a two-way street!

Could there be laws about species?

Several important features of laws prove troublesome for our examples. First, laws can always be expressed as conditional, "If P then (always) Q" or "Whenever P, then Q" statements, or equivalently to the form "All Fs are Gs" (meaning that if anything is an F, then it is a G, or whenever there is an F, there is a G, etc.). In the if–then version, P is called the antecedent, Q is called the consequent, and they are both filled in by sentences. In the "all Fs are Gs" form, the F's and G's are events, things, processes, properties, etc. Second, a law is supposed to be universally true, true everywhere and always, like Newton's law of gravitation, $F = g \times m_1 m_2/d^2$, or Einstein's principle of special relativity that the speed of light in a vacuum is constant in all inertial reference frames. If a law must obtain anywhere its antecedent conditions obtain, then it cannot really mention any particular place, time, or thing. For no particular place, time, or thing has any causal power just in virtue of its spatiotemporal location. This, at any rate, is something that physics seems to have taught us. The universe is uniform in its fundamental causal processes. There are no places or times in which different laws of nature obtain. There could of course be, say, one and only one black hole in the entire universe, but its behavior will be the result of the operation of laws that would affect other black holes, if they existed, anywhere in the universe.

So, there are no laws about Napoleon Bonaparte, or laws true only on the moon, or laws that obtain only during the Jurassic period. Of course Napoleon may combine properties, such as ambition, intelligence, and ruthlessness, never before or since brought together in exactly the same proportions, and these may explain his career. But it is the specific proportions that together with psychological laws (if there are any) explain his actions, not the laws alone. For there to be a universal law about a particular person, he or she would have to have special causal powers that nothing else in the universe has *or could possibly have*. Of course, if there were another person in the universe who combined exactly the same amount of ambition, intelligence, and ruthlessness as Napoleon, he would presumably have to behave in the same way as Napoleon if he were placed under the same conditions. This is just because if there are real psychological laws, they have to work the same way everywhere in the world where their antecedents obtain. The only way they could do this is if their antecedents do not make reference to particular places, times, or things.

One can see that this immediately makes a problem for most of our presumed biological laws. Laws about particular species, even laws about sets of species, laws about higher taxonomic units, laws about genes, about their composition, and how they work, all explicitly mention or implicitly presuppose the existence of particular things, places, or times, namely objects here on Earth. As such they cannot be laws. At most they can be statements about objects and events in a particular stretch of time in the history of the Earth. As such they will be no different from statements of European history such as "All feudal systems practice serfdom," a statement that might look like a law but is not one. (Notice that the point here is slightly different from the earlier claim about singular objects and events, such as the sinking of the *Titanic*. Earlier we said that singular objects and events require laws to explain them. Here the claim is that singular objects and events offer no universal regularities and therefore cannot give rise to laws.)

To see why the vast majority of our biological examples cannot be laws anything like those of physics, consider this one in detail: "Robins' eggs are blue," or more formally, "if something is a robin's egg, then it will also be blue." Could this be a law of nature, one that reports a causal relation, a constant conjunction, between being a robin and having blue eggs? Well, of course, as a generalization it is false, because mutation, the nutrients a robin feeds on, or other conditions may result in robins laying eggs of other colors. Since a natural law must be true, this one cannot be a strict law. But we should not get too hung up on the demand for absolute unexceptional truth at the outset or we will never discover the true natural laws. Let's coin the term "scientific laws" to label our best current guesses as to what the true natural laws really are. So, given mutant and otherwise abnormal robins, we might try again, proposing that the relevant scientific law is: "*Normal* robins' eggs are blue." One thing that we must guard against immediately is the temptation to turn "Normal robins' eggs are blue" into a definition, by defining a normal robin as a bird that, among other things, lays blue eggs. With robin so defined, of course, the law becomes true by definition, just like "A bachelor is an unmarried male" is true by definition. But laws cannot be definitions or the consequences of definitions. The reasons are clear. A law reports a causal relation, and causal relations do not hold by convention or as a matter of linguistic stipulation as definitions do. For a law to tell us anything new about the world, to explain something, it must be possible to *imagine* that it is false. Consider for example, Newton's inverse square law of gravitational attraction. Is it *imaginable* that it is wrong? Certainly. It is easy to imagine a universe in which gravity does not weaken exactly as the square of the distance between bodies, but instead as $d^{2.000000000000000000003512904}$ or some other value. Similarly, as Hume pointed out, it is imaginable that a lit match will ignite water instead of being extinguished by it. By contrast, it is not imaginable that a bachelor be married! The reason is that we have decided to use the description "bachelor" as a label for unmarried adult males. And so long as we stick to that decision, its opposite cannot be imagined to hold at the same time.

So definitions are matters of convention. They cannot be contradicted by the world and do not tell us anything about the world. And therefore they cannot explain. The fact that someone is an unmarried male cannot be explained by the fact that he is a bachelor. Another way to see this is to notice that no observation of events in the world could lead us to doubt that all bachelors are unmarried men. When the well-known former bachelor Sir Elton John married, that did not cast the slightest doubt on the statement that all bachelors are unmarried. The reason is that, as a definition, the statement has no explanatory power for particular facts in the world. But a law must have such power. If it is a law that normal robins' eggs are blue, then that must explain, at least in part, why a particular bird—independently identified as a robin—has blue eggs. Presumably there has to be some contingent fact about normal robins, such that they produce eggs with a composition such that they reflect light of wavelengths characteristic of blue things. This would make "robins' eggs are blue" an explanatory law. But we rob it of its explanatory power if we define robin as a bird that lays eggs of this color.

So let us assume that we do not make that definitional move, that we define robins in such a way that does not include laying blue eggs. Then, could it be a law that all normal robins' eggs are blue? Well, what is a robin? It is any member of the species *Turdus migratorius* (American robin). And what is the species *Turdus migratorius*? Here we find more trouble. Suppose we define the species by pointing to a specimen. Well, aside from the fact that few robins will share all the properties of that specimen, a specimen is a spatiotemporally restricted particular object (perhaps a stuffed carcass in a museum, or a zoo animal). But laws cannot mention or implicitly refer to particular places, times, or things. Suppose we define the species *Turdus migratorius* in terms of location in the evolutionary phylogeny of birds, that is, by reference to its place in the evolution of birds generally. Again our generalization would be about a particular place and time, the Earth during the time birds evolved. Further, what is a species? Suppose we adopt a widely accepted definition attributed to the important evolutionary biologist Ernst Mayr: a species is an interbreeding population reproductively isolated from other populations. Then we could define *Turdus migratorius* in terms of a certain set of birds that interbreed with each other but not with other birds. Notice that our definition has moved us in a circle. We started out asking what makes a particular bird a member of the species *Turdus migratorius*, and now we are defining *Turdus migratorius* in terms of a large set of particular birds. What is more, the definition of "species" that Mayr provided is clearly unsatisfactory, despite being widely accepted. To begin with it will not cover asexual species, of which there are many, and from which sexual ones presumably evolved. Second, there are counter-examples to the definition, animals from undoubtedly different species that can or do interbreed, and members of a single species that cannot do so. But doesn't biology require a well-defined notion of species? This is a problem in the philosophy of biology on which much has been written (see the suggestions at the end of this chapter) but about which we shall have nothing further to say.

If we are going to characterize robins we had better start over. Suppose instead we compile a list of the features that all normal robins share in common. One standard list includes the following features:

> *Physical description* 9–11" (23–28 cm). Dark gray to black above; white, broken eye ring. Red–orange breast and belly; white undertail coverts. Yellow bill; white streaking on throat. *Song*: rising and falling phrases: cheer-up cheerily. *Habitat*: found in forests, woodlands, scrub, parks, thickets, gardens, cultivated lands, savannas, swamps, and suburbs. *Diet*: worms, insects, and other invertebrates dominate spring diet. Fruits dominate fall and winter diet. *Ecology*: builds nest in shrub or human-built structure. Will occasionally nest on ground. Forages on ground. May take food from vegetation. Frequently roosts communally after young fledge. *Reproduction*: females incubate 3–6 eggs (usually 4), for 11–14 days. Young are tended by both parents, and leave nest at 14–16 days. Female usually produces two broods/year. *Distribution*: breeds from portions of Alaska and Canada, south to southern California, southern Mexico, Gulf Coast, and central Florida. Resident in mountains of southern Baja California. Winters from British Columbia and northern USA (irregularly), south to Baja California, Guatemala, and Gulf Coast.
>
> (Adapted from http://imnh.isu.edu/digitalatlas/bio/birds/ sngbrd/thrush/amro/amro_mai.htm)

Of course we will have to eliminate the geographic distribution from the definition, if it is to stand a chance of keeping the law free from spatiotemporal restrictedness. But, even so, the trouble with this definition is that we know perfectly well that there will be many robins that fail to satisfy one or more, indeed several, of these conditions. Indeed, we know this on the strength of the theory of natural selection. For that theory tells us that species' traits change over time in response to environmental changes, to new threats from predators, to changes in the availability of food, to the advent of new diseases, and so on. Eventually everything about robins changes, including egg color. And when egg color changes, there are two possible consequences, neither any good for our prospective law, our "wanna-be" law that robins' eggs are blue. First it could be that our newly evolved bird has not diverged much from the ancestral robin, and we are still inclined to call it a normal robin, despite the change in egg color. And, in that case, our candidate law is just plain false. If something can still be a normal robin and not lay blue eggs, then it cannot be a law that the normal robin's egg is blue. Or it could be that our evolved bird has diverged significantly, to the point that it is no longer a robin but rather some other species, one deserving of a new name. In that case, the law is not false. It is still true that robins, defined by the field guide, always lay blue eggs. But a different problem arises. The law now has an extraordinarily limited domain of application. It applies only to one single and—in geological terms—short-lived species. The law may be true, but accepting it as a law violates the spirit of the enterprise, the search for laws. A law about robins' eggs, or about any other feature of a robin, or about any feature of any species, will be explanatorily useless beyond the momentary existence of that one species, beyond that one geological millisecond in which that species lived, that one flash in the pan. This may not seem reason enough to deny "robins' eggs are blue" status as a law. Recall that it would be acceptable in principle to have a law about black holes even if there were only one in the universe. But here the situation is far worse. If laws can be unique to a species, then every species could be expected to have its own unique laws. And a complete, finished science of biology would have at least as many laws as there have been species in the history of life—and there have been many billions of them! This is a conclusion philosophers might well be prepared to live with. After all, completing the science of biology is not their job. But the problem of species-specific laws is not just that there will be too many of them, as we shall now see.

Clearly the objects of biology are different from the objects of other sciences. In particular, species are quite different from what are called the "natural kinds" of physics and chemistry. Perhaps the most clear-cut natural kinds in physical science are the elements in the Periodic Table of the Elements. This table, first set out by Mendeleev in the nineteenth century, on the basis of the observable affinities of elements to one another, organized about 90 elements into a set of rows and columns we all recall from chemistry class. Mendeleev's Periodic Table was only the last of many taxonomies that had been proposed for the elements since the Greeks introduced the fourfold division of Earth, air, fire, and water. How do we know that Mendeleev's taxonomy is correct? The reason is that atomic theory, and in particular the properties of the component particles, explains the relations among the elements Mendeleev knew, that is it explains their organization into the rows and columns he proposed. Impressively, it enabled chemists to discover the hitherto unknown elements that filled gaps in Mendeleev's original table.

What atomic theory shows is that for each element, there is a set of conditions individually necessary and jointly sufficient for being an atom of that element. For example, to be an oxygen atom, an atom must have eight protons. This is an "essential" property of the oxygen atom, and it is certainly a law of nature that each oxygen atom has this many protons. The moral of the story is that the research program of establishing the correct taxonomy for chemistry was realized and its success was explained by the fact that each of the taxa—in this case, the elements—was a natural kind, that each had a set of essential properties reflected in general laws, and that the laws relating these essential properties to one another explained the organization of the taxa (in the Periodic Table).

But the taxa of biology are not natural kinds, at least not in the same sense. They do not have any essential properties. There is no set of necessary and sufficient conditions for being a robin, and so there can be no strict laws about the features of all and only robins, or any other species, from dodos (*Didus ineptus*) to fruit flies (*Drosophila melanogaster*) to people (*Homo sapiens*).

But, you may say, surely the standard of exceptionless universality is unreasonable in biology? Will there not be inexact, "other things being equal" or *ceteris paribus* laws about species, e.g. "Other things being equal, normal robins' eggs are blue?" And is it not the very function of the qualifier "normal" in that statement to signal that it is deliberately inexact? Moreover, the complexity and diversity of biological phenomena should, it may be argued, lead us to expect that at least to begin with its scientific laws will be inexact, "other things being equal" laws. As in other disciplines, notably in physical science, researchers will first hit upon such laws: "Other things being equal, mercury is a liquid" or "*Ceteris paribus*, electrical conductors produce resistance" or "Normally, oxygen molecules have atomic weight of 16 (eight protons plus eight neutrons)." The task of science is then to fill in these "other things being equal" clauses. For only by doing so can we identify the real, precise causes of phenomena we seek to explain, and only by doing so can we build reliable technologies that exploit the exact, exceptionless laws that underlie the inexact ones. The scientist is suspicious of the claim that an inexact statement is a law only when there seems to be no way to increase its precision by discovering the list of conditions that the "other things equal" clause excludes. It is considerations like this that lead us to reject the "inexact laws" of astrology as pseudo-science. "Normally, Virgos are aggressive," might be a fine law, except that there seems to be no way to further refine it to eliminate the "normally," to understand and list the exceptions, even in principle.

In biology, we also do not expect to be able to increase the precision of any inexact laws about species. For the list of conditions excluded by the *ceteris paribus* clause in "*Ceteris paribus*, robins' eggs are blue" cannot be enumerated in a way that would turn it into an exact law. And the reason again has to do with the theory of natural selection. First, take the notion of "normal." It certainly cannot mean whatever happens to be selected for. For continuously distributed characters such as height, we might be inclined to call the mean of the distribution—the center, for a "normal" bell-shaped curve—normal. But that would make every other character value abnormal. Indeed, most individuals do not have the mean value for any trait, so that would make most individuals abnormal! What is more, in a given environment, at a given time, the mean value of a trait, say height, and all values above it, may be maladaptive for the species. Selection may be favoring lesser height or, under different circumstances, greater height. Indeed it is imaginable that environments vary in such a way as to keep the population close to the mean even when the mean is never the optimal height, the one natural selection favors. In short, natural selection makes it impossible to equate the normal with the mean or to view departures from it as abnormal. So, if normal robins' eggs are blue, it does not follow that a robin laying nonblue eggs is abnormal in the sense of maladaptive. To draw this conclusion we have to add some facts about the local environment.

But this is not the most serious problem for the idea that there are inexact laws about particular species. The real problem is that natural selection is a reflexive process that is always searching for better and better local adaptations. This persistent search makes each species' adaptations a target for selection on all the other species it competes with. An example will illustrate this so-called "arms race" character of natural selection. Robins have blue eggs either owing to selection for blue coloring, or as a by-product of selection for some trait that comes along with blue coloring, or simply as a matter of random drift. No matter why they do so, most robins having blue-colored eggs means that there will be selection for the ability to detect the blue color among animals that make their living by eating robins' eggs. There will also be selection for laying similarly blue-colored eggs among any other species of bird that parasitizes robins by laying its eggs in their nests and letting robins do the work of chick-rearing. The number of such effects on the selective environment of other species that blue robins' eggs produce is indefinitely large. But as other species evolve in response to the effects of blue robins' eggs on their environment, the blue color of robins' eggs will become increasingly maladaptive for the robin! Over the long term, robins could cease to have blue eggs! What's more, the circumstances under which this might happen cannot be enumerated in a way that would turn the inexact generalization that robins' eggs are blue into a more exact law!

There is one more thing to notice. Suppose as a matter of fact that the color of the normal robin's egg in fact never changes throughout the entire time that robins exist, because, say, an asteroid destroys all life on Earth long before an arms race results in any change in the robin's egg color. Once the Earth is destroyed, the robin becomes extinct, so, of course, the generalization that its eggs are blue can no longer be made false by selection. Now a statement can be a law even when there are no examples in the whole universe of its antecedent clause. Newton's first law provides a clearest example: It is true that a body on which no forces are acting moves with constant velocity, even though every body in the universe is as a matter of fact constantly subjected to forces (i.e. gravitational ones from every other body in the universe). The trouble is that even though the robin's egg color did not change, the theory of natural selection assures us that, consistent with all the laws of physics, chemistry and natural selection, *it could have changed* if, for example, the asteroid had not hit, or if owls had become diurnal instead of nocturnal predators, or if cuckoos had switched from parasitizing finches to robins, or if . . . We could add scenarios endlessly. But a statement that we have good reason to suppose could as a matter of natural law have been false, cannot itself be a natural law!

This brings us finally to the most central and the most mysterious feature of laws of nature, a feature palpably absent from our generalization about robins and from any statement about particular species and their members. Laws express some sort of necessity. But this necessity cannot be logical necessity because, as Hume first showed clearly, we must be able to conceive of the contrary of any law, and generally if the falsity of a statement is conceivable it cannot be logically necessary. And we cannot call it physical necessity because that adds nothing new. What is physical necessity? Nor can we simply say that the necessity is nomological, for nomological simply means law-like, and it tells us nothing to say that laws have law-like necessity. Instead, many philosophers have expressed the necessity of laws of nature in terms of the notion of a "counter-factual conditional." A counter-factual conditional statement is one that has the form, "If it were the case that *P*, then it would be the case that *Q*," in which *P* and *Q* are sentences just as in plain indicative conditionals such as "If it rains, then I will get wet." Now compare a law, such as "All objects in free fall in a vacuum have constant acceleration" with a true but accidental generalization that is not a law, such as "All the coins in my pocket are silver." The law will, as philosophers say, "support" the counter-factual that "If the penny in my hand were in free fall, it would have constant acceleration." In other words, the counter-factual is an implication of the law, or follows from it. But the merely true accidental generalization will not support the counter-factual conditional, "If the penny in my hand were in my pocket, it would be silver." In fact, we believe this statement to be false! This difference between supported counter-factual statements and unsupported ones is at least a symptom of the fact that laws express some sort of necessary connection between their antecedents and their consequents that is missing between the antecedent and the consequent of true but merely accidental generalizations. Notice that support for counter-factuals is not what the necessity of laws *consists in*. Rather, their necessity is supposed to explain the fact that they support counter-factuals. Supporting counter-factuals is a mark, sign, or symptom of a general statement's being a law. Nomological necessity is a feature of laws that is revealed by a generalization's support of counter-factuals.

Now it is pretty clear from what has already been said that the statement "Robins' eggs are blue" will not support counter-factuals. That is, if any particular nonblue egg that is not a robin's egg were to become one, it would not necessarily be blue. And the reason it would not is not too different from the reason that "All the coins in my pocket are silver" will not support "If this penny—a nonsilver coin not in my pocket—were in my pocket it would be silver." That all the coins in my pocket are silver is a mere historical contingency. Consider first the counter-factual supposition that the nonblue non-robin's egg is somehow transformed into a robin's egg. It could turn into the egg of a mutant robin (one that is still a robin), or one that had been on a special diet that discolors the eggs. The point is that the blueness of robins' eggs is merely a historical contingency, a kind of accident, with no physical necessity to it, albeit a contingency that lasts longer and is more widespread than the one about the silver coins in my pocket just now.

Our exploration of whether a regularity about the members of a species could be a law or not has led to a negative conclusion, but it has enabled us to identify several of the components of the philosopher's standard account of what it is to be a law. Laws report and often explain causal relations between types of events, states, facts, and processes. They are universal in scope and are conditional in logical structure. Thus we can express them as having the form of an "If P then Q," where the P and Q are facts that can obtain any-where or at any time, or laws can take the form "All Fs are Gs," where it is understood that anything at all that comes to have the property F will also have immediately or eventually the property G. This universality of form reflects our belief that laws report fundamental or derived truths about the underlying machinery of nature, machinery that always operates in the same way everywhere. For that reason, we prohibit laws from mentioning specific places, times, or things. A causal statement that does so is no law, though it might be true and if true will be true in virtue of actual law or laws. Thus it is true that the *Titanic*'s striking an iceberg caused it to sink, but there are no laws about the *Titanic* and icebergs. Similarly, as we have seen, being a robin's egg does in fact cause an egg to be blue, but there is no law connecting robins to blue eggs. In each of these cases, of course, the laws that underwrite the causal claims are numerous, often unknown, and often difficult to weave together into an explicit explanation.

What makes laws explanatory is not their universal form, for this is some-thing they share with accidentally true generalizations such as "All gold solids are less than 1000 kg in mass," which is probably true but just as certainly not a law! Rather their explanatory power derives from some strange kind of necessity that they bear, not logical necessity, but some other ill-understood kind, which reflects itself in the support of counter-factual conditionals such as "If this rubber rod were made of copper, it would be a conductor." So, in addressing the question of whether a candidate for a law in biology is in fact one, we now have a kind of litmus test:

1 Is the candidate a true universal conditional that makes no mention of specific places, times or things?

2   Is the candidate a contingent statement the denial of which is conceivable, as opposed to a definition or the consequence of definitions that cannot report causal relations?
3   If the candidate is true only because of a *ceteris paribus* statement, can we expect to narrow the range of its exceptions by empirical means?
4   Does the candidate support counter-factual conditional statements?

If the answers to all of these are yes, we have a law. To this list we may add one more feature, though it may not be independent of the other conditions listed. Scientific laws are those generalizations in which we come to have great confidence after only a relatively small number of observations. How many times did Galileo need to drop large and small cannon balls from the Leaning Tower of Pisa to establish the law of constant and mass-independent acceleration of free falling bodies? How many times did Faraday have to run his experiment proving that magnetic fields are accompanied by electrical currents? By contrast, establishing the truth of the statement that no mass of gold weighs more than 1000 kg requires us to travel to a great many bank vaults. Why is this? Presumably it has something to do with the necessity we attribute to laws, and something to do with our confidence that the particulars of the few known demonstrations of the law are not special in any way or, in other words, that the small sample of conditions studied is representative of the much larger set of possible conditions.

Models in biology: Mendel's laws, Fisher's sex ratios, the Hardy–Weinberg equilibrium

Mendel's laws are the cornerstone of much of the genetics taught in schools and universities. We can all remember learning how to fill in Punnett squares, following Mendelian principles of segregation, independent assortment, and dominance. What one goes on to learn, in more advanced courses in genetics are the exceptions, complications, and corrections one needs to make in the use of Mendel's laws to fill out these squares.

It does not take much more examination than that to conclude that Mendel's laws are not, after all, really laws at all. Mendel did his famous experiments on pea plants in the mid-nineteenth century. His published results went unnoticed until rediscovered in the early twentieth century and, since then, a major theme of the history of genetics has been the discovery of more and more exceptions to his laws. Luckily for Mendel and for genetics, the traits he first studied did not happen to involve genes located close together on the same chromosomes. Had they been so "linked," that is lying close together on the same chromosome, they would not have assorted independently. Once linkage was detected, it became clear that the second law is a rough and ready generalization with enormous numbers of exceptions, such as those arising from linkage. As for the law of segregation, geneticists now know cases in which segregation is unequal, in which one of the two alleles is preferentially transmitted to the next generation, the so-called segregation distorter alleles.

Of course, just because Mendel's principles are not laws does not mean that they are not important in biology. What it does mean is that when they are successfully applied in prediction, and when they are not, is a matter to be explained by appeal to other more fundamental regularities. In the case of Mendel's laws, these will be regularities about meiosis and other details of cell physiology. Is that where the laws are? Somewhere in these lower level processes, is that where we will find the fundamental causal laws of biology that explain Mendelian generalizations and their exceptions?

The answer is almost certainly not. Again, the reason goes back to Darwinian theory. For the theory tells us that meiosis, segregation, and assortment are—like other features of organisms such as genes, chromosomes, and sexual reproduction—the result of a long evolutionary history. In the course of that history, natural selection produced adaptation, including both the Mendelian processes themselves—such as meiosis that produces segregation—and other non-Mendelian processes, some of which—such as segregation distorters—take advantage of Mendelian processes. Future environmental changes could modify meiosis further, or even do away with it altogether. Similarly, if natural selection is operating on other worlds circling other suns, we have some reason to suppose that there will be replicators and perhaps also interactors on these worlds but little reason to suppose that they will reproduce by meiosis, or that anything like Earthly sexual physiology will have emerged. The domain of any laws that we discover about sexual processes, or about anything else in biology, could well be quite limited, that is to say limited to a single instance of biology here on Earth and further limited to a particular time range in Earthly evolutionary history.

Some philosophers of biology and some biologists have argued, in the light of considerations like these, that biological laws are really quite different from laws in physical science, and therefore biological theories and explanations must be quite different from those in chemistry or physics. These philosophers and biologists note that principles such as the Hardy–Weinberg "law" or Fisher's "sex ratio model" play important roles in biological explanation, indeed they play many of the same roles that laws play in physical science. But for well-understood reasons, these models are quite different from the causal laws of chemistry or physics. From this it is inferred that biological laws are fundamentally different from physical laws, and that therefore biological explanation and biological theories are different as well.

Recall the statement of the Hardy–Weinberg law: If four conditions obtain, in an infinitely large population, given an initial set of allele frequencies, then genotype frequencies remain constant. The four conditions are: no immigration or emigration, random mating, no mutation, and no natural selection. Given these conditions, it only takes a bit of elementary algebra to deduce that if in generation 1 the proportion of allele P in the population is p, and the proportion of allele Q is q, then in the ratio of genotypes

PP, QQ, PQ in the next generation will be p^2, q^2, and $2pq$. Weinberg was a physician, a biologist of a sort. But Hardy was a mathematician and he always claimed to be embarrassed that the "law" should bear his name, because it is nothing more than a trivial mathematical deduction. Hardy was right. The Hardy–Weinberg "law" has no more empirical content than, say, $2 + 2 = 4$ or a definitional truth such as "All bachelors are unmarried males."

Now in the previous section we noted that such definitionally necessary truths cannot report contingent causal connections, have no explanatory power, cannot support counter-factuals, and therefore cannot be laws, at least not of the sort we are familiar with in other natural sciences. If biology is different, if the Hardy–Weinberg law really is a biological law, if it will really do explanatory work for biology in spite of its status as a definition or a "tautology," then a great deal of philosophy of science will have to be overturned. To begin with, it will turn out that a priori, nonexperimental, nonobservational knowledge is a source of biological theory. This will be deeply troubling to those who wish to contrast empirical science with non-empirical subjects, such as mathematics or revealed religion. We will also have to give up the notion that laws report causal relations or, even more radically, the conclusion that causal relations could as a matter of logic have been different from what they are. For after all, the Hardy–Weinberg "law" is a logical truth. If it is a law or reports causal relations, then the relations it reports could not have been different from what they are. Mathematical statements are normally considered necessary truths. Empiricist philosophers and empirical scientists—not to mention opponents of creationism—will be greatly troubled by this conclusion.

So let us consider exactly what the role of the Hardy–Weinberg "law" is in biological explanations. Suppose we find a population in which gene and genotype frequencies appear to remain the same over a period of time. Can we then infer from the law that all of the four conditions mentioned in its antecedent obtain? Not quite. The Hardy–Weinberg law allows us to infer either that: (i) all four conditions obtain, or (ii) one or more do not, but the resulting deviations just balance each other out. Suppose, for example, that there is as much emigration as immigration (and the emigrating and immi-grating groups have the same allele frequency), or that there is mutation but natural selection weeds the mutants out, or that mating is nonrandom but the offspring of the assortative matings emigrate, or some other combination of factors is keeping gene ratios and genotype ratios constant. These may seem improbable for one reason or another, but we cannot rule them out ahead of time.

Suppose, on the other hand, that we find genotype frequencies changing over time. Then can we infer that at least one of the four conditions in the antecedent does not obtain? Yes, but only if we add the stipulation that the four factors mentioned in the antecedent of the Hardy–Weinberg law are the *only* factors that can change gene and genotype frequencies in a population. This claim is however not part of the Hardy–Weinberg law as we stated it. It is a much stronger claim, which most certainly is not a mathematical truth, a tautology, a trivial consequence of our definitions. It is a different law, or at least a candidate for one: "Whenever genotype frequencies change in an infinitely large population, the only cause will be some combination of changes in immigration or emigration, mutation, random mating, or natural selection."

So the portion of the Hardy–Weinberg law that enables us to move from gene frequencies to genotype frequencies is just pure algebra without any implications for the course of nature at all. If we modify it to make it explanatory, so that it identifies the causes of change in gene or genotype frequencies, it is going to be a contingent claim after all and not a mathematical model.

To make things clearer, let's consider R.A. Fisher's sex ratio model, which is widely used to explain why almost all sexually reproducing species have a 1:1 female-to-male sex ratio. This is a very convenient state of affairs, once widely thought to reflect the wisdom of the Designer, who arranged matters so that there would be just enough men and women to go around, so that almost everyone could expect to have one and only one spouse. Fisher harnessed Darwinian natural selection to provide a better explanation, better in part because it also explains the rare cases of sexually reproducing species in which females heavily outnumber males. The sex ratio *model* is so called because of two features: (i) it begins with a number of assumptions, which may or may not be true for any given sexually reproducing species, and (ii) it derives by logic alone the conclusion that the sex ratio is 1:1. (Actually, it is not just that the assumptions might not be true for a given species, but that some of them cannot be perfectly realized in fact by any species. Fisher's model is an idealization.) What are the assumptions? Like Hardy–Weinberg, it assumes that the interbreeding population is infinitely large and mating randomly. The model assumes also that individuals differ in a particular heritable trait: the trait of giving birth disproportionately to females or to males. Now, if in any generation, there happen to be more males than females, then those males and females with the trait of producing disproportionately more female offspring than male offspring will be fitter, for their offspring will have more reproductive opportunities, on average. As a result they will have more offspring, and to the extent that their offspring have the same hereditary disposition to larger numbers of female offspring, this trait will spread in the population until the sex ratio shifts to more females than males. At this point the hereditary disposition to have more male offspring than female ones becomes fitter, and so on until the sex ratio reaches a stable equilibrium at 1:1.

Interestingly, under some circumstances this same mechanism can produce a sex ratio that permanently favors one sex over the other. In many sexual species, the female has a limited number of ova and the male has a vastly larger number of sperm, so that one male can successfully mate with many more partners that one female can. Thus, in principle, one male can fertilize many females, but not vice versa. Now imagine a species in which a female controls the sex ratio of her offspring and also in which her offspring stay together after birth and mate with each other before dispersing into the larger population. (There are in fact such species, for example the parasitic wasp, *Nasonia vitripennis*.) From the perspective of a mother in such a species, it will be to her advantage to produce a large number of daughters and very few sons. Producing more daughters gives her more grand-offspring but producing more than a minimal number of sons will not. Under these circumstances, selection favors a strongly female-biased sex ratio, and in *Nasonia* that is in fact what we see.

The model works, but it actually needs a further refinement. Among *Homo sapiens*, the sex ratio is not 1:1 but rather about 1.05:1, that is 1.05 males to each female. This does not refute Fisher's model, because the model is a mathematical truth, a logically necessary argument in which the 1:1 sex ratio follows validly from its premises or assumptions. The most the 1.05:1 ratio can show is that the model is not applicable to *Homo sapiens*. Why is it not applicable? It must be that some assumption of the model is not realized by this species. The answer is enlightening not only for biology but also for the question of how models explain and whether in doing so they displace laws or constitute laws. It seems that between birth and sexual maturity, males have approximately a 5 percent higher mortality rate, so in order to supply a 1:1 ratio of males to females at sexual maturity, nature has to provide 1.05 males to each female at birth (note the expression "in order to"). In other words, natural selection favors a slightly skewed sex ratio in *Homo sapiens*.

So the Fisher sex ratio model is always true, in the same way that $2 + 3 = 5$ is always true, but there is a range of cases to which it applies and a range of cases to which it does not. About each of these former cases, it will turn out to be an empirical truth that the Fisher sex ratio model applies to it, but of course this will no more be a law than "robins' eggs are blue." And there will be a range of species to which it does not apply. What is more, there will be a more general model, with an additional term to accommodate pre-reproductive mortality, that applies to all the cases in which the original Fisher's model applies and also to cases such as *Homo sapiens*. And of course there will be an even more general model, in which there is also a variable for the frequency of sibling mating to accommodate species with female-skewed sex ratios. But will this even more general model be a biological law?

Well, we can call it a law, of course, but as Lincoln said, calling a dog's tail a leg does not make it one. All of these models are *necessary truths*. Their empirical core, which gives them a role in the explanation of the sex ratio of a species, is the claim that the species satisfies the assumptions of the model. Once we establish that the assumptions are satisfied, logic alone suffices to conclude that the model's implications must be true. Of course, strictly speaking, no actual population ever fully satisfies either the assumptions of the Hardy–Weinberg law or Fisher's sex ratio model. There is almost always a little emigration and immigration, a little mutation and some nonrandom mating. Even more potentially serious is the fact that no populations are infinitely large and some are quite small. The most we can demand when we apply a model is that the actual population the behavior of which we seek to explain satisfies the model's assumptions "closely enough." But what does "closely enough" mean? That will vary with the context of inquiry. If our aim is prediction of outcomes on which human lives are dependent, we will demand a very close approach to the asymptotic limit of infinite population size. If our aim is explanation of an outcome as an approximation of the ideal case, our standards will be lower. In this respect models in biology are no different from models in physical science. The billiard ball model of a gas explains why real gases approximate the ideal gas law, $pV = nRT$, to the extent that they realize the assumptions of the model that molecules are infinitely elastic point masses exerting no gravitational or other forces on one another.

The interesting difference between biology and physics appears to be this: physicists seek models with highly idealized assumptions and limited domains of application in order eventually to build general theories in which the idealizing assumptions are relaxed and the domains of application broadened. In other words, they seek theories composed of laws about real systems that underwrite and explain why the idealized models work well enough and also explain when and why they fail. This does not seem always to be the case in biology. Biologists are satisfied to generate a wide range of models, and sometimes, as in Fisher's case, they seek to generalize them. But they do not appear to seek general laws that would underwrite them. Is this because biology does not require such laws, or because they have already discovered the general laws of the fundamental underlying theory?

Fitness and the principle of natural selection

To recapitulate, there is good reason not to expect laws about individual species or, for that matter, groups of species. But perhaps there are broader generalities, applying to all or most species over the history of life. Consider a principle formulated in the nineteenth century by Karl von Baer on the basis of embryological observations across many species. (We update the principle here, formulating it as an evolutionary principle in a way that von Baer never did.) The principle states that as a species develops, from embryo to adult, it progressively diverges from the pathways followed by its evolutionary relatives, with the result that early embryonic stages are shared by large groups of more distantly related species while later stages are shared only by smaller closely related subgroups. Thus the species in our own larger group, the chordates, pass through a common embryological stage called the pharyngula stage in which structures similar to the gill slits of adult fish are present. In fish these structures are later elaborated in development but in mammals they disappear as development proceeds. And the divergence continues, fish acquiring adult fins and mammals acquiring limbs. Development, according to von Baer, is a story of progressive divergence. (Notice that the claim is not that mammal development is just a continuation of fish development, that mammals pass through all fish stages, up through the adult, and then proceed further. This was the prediction of a very different law, proposed in the nineteenth century by Ernst Haeckel, that "ontogeny recapitulates phylogeny." This "biogenetic law," as it has been called, is now known to be completely false. von Baer's law is still widely accepted, although exceptions to it are known.)

What is of interest in von Baer's law is that, to the extent that it is true, it may be explainable as a consequence of natural selection. It may arise from the fact that variation in early developmental stages is more likely to damage fitness than variation in later stages. The reason is that development is at least partly a cumulative process with later stages building on the results of earlier stages. Thus any variation arising in an early stage will affect all of development lying "downstream," so to speak, while later stage variation will have fewer effects. Analogously, in the building of a house, an architectural decision to modify the foundation could have consequences for the whole structure, whereas a modification to a window has fewer consequences. So, as a result of the cumulativeness of development, selection can be expected to favor mechanisms that reduce the likelihood of variation occurring, or at least expressing itself, early in development. The expected effect of such "canalizing" mechanisms, as they are called, is that in all groups early development should be more conserved. The reasoning here is somewhat speculative, but the point is that it is easy to see how von Baer's law could be merely a consequence of natural selection.

Let us take for granted that it is, and further suppose that all similar general patterns in evolution that relate to adaptation can also be understood as a consequence of natural selection. In other words, let us suppose that all of the apparently universal, or near universal, patterns in adaptive evolution that have been proposed, or will be proposed in the future, are a consequence of natural selection. This might sound like a huge assumption, given how little has been said about such patterns here, but it really is not. Recall that for explaining adaptation, natural selection seems to be the only game in town. And therefore it is not unreasonable to expect that any pattern observed in adaptive evolution has something to do with natural selection or, more boldly, that it has natural selection at its core. If so, then the obvious next question is whether natural selection is itself a law and, if so, perhaps the only law of adaptive evolution.

Here it is worthwhile reconsidering a different version of Darwin's theory than the one offered earlier in terms of replicators and interactors, namely the version in the first edition of *On the Origin of Species*. Schematically, it goes like this:

1   Reproducing populations increase exponentially.
2   The capacity of any region to support any reproducing population is finite.

Therefore:

3   There will always be a struggle for survival and reproduction among competing populations.

Also:

4   There is variation in the fitness of members of these populations and some of these variations are heritable.

Therefore:

5   In the struggle for survival and reproduction, the fittest variants will be favored and will survive and have more offspring.

And therefore:

6   Adaptive evolution will occur.

Notice first that the theory requires very little in the way of data. We need only observe that reproduction is exponential, survival is limited, and heritable variation in survival and reproductive ability exists. In other words, Darwin need not have spent five years circumnavigating the globe—his voyage of discovery on the HMS *Beagle*—to hit upon the principle of natural selection.

Notice too that this way of expressing Darwin's theory makes its law-like structure easy to see. At the core of this structure is statement 5. Whenever and wherever the factual conditions outlined in statements 1 through 4 are met, the theory claims that statement 5 will be true. Statement 5 articulates what is often called the "principle of natural selection" or PNS, which we may state more formally as follows:

> *PNS*   For any two individuals, x and y, if x is fitter than y in environment E, then, probably, x will have more offspring than y in E.

Two concepts required to express this principle are controversial: fitness and probability. The one on which the most ink has been spilled is "x is fitter than y," or relative fitness (or usually just "fitness" for short). It is held by some that theory requires a definition of fitness, and that the only definition of fitness under which the theory of natural selection as a whole is true renders the PNS true by definition! In other words, the claim is that the PNS has no more causal, explanatory power than the mathematical models we have already denied scientific status to.

Here is the problem. Biologists typically measure fitness differences by measuring differences in reproduction. If their measurement reflects the meaning of the words, then the words "x is fitter than y," mean that x has more offspring than y. Now, plug this definition into the PNS and the result is the obvious triviality:

> For any two populations, if x has more offspring than y, then, probably, x has more offspring than y.

One wonders what the point of the "probably" is in this expression, as the statement will also be equally, trivially true if we leave the "probably" out.

One conclusion sometimes drawn from this result is that on this definition of fitness the theory of natural selection is "unfalsifiable." A theory is unfalsifiable if no possible evidence could disconfirm it. Euclidean geometry, for example, is unfalsifiable: An astronomer's calculation that the angles between three stars do not add up to 180 degrees would not cast the slightest doubt on the theorem of geometry that a triangle's internal angles equal 180 degrees. Rather, it casts doubt on the applicability of Euclidean geometry to that region of space. As we have seen above, the same holds true for a mathematical model such as Fisher's or the Hardy–Weinberg "law." By contrast, scientific theories are held to be falsifiable. That is to say it is a hallmark of scientific claims that we can imagine experimental data or observations that would lead us to surrender them. Theories that are unfalsifiable by any imaginable data rule out no course of events at all and so cannot explain a course of events that actually does happen. Suppose fitness were defined in terms of actual offspring produced, as above. Then, even if short-necked giraffes began having more offspring than long-necked ones, and eventually the average length of giraffes' necks were to decline, while nothing else changed, including the role of leaves at the top of trees as the preferred source of giraffe nutrition, the theory of natural selection would remain unchallenged. For the increase in offspring of short-necked giraffes is by definition equal to an increase in fitness by these giraffes and so does not refute the theory of natural selection. In other words, on the definition of fitness as relative rate of reproduction of x compared with y, no change in relative population proportions of x and y could falsify the theory. But the theory is about such relative changes. So nothing could falsify the theory. Ergo, it fails to be a scientific theory!

Of course the response most evolutionary biologists give to this charge is that they do not define fitness in terms of reproductive rates, even though such rates are what they employ in order to measure fitness differences. Measurement is not the same as definition. Inches and centimeters measure space, they do not define it. Seconds and years measure time, they do not define it. Centigrade and Fahrenheit degrees measure heat, they do not define it. The same goes for fitness and reproduction. What is more, fitness needs to be measured in different ways under different circumstances. Consider what we learned about sex ratios above. If we just counted offspring we would be unable to discriminate the fitness of two organisms that gave birth to the same number of offspring, when one gave birth only to males and the other only to females. Yet, depending on the current sex ratio, or other factors such as sibling mating, at the times of birth they would have quite different fitnesses. Sometimes a better measure of fitness is given by counting only male offspring or female offspring or grand-offspring, or granddaughters or grandsons. Sometimes the fittest will be those who have fewer offspring in a harsh season and more offspring in a lush one. Which will be the "right" measure depends on the environment in which organisms find themselves.

This may suggest that fitness should be defined as a relationship between organisms and environments, not as a head count of offspring or descendants. In fact, one natural way of defining fitness invokes the notion of environmental "design problems" mentioned in the first chapter. Suppose we view adaptation as the solution to metaphorical "design problems" set by the environment (metaphorical because there is no literal designer, just environmental changes and randomly produced variations that may or may not enable the organism to survive in the face of these changes). Then x is fitter than y might be defined as "x solves design problems posed by the environment better than y does." This definition has some intuitive advantages but many practical difficulties. Most of them are difficulties of applying the definition, that is problems of converting the definition into measurements.

First, for a given design problem—e.g. camouflage, or keeping warm, or fighting parasites, or building nests—how do we tell which of two organisms under comparison is better at solving the problem? One answer immediately suggests itself: count offspring. But we already know that this answer is not generally adequate. Second, given two organisms, each solving a different design problem—say one solves the problem of staying warm while the other solves the problem of finding water—how do we tell which solves its respective problem better? And how do we take into account what Olympic judging rules call the "degree of difficulty" of each organism's achievement? Suppose one zebra is better at out-running lions and swatting away disease-bearing flies than another but the second is better at hiding from lions in the tall grass and stores water better than the first. Which is fitter? Again, the only way to solve this problem seems to be to count offspring. Third, how many "design problems" do organisms face? It is very hard to count them up, so we cannot even begin to deal with the problem of aggregating them into some overall directly measurable definition of fitness.

One conclusion to draw from this discussion is that definitions must be distinguished from measurements, but a definition that does not easily lend itself to measurement will not have much of a role in quantitative explanation and prediction. And one that cannot be measured at all cannot figure in statements that are falsifiable. It is perfectly acceptable to change one's measurement methods depending on the circumstances. Physicists and chemists have a half-dozen or more different ways of measuring heat. But, in principle, alternative measurement devices and units should all be measurements of the same property, one that can be specified independently of them. That is our problem here: What exactly is the relationship of "x is fitter than y?" Fitness does not seem to be a unitary or constant thing, one that can be measured in alternative ways under different circumstances.

Some philosophers—notably Robert Brandon—have tried to solve the problem by exploiting the way in which fitness is measured while avoiding trivializing it by turning the PNS into a disguised definition. They adopt the so-called "probabilistic propensity" definition of fitness. In general, a propensity, capacity, disposition, or ability is a trait, like being magnetic, or being fragile, that an object has but does not manifest except under certain circumstances. Thus, fragile objects do not break unless struck. But we often explain why a glass broke by citing its fragility, its propensity to break when struck. Until the advent of material science in the twentieth century, there was no good theory for why some things are fragile and others not. The advent of such theories did not deprive fragility of its explanatory power, even though it is hard to define fragility except through its effects: "If x is struck, then if x is fragile, it will break apart." This "definition" has many problems. For one thing, fragile object sometimes withstand striking. We would like to know exactly how strongly something must be struck for its fragility to be revealed by its breaking. Propensities we identify in ordinary life have an inevitable vagueness about them. But there are propensities identified by natural science, such as electrical resistance, which can be measured in precise units, e.g. ohms. Typically propensities or capacities, like almost all scientifically interesting quantities, are measured in units that reflect their effects. Thus, heat is measured by its effects on liquids such as alcohol or mercury enclosed in tubes. And, of course, some propensities are probabilistic: two dice have the probabilistic propensity to come up snake eyes in 2.777778 percent of their tosses.

So, applying all this to a definition of fitness, we could proceed as follows:

x is fitter than y in environment $E =_{df} x$ has the probabilistic propensity to leave more offspring than y in E.

Notice that this definition of fitness leaves it a contingent truth that in any particular generation, the fitter of two organisms actually leaves more offspring. For, as we well know, the most probable outcome is not always the actual outcome. Just as a pair of dice can come up snake eyes twice in a row, even though the probability is on the order of one in a thousand, it does happen from time to time. So the less fit organism can have more offspring. It just should not happen very often, according to the theory!

Unfortunately, this stratagem for defining fitness faces problems, two especially worth mentioning. First, the definition is incompatible with some potentially important evolutionary processes. In some cases, nature will not select for organisms that are most likely to leave more offspring. In some environments, it will select for the one who leaves the most grand-offspring (the so-called grandmother effect). One solution would be to change the word "offspring" in the definition above to "descendants." x may be more fit than y if it has a probabilistic propensity to leave more descendants on a short timescale (e.g. offspring), while y may be more fit if it has a propensity to leave more descendants on a long timescale (e.g. great-great-great-grand-offspring). There is no contradiction here. It is simply that fitness is a timescale relative property. Another fix might be necessary to take into account the possibility that two organisms can have the same probability of leaving the same number of descendants on the same timescale and yet have different levels of fitness. Suppose, for example, one organism had a probabilistic propensity to leave two offspring per year and another to leave one in even years and three in odd years. They both have a propensity to leave two offspring per year, on average, but after nine generations the first would have 512 descendants and the second 243 (for details see Brandon 1990). Thus, the definition of fitness might have to be adjusted to take into account the variance in propensity to produce offspring, as well as the average.

A more serious problem faces any such definition when we recognize that the PNS is itself a probabilistic statement. Were we to plug the probabilistic propensity definition into the PNS, the result would surely be supposed by most people to be a truth with all the explanatory power and falsifiability of "all triangles have three sides." Here is how it would read:

> *PNS + propensity definition* If x has a probabilistic propensity to leave more offspring than y in environment E, then, probably, x will leave more offspring than y in E.

However, whether it is a trivial definitional truth or not depends on whether the term "probably" in the antecedent shares the same meaning as the concept of probabilistic propensity in the definition of fitness. There are, as we shall see, several definitions of probability, some of which might turn the PNS + propensity definition into a contingent statement.

Alas, this will not solve all of our problems. The probabilistic propensity definition of fitness is every bit as difficult to apply in practice as the "design problem solution" definition. How shall we measure the probabilistic propensity of a species to leave descendants in a way that is independent of the actual number of descendants it leaves?

Some argue that these problems with the design criterion and probabilistic propensity view of fitness should be treated as practical problems of application of a general concept of fitness as probabilistic propensity. In principle, there is no barrier to biologists understanding the design aspects of survival and reproductive success sufficiently to craft the correctly qualified probabilistic propensity for each different evolutionary process, and then to estimate the relevant probabilistic propensity from empirical data. And, they argue, as there is no in-principle barrier to doing so, there is no in-principle barrier to testing Darwin's theory. If so, these approaches do render the theory falsifiable in principle, if not presently in fact.

But others argue that these problems are fatal to the project of identifying a PNS law in biology, at least if we insist on laws like those in the physical sciences. They conclude that we need to completely reconsider the structure of the theory of natural selection and its component parts, that the attempt to force the theory into a mold drawn from physical science just will not do its character justice.

Darwinism as a historical research program

More than one influential philosopher of biology has rejected the search for biological laws as deeply misconceived. The reason is not that there is no such thing as the theory of natural selection, still less that Darwinism is not "scientific." It is just that not all sciences proceed in the same way and, in particular, some sciences—such as biology—do not require their own "proprietary" laws for explanation and prediction (e.g. Philip Kitcher). Rather, they borrow laws from other sciences, employ mathematical models that illuminate particular processes, and offer methodological prescriptions about how to illuminate biological processes. In this view, there is no virtue in attempting to meet the standards of law in the physical sciences. The objects of inquiry in biology simply are not of the sort that allow that level of generalization and abstraction.

Some of these philosophers (e.g. Elliott Sober) emphasize the historical character of Darwinism, and—adopting Dobzhansky's dictum that nothing in biology makes sense except in the light of evolution—the historical character of all biology. Thus, consider the plethora in biology of local and temporary properties, naming particular places, times, or things. In biology, this is no weakness or defect that one should seek to eradicate or avoid. These particulars characterize life on this planet! They are history! Darwin's great insight was twofold. First, life on this planet is a branching tree of descent, and second, the adaptive characteristics of all living things on this tree are in large part the result of a natural selection process. These two insights virtually guarantee the local and temporary character of properties of organisms. And they also justify a research tactic that involves helping oneself to a great deal of physical science and, for that matter, sometimes a bit of social science and some mathematical models, but do not eventuate in special biological laws in the philosopher's sense described in the first section of this chapter.

Examining the myriad case studies in which Darwinian theory is exploited and its explanatory strategies vindicated enables us to turn the charge of vacuity, triviality, and unfalsifiability, often lodged against the theory, on its head! The philosopher who first charged Darwinism with unfalsifiability, Karl Popper, never recanted this charge, but did eventually concede that unfalsifiability does not render it trivial pseudo-science, as it does astrology or homeopathy. Rather, he argued, Darwinism is a "metaphysical research program." It is a set of methodological rules or principles that guides biological research and that are justified not by any particular body of evidence but more broadly by all of the biological evidence and, indeed, by the argument that seems to show that blind variation and selective retention are "the only game in town," the only way to explain adaptation in nature.

That it will be hard to cash this research program in for a set of specific proprietary biological laws, special to biology, reflects a distinctive feature of the theory that another philosopher, Daniel Dennett, has noticed. The "mechanism" of blind variation and selective retention is what he calls a "substrate-neutral algorithm." An algorithm is more easily illustrated than defined. We are all acquainted with the simple algorithms of arithmetic, such as addition, subtraction, multiplication, division, and all the combinations of these procedures. Take addition: for any two numbers as inputs it gives one and only one number as an output. Multiplication differs from addition in that for the same two numbers it gives a different number as output. In general, an algorithm is a rule the application of which requires no thought, interpretation, or judgment. Anyone—or for that matter any of a variety of different physical systems—can implement an algorithm. That is they can realize an algorithm, or be an instance of it. Thus, computers, calculators, adding machines, abacuses, and so on are all different sorts of devices, but they can all implement the addition algorithm. For that matter, tree ring growth implements the addition algorithm. If any of a myriad different physical systems—from tree rings to brains—can implement the addition algorithm, then the algorithm is "substrate neutral." It follows that knowing something to be an implementation of a particular algorithm cannot tell you what it is made of or exactly how it works. Notice also that there are many algorithms implemented by purely mechanical systems that no one has ever thought of, and which have no useful application in human life. Consider the algorithm: "Take a number to the twelfth power and add 31,081,946 to it." No one ever thought of this algorithm until now and presumably it is of no use to anyone but, nevertheless, there is such an algorithm. To identify a physical process as implementing an algorithm is not to identify it as having a purpose or fulfilling any interesting need, end, or goal. It is just to say that the system gives the same specific output for a specific input every time. Consider the algorithm that implements Ohm's law: "Take the voltage across an electric circuit (E) and divide it by the resistance of the circuit (R). The result is the current flowing through that circuit (I)." In other words, $I = E/R$. Electrical circuits were mindlessly implementing the algorithm $I = E/R$ long before anyone realized they could be used as (analog) computers to do simple division.

Could blind variation and selective retention be such a substrate-neutral algorithm? That it is substrate neutral seems relatively easy to show. After all, many different physical systems implement natural selection, from self-replicating lines of DNA molecules to reproducing individuals to reproducing species. Darwinian evolution takes as inputs any number of such lineages at a given time, and then gives a probabilistic output, the lineages that have the highest probability of leaving descendants in the future. The gory details of how natural selection is implemented in particular cases will be complex and variable from case to case, and will take quite different amounts of time to process inputs into outputs. The source of the complexity, the variation in the way the mechanism works, and the amount of time it requires are all matters that vary among lineages and the environments in which they find themselves. And each lineage plus its environment is the mechanism that implements the algorithm.

But is natural selection just an algorithm? One objection to the idea that it might be is the claim that its "output" is not a particular event, state, or process, but rather the probabilities of each of a number of different outcomes. But that is no objection, because algorithms can be probabilistic. Indeed, computer scientists have developed many such algorithms for encryption, gambling, and simulations of various kinds. Why should nature not have done so as well?

The idea that natural selection is such a substrate-neutral algorithm has many attractions. To begin with it will be pretty obvious that that the view can both nicely delimit the domain of the biological (as per Dobzhansky's dictum) while making the search for special biological laws otiose. Consider a simple algorithm such as addition. No one will suppose that all systems that implement addition do so in accordance with a single or even a small number of laws of nature. After all, what do tree rings have in common with Pentium processor microchips? No physical commonality explains why they both do addition. Similarly, why suppose that all systems that implement the blind variation and selective retention algorithm (if it is one) do so in virtue of the same law or laws of biology or any other science? This insight is the flip side of the idea that, like other algorithms, Darwin's is substrate neutral. The more different ways an algorithm can be implemented, the less likely its implementation by a set of physical systems reflects the operation of any law or, for that matter, a small number of laws, biological or physical.

There will of course be a research program associated with this algorithm. It will be the search for the detailed mechanism that underlies and implements the algorithm in each and every case of biological interest. Of course, it will not be easy to identify the exact features of every system that does implement the natural selection algorithm. Sometimes the evidence will be lost (as with the dinosaurs). Sometimes the system will be too complex, too hard to separate from other systems, or too difficult to experiment on (human brains). Sometimes the problem will simply be that organisms of interest live much longer than experimenters do (giant tortoises or bristlecone pines). But these problems will be treated by the research program as tests of the creativity and ingenuity of biologists, not counter-evidence against the existence of general principles in biology.

Each of the successful studies of how the natural selection algorithm is implemented will of course be component parts of the theory of natural selection, and some of these components will be grouped together under other algorithms as well. Which ones? Well, the mathematical models such as the Hardy–Weinberg "law," Mendel's "laws," or Fisher's sex ratio model. For, despite the heterogeneity of systems that implement the natural selection algorithm, there will be some common features that many of the implementing systems share, especially if these systems are related by descent! And that is where we came in, so to speak, with the realization that Darwin's great insight was that biology is a historical science, a science that illuminates natural history in part by showing how it implements the Darwinian algorithm.

Like many other algorithms, the "random variation and selective retention" algorithm may turn out to be a necessary truth. The algorithms that arithmetic consists in are unfalsifiable statements, often defended as giving the meaning of the mathematical operations they are named for. Addition just is whatever the addition algorithm does to two numbers. Similarly, the PNS may perfectly well be the only thing that we can say in general about fitness, and one of the core missions of evolutionary biology is making complex nonalgorithmic judgments about how different biological systems implement fitness differences.

Treating natural selection as an algorithm with indefinitely many implementations, among which there may be nothing else in common, seems to solve a lot of the problems about what the theory says, how it works, and what its relation can be to the rest of biology and physical science. But it does raise a worry. If natural selection is an algorithm that applies universally, explaining all adaptation whenever and wherever it occurs, and if it is the only algorithm that can do so, if natural selection is truly the only game in town, then it would seem once again to be a law (or at least there is a law that the algorithm operates always and everywhere). And it was to avoid the conclusion that there are laws of evolution that we began to explore the idea that natural selection is an algorithm, variously instantiated owing to the operation of a vast and heterogeneous set of physical laws operating on initial conditions of whatever kind are to be met with in the universe. We have come full circle. If the algorithm is instantiated just as a result of the operation of physical law, then this reflects the operation of a law, albeit one derived from physical laws.

One last notion needs to be mentioned here, a much more radical way to think about the absence of law in biology. We could consider the possibility that the same limitations on laws in biology also limit laws in the physical sciences. Some cosmologists think that the laws of the universe are not quite as timeless as we have imagined, that they have changed over time, especially in the first few moments of the universe, in the Big Bang, but also afterward, if more gradually, in its aftermath. It is not just that the physical substance of the universe has changed, the number and types of particles in existence, for example, but also the regularities that govern that substance, such as the inverse square law of gravitation. Perhaps the value of fundamental parameters or constants in physical laws is changing, evolving over time. Further, the notion that laws may be changing over time raises the possibility that they vary in space as well. There is no certain evidence for this now, but neither is there any logical obstacle to it. Such possibilities challenge the traditional philosophical analysis of a physical law. If there is evolution in the laws of physics, then our inability to find laws in biology might be a symptom of a more general problem with laws. If physical laws in fact vary over time as their parameters and constants change or, more radically, if their mathematical, functional forms change over time, physics will turn out to be a historical science. But it will not be one in the same way biology appears to be. For biology is a historical science owing to the indispensable role of both initial conditions here on Earth and timeless nomological truths in the explanation of its apparent regularities. Were physics to be historical, that is were initial conditions—dates and locations—to play a role in the explanation of when and where its generalizations obtained, there would be no fundamental timeless exceptionless laws available to explain these local generalizations. The absence of fundamental fixed laws in physics would not so much absolve biology of the need to seek explanatory laws as it would undermine explanation throughout the natural sciences.

In any case, according to some biologists and philosophers, the absence of strictly timeless and universal laws in physical science would require us to completely rethink the character of biological theory and explanation. For these thinkers hold that physical science constrains and underwrites biological theory. We shall consider this view in Chapter 4.

Summary

Our search for uniquely biological laws has been so far unsatisfactory. We began at a high level of specificity and a low level of explanatory significance—robins' eggs are blue—and moved to generalizations with successively greater generality and explanatory importance. But at each level we have found serious obstacles to the conclusion that biology has distinctive laws. And the problem has not been simply that there is nothing in biology like the strict laws of Newtonian mechanics. Even inexact, "other things equal" laws seem to be ruled out in biology.

Worse, even the core principles of Darwin's theory—which we argued in the last chapter are what makes biology a science—do not seem to noncontroversially satisfy requirements for being laws of nature. This is important, for scientific explanation would seem to require, presuppose, or assume laws—or statements similar enough to laws—to underwrite the causal claims these explanations report.

The difficulty of identifying unambiguous biological laws leads some philosophers to argue that there is no need for unique or proprietary laws, distinctive of the science. Perhaps algorithms, appropriated from mathematics, will suffice. We have seen that purely mathematical models lack the empirical content that the explanation of a particular fact or set of them requires. This problem of empirical content indeed vexes the most obvious candidate for being a distinctive biological law—the PNS. No matter how expressed, the PNS has long been stigmatized as unfalsifiable and indeed it appears that the various remedies for the problem this charge turns on—the definition of comparative fitness differences—have their own problems. We will come back to these matters later.

Suggestions for further reading

Elliott Sober defends the claim that models function in biology in the same way that laws do in physics in *The Philosophy of Biology*, which also provides an accessible account of the three models discussed above. Among the most well-known discussions of biological models is Richard Levin's paper "The strategy of model building in population biology." Sober and his co-author Steven Orzack subject Levin's paper to criticism in "A critical assessment of Levins' 'The strategy of model building (1966)'," and "A response to Sober and Orzack: formal analysis and the fluidity of science" is Levin's rejoinder.

The principle of natural selection and the definition of fitness have been a focus of a good deal of work in the philosophy of biology over the last half-century. Popper's argument that the definition makes Darwin's theory unfalsifiable is expounded in "Darwinism as a metaphysical research program" and is reprinted in Rosenberg and Balashov, *Philosophy of Science: Contemporary Readings*. It is immediately followed by an excerpt from Darwin, "Difficulties of the theory" which shows that Darwin certainly never treated his theory as unfalsifiable. Brandon's *Adaptation and Environment* defends a propensity definition of fitness and identifies the problems of giving an account of fitness that makes the PNS a law. Bouchard and Rosenberg's "Fitness, probability and the principles of natural selection" defends the claim that the principle of natural selection is a law of nature and explores alternative accounts of the nature of fitness that are compatible with this thesis. Campbell and Robert's "The structure of evolution by natural selection" summarizes much of this literature and provides a novel interpretation of the PNS as a law.

Natural selection as a substrate-neutral algorithm is an idea elaborated in Daniel Dennett's *Darwin's Dangerous Idea*. Elliott Sober argues that the Darwinian theory of evolution must be understood in large part as a claim about the history of life on the Earth in *The Philosophy of Biology*, a thesis earlier defended in a more radically "historicist" version by T.A. Goudge, in one of the earliest works of the philosophy of biology, *The Ascent of Life*.

In *The Advancement of Science* Philip Kitcher defends an account of the theory of natural selection and its application to explanation that is independent of any need for laws or substantive generalizations about biological processes.

One of the first philosophers to deny the existence of biological laws, especially about particular species, was J.J.C. Smart in *Philosophy and Scientific Realism*. Some philosophers of science have defended the notion that there can be laws about particular species, for example Marc Lange, in *Natural Laws in Scientific Practice*. Others have held that all laws, including the laws of physical science, have "other things being equal," *ceteris paribus* clauses. See, for example, Nancy Cartwright, *How the Laws of Physics Lie*. For an introduction to the problem of defining species and species names, see David Stamos, *The Species Problem*.

3 Further problems of Darwinism

Constraint, drift, function

Overview

The best-known challenge to Darwinism from within biology was, ironically enough, framed by two eminent evolutionary biologists who between them made some of the most influential contributions to the philosophy of biology, Stephen J. Gould and Richard Lewontin. The challenge was advanced in a paper published in the *Proceedings of the Royal Society of London* and entitled "The spandrels of San Marco and the Panglossian paradigm: a critique of the adaptationist programme" (Gould and Lewontin 1979). At the time of publication even the title required decoding, but now almost everyone who pursues the philosophy of biology knows what a "spandrel" is and who Dr. Pangloss was. It is easier to first sketch the drift of their argument and then explain its title. Much of our understanding of the current research program of evolutionary biology is owed to this paper and the responses it elicited. For the paper focuses on adaptationism—the explanation of biological traits as evolutionary solutions to design problems—and on the errors and temptations into which biologists and others following this research program have fallen.

Every biologist, no matter how strongly committed to adaptationism, recognizes the role of genetic drift in evolution. Drift is a chance factor in evolution, and it is recognized by all the textbooks on the subject. But recognizing the role of drift is not the same thing as agreeing on what it is, how it works, and what its relation to adaptation is. These are some of the hardest questions in the philosophy of biology, and they turn on differences in interpretation of probability that have vexed philosophers of science for at least two centuries. In this chapter we identify a number of different interpretations of probability, consider which has a role in biology, and whether any of them can enable us better to understand genetic drift. Perhaps more fully than any other problem at the foundations of evolutionary theory, the problem of how to combine drift and selection shows the relevance of philosophy to biology.

This chapter ends by returning to the purposes, goals, and ends—the teleology implicit in the vocabulary of biology. By applying the theory of natural selection to the analysis of terms such as enzyme, gene, neuron, flipper, or hive—words that name structures in terms of their *function*—philosophers have tried to render their teleology harmless. This enterprise has met with resistance. Some of the resistance stems from the belief that biological functions cannot be cashed in for adaptations, as we need a prior concept of function in order to express and assess claims about adaptation itself.

Adaptationism—for and against

Chapter 2 reported the debate about the unfalsifiability of the principle of natural selection when fitness is defined in terms of reproductive success. The practical problems arising from a definition of fitness differences in terms of alternative packages of design problem solutions also became apparent. Gould and Lewontin's famous paper carries these criticisms further. It defines "adaptationism" as the research program in biology which "regards natural selection as so powerful and the constraints upon it as so few that direct production of adaptation through its operation becomes the primary cause of nearly all organic form, function and behavior" (Gould and Lewontin 1979: 584). Adaptationism begins by "atomizing" organism into separate traits, and then seeks the design problem that each of these traits optimally solves. When it fails to show the optimality of a trait with respect to a single design problem, adaptationism seeks conflicting design problems which the organism's lineage faced and which favored these suboptimal traits as "trade-offs" in an optimal package. This is where Dr. Pangloss and Panglossianism emerge. The eighteenth century philosopher Voltaire introduced Pangloss as a caricature of Leibniz, the German philosopher who held that everything has a function, a role to play in making this the best of all possible worlds. Thus, for example, Dr. Pangloss explained the existence of the bridge of the nose on humans as owing to its function in supporting eyeglasses. One problem here is that the bridge of the nose is not a separate trait, in the sense that it was never acted upon by natural selection. The nose as a whole perhaps is a trait but, even if so, the bridge is nothing more than an arbitrary aspect of it. Another problem is that eyeglasses came long after nose bridges so could not be part of their cause. More generally, Gould and Lewontin argued, it is impossible to tell just by looking at a few generations whether a particular feature of an organism is an adaptive trait. Such speculations, based on "reverse engineering" of function and plausible selective histories, are not science; they are "just so" stories. (Readers may recall Rudyard Kipling's *Just So Stories*—fables about how the camel got its hump, how the elephant got its trunk, how the leopard got its spots, etc.) What has this to do with "spandrels?" As Gould and Lewontin tell us, spandrels are the curved triangular areas in the raised corners of the square structure supporting the central dome in cathedrals like the Basilica of San Marco. They are typically decorated with mosaic religious iconography, often well integrated into the much larger mosaics of the dome itself. The mistaken treatment of traits not actually selected for as adaptations is likened by Gould and Lewontin to the mistake of treating spandrels as design features, specifically as spaces intended by the architect for the support of the corner mosaics. In fact spandrels are the result of an architectural constraint, the inevitable consequence of fitting a dome to a square, an inevitable consequence that the mosaicists merely put to good use.

Gould and Lewontin go on to trace the adaptationist program through several "common styles of argument":

1   "If one adaptive argument fails, try another." If antlers do not really protect against predators, then perhaps they are selected for interspecies competition. If neither protection nor interspecies competition works, try sexual selection.
2   "If one adaptive argument fails, assume that another as yet undiscovered exists." Disconfirmation is only a reason to look further for another design problem the trait solves.
3   In the absence of a good adaptive argument in the first place, attribute failure to ignorance of the organism's structure and behavior.
4   "Emphasize immediate utility and exclude other attributes of form."

They conclude:

> We would not object so strenuously to the adaptationist programme if its invocation, in any particular case, could lead *in principle* to its rejection for want of evidence. We might still view it as restrictive and object to its status as an argument of first choice. But if it could be dismissed after failing some explicit test, then alternatives would get their chance.
>
> (Gould and Lewontin 1979: 587)

So, the hypothesis that *the* cause, or the most important among the causes, of the structure of most organisms and their behavior is natural selection, turns out on Gould and Lewontin's view to be one that many evolutionary biologists have been reluctant to surrender, come what may. This charge is different from the claim that the theory of natural selection is unfalsifiable owing to a circular definition of fitness. But it has a similar upshot. Gould and Lewontin argue that evolutionary biologists believe that their theory—adaptationism—makes contingent, empirical, causally explanatory claims about the world, but by refusing to accept any evidence as disconfirming it, some of them deprive it of this status as a claim about how the world works. There are several parts of this charge that need to be sorted out. First, is it true that evolutionary biologists embrace adaptationism as defined, and as the research strategy Gould and Lewontin describe? Second, is some form of adaptationism a defensible strategy? Third, are there other defensible strategies, in which nonselective factors, in particular constraints, take the central role? Fourth, how shall we understand the relationship between selection and constraint, and what is the proper role of each in evolutionary explanation?

The first question has two answers. One is that times have changed. If evolutionary biologists used to be unqualified adaptationists, since 1979 they have for the most part taken the Spandrels critique to heart, with the result that adaptive hypotheses are typically framed more carefully, more falsifiably, and alternative nonadaptive explanations are more often considered, than in the decades before Spandrels. Gould and Lewontin produced a real cultural change in evolutionary studies.

The second answer is that evolutionists were never really unqualified adaptationists. While not always as careful in their thinking and writing as Gould and Lewontin would like, they have always known that adaptation is constrained, that form, physiology, and behavior cannot be due to adaptation alone. For example, some biologists, such as Francis Crick, believe that the genetic code is a "frozen accident," that the code could easily have been other than it is. And there is no consensus among evolutionary biologist that selection is responsible for the African rhinoceros having two horns whereas two of the three Asian species have a single horn. This could be a matter of "drift" (a concept to which we shall return later in this chapter and the next). And then there is a huge category of commonly acknowledged examples of poor adaptation that are sometimes called imperfections of "design." Two occur in the organ we often think of as perfectly adapted, the vertebrate eye. There is the blind spot that arises from the fact that the optic nerve enters the retina from the front. And the fact that we blink both eyes simultaneously is a maladaptation that must blind us to threats occasionally. These probable frozen accidents and imperfections are constraints on selection and have long been readily accepted as such by adaptationists. And they reflect the widespread recognition that traits are the products not just of selection but of the interaction of natural selection, constraint, and chance.

Thus, today, most evolutionists would cheerfully plead guilty to the charge of being adaptationists, albeit with appropriate caveats to accommodate Gould and Lewontin's critique. These caveats would include acknowledgment of the possible contributions of constraint and drift, and the importance of framing hypotheses so that they are falsifiable.

Our second question is whether biologists are right to be suitably qualified adaptationists. Is a persistent, even dogged, search for adaptive explanation, of the sort decried by Gould and Lewontin, justified? In some cases, at least, it certainly seems to be. Take, for example, the problem of explaining sexual reproduction. This is no peripheral issue in evolutionary biology. The vast majority of animals reproduce sexually and only a very small number asexually. Indeed, the most widely accepted definition of species presupposes sexual reproduction: an interbreeding population reproductively isolated from other populations. (As discussed, asexual species make this definition somewhat problematic.) So sexual reproduction is considered biologically significant. And it is also probably the best example of the adaptationist's refusal to consider alternative explanations. Paradoxically, the reason is that there are features of sexual reproduction that are on their faces extremely difficult to reconcile with the theory of natural selection.

Here is the problem that sex poses for selection theory. Sexual reproduction involves meiosis, and meiosis produces gametes with only half the organism's genes. Therefore only half of each organism's genes are passed to the next generation in each offspring. If the number of offspring, or equivalently (in most cases) the number of gene copies in the next generation, is a function of fitness, then the cost to an animal of sexual reproduction, in terms of fitness, must be very high indeed! Other things being equal, there is a continuing invitation to alternative means of reproduction, for example parthenogenesis (a form of asexual reproduction), which has lower genetic fitness costs. And yet parthenogenesis is rare in animals, and does not persist for more than a few generations (except in a small number of species, for example in certain rotifer and insect species). Thus, either sexual reproduction is not an adaptation, meaning that it is the result of constraint or chance, or it confers benefits so large that they swamp the fitness costs of meiosis. The adaptationist points out that these huge costs strongly suggest that sex is an adaptation. It is difficult to imagine that either constraint or chance could maintain sex against so strong a disadvantage.

Following the adaptationist program, evolutionary biologists have hypothesized alternative benefits that sex might accord and sought evidence that supports these hypotheses. None have as yet been sufficiently well confirmed to be accepted or to reconcile sexual reproduction with natural selection. Almost all suggest that it is the recombining—i.e. shuffling—of genes that makes sex an adaptation. One attractive hypothesis was advanced by the theorist William D. Hamilton, who suggested that recombination helps animals to resist parasites. Parasites reproduce fast and mutate quickly, thus exploiting any opportunity to invade a host. One long-term strategy against them is to change the traits to which parasites are adapting to exploit faster than the parasites are able to adapt. And recombination among the genes of two genetically different parents provides the rapid trait variation needed to win this evolutionary arms race.

For the adaptationist, the hypothesis presents two problems. First, it is not obvious that sexual reproduction confers only one adaptive advantage, as opposed to several, all of which when added up counter-balance the cost. Against this, one might argue that sex is ubiquitous in animals across a huge range of environments. Surely if sex is the solution to a large number of smaller design problems, there would be more than just a few environments (e.g. that of a few rotifers and insects) in which all or most of these problems were absent so that asexual reproduction would have a chance to arise and persist. In any case, multiple advantages is not an argument against the adaptationist's program of searching for an adaptive answer. If true, it simply means that the answer is going to be harder to find.

Second, given the complexities involved in tracking the arms race move and counter-move of parasite and host across all the different lineages of animals (and then of plants, fungi, and microorganisms), it will be very difficult to find decisive evidence to support the hypothesis. Finding evidence for or against Hamilton's hypothesis about why sex exists is going to be a long and hard task without the expectation of any "silver bullet" or crucial experiment. But again this does not disconcert the adaptationist. The difficulty of the task is no reason not to try.

For the problem of sex, evolutionary biologists have essentially adopted all four styles of argument that Gould and Lewontin condemn: "If one adaptive argument fails, try another," "If one adaptive argument fails, assume that another as yet undiscovered exists," and so on. The adaptationist has to admit the possibility in principle that this approach could lead nowhere, that sex could—again in principle—be the result of some unknown constraint. But given the huge fitness costs sex seems to entail, along with its ubiquity in nature, a determined search for adaptive explanation seems well justified.

It is worth saying that, despite the stridently condemnatory tone of the Gould and Lewontin argument, it is not clear that they would object to adaptationism pursued in this fashion, with the appropriate acknowledgment of alternative explanations. Indeed, it is possible to read Spandrels not as a blanket condemnation of the adaptationist program, but of the incautious, superficial, and complacent application of it.

Constraint and adaptation

Our third question was whether there is a defensible alternative to an adaptationist research program, and the answer is yes. Several subfields of biology are nonadaptationist in the sense that their primary mission is not finding and explaining adaptations. Instead, what we find at the core of their mission is constraint, either as a central operating assumption or as a direct target of investigation.

Darwin saw a central role in evolution for constraint, or what he called "unity of type," and which he understood mainly as a limitation on the ability of natural selection to effect change. Gould and Lewontin use the example of the body plan, or *bauplan* from the German for "building plan." For example, all insects have three body regions: head, thorax, and abdomen. All vertebrates have a spinal column. All crustaceans (including crabs, shrimps, pillbugs, and their relatives) have the same number and sequence of appendages on their heads. These *bauplan* features are universal (or nearly so) in their respective groups and apparently so constrained as to be immune to removal by natural selection, or removable only with difficulty. Are three body regions optimal for all of the tens of millions of insect species, in all of the environments they inhabit? The constraint argument says probably not. More likely, the variation necessary to generate an insect with two or four or some other number of body regions simply cannot arise, or does not arise very often. Or, when it does arise, it disrupts the basic organization of the organism to such a degree as to render the organism tremendously unfit. As Gould and Lewontin put it, the body plan as a whole is:

so integrated and so replete with constraints upon adaptation . . . that conventional styles of selective arguments can explain little of interest about them. It does not deny that change, when it occurs, may be mediated by natural selection, but it holds that constraints restrict possible paths and modes of change so strongly that the constraints themselves become much the most interesting aspect of evolution.

(Gould and Lewontin 1979: 594)

Importantly, the constraint argument does not say that body plan features could not have been adaptive at their time of origin, although some body plan features did undoubtedly arise and become fixed by chance. But many may have been adaptations originally, in some ancestral environment, and later become fixed, in effect becoming frozen accidents. In either case, whether originally adaptive or not, the implication is that a constraint arising earlier limits adaptation to the *immediate* environment in which the organism finds itself later.

Notice too that constraint has a flip side. It can act as an aid to adaptation as well as a limitation. Recall the point from Chapter 1, that later-arising traits build on earlier traits, allowing complex adaptations to be built up step-wise. Constraint on early arising traits, imposed by the need to preserve later ones, is one of the mechanisms that makes such cumulative evolution possible. And constraints are involved in adaptation in another way, in what Stephen J. Gould and the paleobiologist Elizabeth Vrba (1982) have called "exaptations." These are traits originally adapted to solve one "design problem" that are subsequently co-opted by selection to solve quite a different one. ("Exaptations" have in the past been called "preadaptations," but this label misleadingly accords natural selection a sort of foresight that no evolutionary biologist accepts.) Thus, the wrist bones and digits of bat ancestors are exaptations, in that they evolved originally as solutions to one design problem, and were later co-opted in the solution to a new one, supporting a wing structure. Recall the point made in Chapter 1 that evolution is opportunistic, often exploiting quick and dirty solutions in preference to optimal but slow-to-emerge solutions. Constraint is one reason that optimal solutions might be slow to emerge, or even unavailable. For the ancestral bat, an ideal wing might not have involved the digits at all (indeed, bird wings evolved differently). Constraints on variation prevent natural selection from optimizing. Instead, natural selection improvises, using the variation available.

And then there is the type of constraint that Darwin called "correlation of parts." Sometimes, a body part is not itself the result of selection as an independent solution to a design problem but rather the result of selection acting on another part with which it is correlated. One of Gould's favorite examples is brain size, which increased over evolutionary time in the human lineage. Are large brains the result of selection for superior intelligence? It could be that a great deal of the increase in brain size is simply a result of the connection in development between brain size and body size. In this view, selection is involved in the trend, driving the underlying increase in body size. But the brain's enlargement itself is the result of correlation of parts—brains and bodies—and therefore is not an adaptation. Notice here too that constraint has a positive as well as a negative aspect. Body size constrains brain size, in the sense of causing it to change even in the absence of selection pressures for change. But it also offers opportunities, producing change even when the change may have no immediate selective advantage. Selection increases body size, and constraint gives the organism a larger brain *for free*, so to speak.

All of the above constraints fall into a broad category of what are called phylogenetic constraints, or limitations on change arising in the evolutionary history—the phylogeny—of a group. Ordinarily, these are expressed as limits that are internal to the organism, arising in its development, and in that case they are also called developmental constraints. Correlation of parts is a developmental constraint. The study of constraints on development, or more generally the relationship between development and evolution, was central in nineteenth century biology (especially in biology in the German-speaking world: e.g. Haeckel). But in the twentieth century, breakthroughs in population genetics moved biology more toward the study of adaptation, leaving what some saw as a gap in the Darwinian research program. "The spandrels of San Marco" drew attention to this gap, and indeed since Spandrels the study of developmental constraints has seen a resurgence, under the label of evolutionary–developmental biology, or "evo–devo."

The focus of evo–devo is the molecular mechanisms underlying evolutionary change in developmental programs, i.e. in ontogeny. A key finding that helped launch this field was the discovery of certain genetic control units, the *Hox* genes, which seem to be present in almost all animals and which in many control the differentiation of regions along the body's major axis. These genes seem to be critical components in a larger developmental process that produced the great diversity of body plans we see among animals and therefore represents a major constraint on animal organization.

Constraints are also crucial in the project of phylogenetic reconstruction, the reconstruction of the family tree of relationships among species in a group. Constraints make it possible to determine who begat who, so to speak, at the level of species. To see why constraints are essential to this project, consider how the world would look in their absence, if natural selection were omnipotent and able to modify every species optimally. The effect would be to erase all homology, that is to erase all similarity due to descent from a common ancestor. For example, suppose for the sake of argument that modern fish are optimally designed. In that case, modern whales—which evolved their aquatic life habit independently, from land mammals—would be indistinguishable from fish. Whales would have evolved scales. The tail fin would have rotated 90 degrees to lie vertically (instead of horizontally as it does in actual whales). Whales would also have lost the ability to nurse their young. (We would never know they were mammals.) And they would resemble fish not just at the gross structural level but in every detail, down to the level of tissue morphology and molecular physiology. The technical term for selection-driven similarity is "convergence," and the argument is that without constraint, convergence would be massive, pervasive, perfect. In fact, however, we think such perfect convergence does not occur (although consider: if it did, how would we know?). And the barriers constraint imposes on adaptation is the reason we can trace the true ancestry of whales. Constraint preserves history. Indeed, in one of the methods employed in modern phylogenetic reconstruction, the parsimony method, the assumption is that change is highly constrained, and that convergence from different traits to similar ones in different species through selection is rare. The method finds the phylogenetic tree with the minimum number of changes, the minimum number of convergences. In one phylogenetic reconstruction method, constraint— not adaptation—is the default assumption for explaining shared traits over long periods of evolution.

Importantly, there is no suggestion here that constraint is the only possible cause of constancy, of the absence of evolutionary change. Selection too can produce constancy. The great similarity in structure in the protein cytochrome-c across many plants, animals, and protists is likely the result of strong selection for it to perform a similar function in metabolism. Rather, the claim is that constraints of various kinds are among the possible causes of constancy. Further, constraint is likely to be involved in cases where function is known to have changed. For example, the persistence of hip bones in whales could be the result of a constraint, on the assumption that—lacking legs—hips are not functional in whales.

There are three other categories of constraint that are known as formal, physical, and architectural constraints. Formal constraints are those imposed by the restrictions of mathematics or geometry. The hexagonal shape of cells in honeybee hives is probably not the result of natural selection, but of a geometric inevitability arising from the way the honeycomb is built. Cells start circular in cross-section and become hexagonal as a result of close packing, of the minimization of spaces between them. Physical constraints are those imposed by the physical and chemical laws. All organisms are constrained by the laws of gravity, diffusion, thermodynamics, etc. And architectural constraints are those imposed by the properties of the materials of which the organism is built or, more generally, by the organization or structure of the organism. All of these last three categories of constraint are central to a subfield of biology called biomechanics. Biomechanics is interested, for example, in the tensile properties of the material that a seaweed uses to attach itself to a rock and to survive the stresses of a turbulent surf. It is interested in how the shapes and orientations of the bones in the leg of a heavy land animal enable it to walk or run without serious risk of breakage. Generally speaking, the presumption is that the organism is well adapted, if not optimal, but the focus is on the constraints imposed by geometry, physics, and material properties of organisms and their components.

Nothing in the various constraint-driven research programs could be called *anti*-adaptationist. Indeed, phylogenetic reconstruction is an important route for discovering adaptation. In a genealogical tree in which convergences have been minimized, those remaining are likely adaptations. Biomechanics could be construed as the study of the materials and the configuration of those materials that are immediately available to evolving lineages to solve the design problems the organisms in these lineages face. The constraint research programs are alternatives to the adaptationist program but only in the sense that they have different interests, a different focus. There is no conflict. In a common misreading of Spandrels, Gould and Lewontin are thought to be saying that selection and constraint offer alternative routes to adaptation. Were they to have so argued, Gould and Lewontin would have in fact been rejecting Darwin! But, to the contrary, they acknowledge that selection is the only explanation available for adaptation, when it occurs. Nothing in Spandrels challenges natural selection's monopoly on explanation of the fit of organisms to their environment, its explanation of the origin of function in nature. Their claim is rather that there is more to organisms than their adaptations, other aspects worthy of study.

Our fourth and final question was how the relationship between selection and constraint is to be properly understood. An elegant heuristic has been offered by Elliott Sober, later elaborated by Roger Sansom (2003). The essence of the heuristic is this: constraint "proposes" and selection "disposes." Suppose that the major selection pressure on zebras is pursuit by predators such as lions. Now consider the full range of form, physiology, and behavior that is *conceivable* for zebras. Imagine not only zebras as they are, but zebras that are faster, or bigger, or have tougher hides, and so on. But don't stop there. The range of the conceivable includes zebras with vertical take-off ability, zebras with rear-mounted AK-47s, and zebras with predator-mind-control capability. The conceivable includes the full range of what is thinkable, however unrealistic or absurd.

The role of constraint, then, is to reduce the range of the conceivable to what can actually be generated by natural variation. Zebras with vertical take-off ability, and such, are developmentally unavailable, and probably impossible for physical, architectural, and material properties reasons as well. In other words, they are ruled out by constraint, leaving only the more realistic natural variants, zebras that are faster, bigger, and so on. Of course, constraint limits these too. Given the constraints of zebra organization, it might be that natural variation cannot deliver both size and agility at the same time. Bigger might mean less maneuverable. It is not just the absurd that constraint rules out.

Now natural selection enters the picture. And the role of selection is to reduce the range of what natural variation offers to what can actually survive and reproduce in a given environment. That is to say selection takes the offerings remaining after constraint acts, the offerings available by natural variation, and leaves the few variants that are more fit, perhaps zebras that are larger and therefore better able to fend off lions, despite being less maneuverable. In sum, the heuristic works like this: constraints culls the (truly enormous) range of the conceivable and offers up to selection the (much smaller) range actually available. Selection then culls the range of natural variation leaving the few that are more fit. Constraint proposes, and selection disposes.

The great value of this heuristic is that it shows clearly how certain sorts of explanations in evolution depend equally on both selection and constraint. In particular, this is true for questions about the cause, or origin, of a trait. What is the cause of large body size in zebras? For such questions, constraint alone is obviously insufficient. In the absence of selection, not just large zebras would survive but medium and small ones too. More broadly, without selection, every developmental oddity survives and reproduces. And this is clearly not the case.

But for questions about cause or origin, selection is also insufficient by itself. Worse, it is not clear that the notion of constraint-free evolution is even intelligible. For example, without constraints, we cannot say that the cause of zebras being large is that large size is fittest, partly because without constraints, this would be untrue. It would enhance zebra fitness even more if they had rear-mounted AK-47s. Alas, there are constraints that exclude this option. Even more troubling is that the notion of "fittest" is not meaningful unless applied to a specified, or in principle specifiable, range of possibilities. Without constraint, the range is infinite, or at least unspecifiably large. To put it another way, selection acts on what is available, and constraint is needed *as a matter of logic* to specify what is available. Thus the Sober–Sansom heuristic reveals an asymmetry in the roles of selection and constraint in explaining the evolutionary origins of traits. Selection without constraint seems meaningless. Constraint without selection is merely unrealistic.

This logical dependence of selection on constraint is widely understood, and may in part account for the outrage with which some adaptationists answered Spandrels. Gould and Lewontin seemed to be saying that adaptationists overlook constraint. But for arguments about cause or origin of a trait, it is clear that constraint *must* be part of the argument, if only implicitly, because the notion of selection without constraint is meaningless. To some, it must have seemed as if Gould and Lewontin were accusing them of arguing, absurdly, against something logically required by their explanatory strategy.

But constraint and adaptation can sometimes compete. And when they do, Gould and Lewontin's complaint that adaptationists sometimes ignore constraint does make sense. Consider, for example, evolutionary questions about difference making. For zebra body size, we can meaningfully ask what accounts for the change in body size from the much smaller zebra ancestor, *Hyracotherium*, living tens of millions of years ago. In other words, we can ask what made the difference in zebra evolution between some trait (here, large body size) and some alternative (here, small body size). For questions formulated this way, either selection or constraint could be the answer. The difference maker could be selection, its directly favoring large size. Or it could be, for example, that selection favored long legs, that leg length and body size are correlated in zebra development, and therefore that the increase in body size was the result of a constraint. In that case, one is inclined to say that the difference maker was a constraint, the correlation in development. Of course, it could also be a combination of selection and constraint. Nothing in this reasoning demands single factor causes. The point is that for difference-making questions, selection and constraint can be opposed.

What is genetic drift?

We have left for separate discussion the first alternative to adaptationism that Gould and Lewontin mention, and that has itself been the source of controversy in both evolutionary biology and its philosophy for much of the last century. This is the concept of random drift. Gould and Lewontin write:

> At present, population geneticists are sharply divided on the question of how much genetic polymorphism within populations and how much of the genetic differences between species is, in fact, the result of natural selection as opposed to purely random factors. Populations are finite in size and the isolated populations that form the first step in the speciation process are often founded by a very small number of individuals. As a result of this restriction in population size, frequencies of alleles change by *genetic drift*, a kind of random genetic sampling error. The stochastic process of change in gene frequency by random genetic drift . . . has several important consequences. First, populations and species will become genetically differentiated . . . in the complete absence of any selective force at all.
>
> Secondly, alleles can become fixed in a population *in spite of natural selection* . . . .
>
> Thirdly, new mutations have a small chance of being incorporated into a population, even when selectively favoured . . . .
>
> (Gould and Lewontin 1979: 156–157)

Random drift, genetic drift, or just plain drift labels the statistical or stochastic or probabilistic character of evolution by natural selection. Recall the principle of natural selection (PNS; Chapter 2) which tells us that fitness differences *probably* result in population differences. The "probably" in the PNS reflects the fact that when populations are small, chance will sometimes result in the less fit increasing. For the same reason, chance allows for a fair coin coming up tails six times in a row. Of course contemporary evolutionary biology denies none of Gould and Lewontin's claims about drift. The biological problem is to what extent random drift—probability, chance, luck—is a factor in the actual course of descent with modification that constitutes evolution here on Earth. Some biologists have argued that explaining the actual course of evolution demands a significant role for drift. Others have denied this. Lewontin and Gould are just two of the biologists in the first group. But even among those who doubt that drift is generally an important factor, it is considered likely to be important in certain evolutionary processes, like speciation. One recognized mechanism of speciation is geographic isolation. In one version, the process begins with the emergence of some new geographic barrier, perhaps a new seaway or mountain range that separates a small number of members of one species from the rest of a large population. This small population then reproduces in isolation from the larger parent population, owing to the barrier that separates them. If the founder population is small it probably does not carry the full range of genetic variation in the large population. Further, in small populations new combinations of genes are likely to arise, producing new phenotypes, which may become fixed by chance. Eventually, given sustained isolation of the founder population, a new species emerges. More generally, in populations of any size, chance can change the distribution of traits from generation to generation. Such changes that do not take populations in the direction of greater adaptation are often described as resulting from drift. That such changes can and do occur is uncontroversial. But their importance in determining the evolutionary trajectories of most species, most of the time, is an empirical issue that is much debated.

The philosophical problems of drift arise from competing understandings of how drift works and what its sources are: Is drift a separate evolutionary force or cause that combines with selection, a second independent force, to determine evolutionary trajectories? Biologists often assume this interpretation of drift, especially when they accept the role of drift as running counter to that of selection, slowing it down, or preventing it from working altogether in determining evolutionary outcomes. Another view treats drift not as a distinct factor in evolution, but as an inseparable reflection of the character of natural selection as a population-level process. In this conception, drift is always present in evolution, even in a fully deterministic world, owing to the fact that natural selection is a statistical process that operates only on populations and is not reducible to the heritable fitness differences between individual competing organisms. On this view, drift, like entropy in thermodynamics, is a property of ensembles or populations that disappears when we focus on individual organisms (just as entropy disappears when we focus on the individual particles of a gas enclosed in a container). Still a third view we should consider, if only to illustrate the problems drift raises for the theory of natural selection, treats drift as a reflection of our ignorance of all the selective forces that together determine unique evolutionary outcomes. These utterly different understandings of drift make for very different interpretations of how the theory of natural selection is to be understood, as we shall see.

One way to begin to deal with these questions about drift is to return to the PNS, introduced in Chapter 2:

> *PNS* If x is fitter than y in environmental E, then, *probably*, x will have more descendants than y in E.

The qualifier "probably" in the PNS is the point of entry for drift, and it is essential to the truth of the PNS and its explanatory/predictive powers. For example, we know that the larger the fitness difference between x and y, the more probably x's descendants will outnumber y's, and the more probably this will happen earlier rather than later. We can also be confident that the larger the populations of x and y, the higher the probability that x's descendants will outnumber y's. And, when the population is large, as it is in so many species, the greater the variance in fitness differences, the sooner these demographic differences show up. Indeed, this is the thought behind R.A. Fisher's "fundamental theorem of natural selection," typically expressed as follows: "The rate of increase in fitness in any organism at any time is equal to its genetic variance in fitness at that time." The theorem follows from the PNS, along with certain further assumptions about population size—it must be very large, effectively infinite—and from assumptions about the phenotypic effects of individual genes—that they are small and gradual.

In general, if populations were always infinitely large or lasted for an infinite amount of time, we would not need the "probably" in the PNS. (As the poet Andrew Marvell once said to a coy mistress, "had we but world enough and time . . . .") But they are not, so the qualifier is required, just to make the PNS true! Notice that this same qualifier raises the problem we faced in Chapter 2, namely that it insulates the PNS against falsifying evidence. A counter-example to evolutionary theory can always be written off as a chance event, fully consistent with the theory. How can we be sure that a change in the traits in a lineage is the result of adaptation and not a result of chance events? It seems that invoking drift in evolutionary explanation may expose evolutionary theory to the same charge of untestability that Gould and Lewontin raise against excessive adaptationism.

Let us begin by asking what kind of probability the PNS invokes. There are at least two broad conceptions of probability: subjective and objective. The term "objective" in this context is used to label probabilities in the world independent of the mental states—independent of preferences and expectations, beliefs and desires—of cognitive agents like us. "Subjective" probabilities are those that do depend for their existence on the states of mind of actual or possible cognitive agents. There are at least three different kinds of objective probability, but really only one sort of subjective probability. Moreover, the distinction is somewhat misleading, for both objective and subjective probabilities are "objective" in one sense: they both obey the axioms and theorems of the mathematical theory of probability.

Very roughly, a subjective probability is the odds a rational agent would give in making bets on whether a particular outcome will occur, given the available evidence. This sense of probability is sometimes called Bayesian probability because it requires rational agents to use a certain formula to change the strength of their beliefs (their subjective probability judgments) about the world as new evidence comes in. This formula was first derived from probability theory by Thomas Bayes in the eighteenth century. For this reason, subjective probabilities—betting odds that are recalculated in accordance with this formula as new evidence comes in—are also known as Bayesian probabilities. These probabilities are subjective in that they will exist only if rational agents exist to make bets, or else they exist only on the condition that if there were rational agents, they would make bets. Bayesian probabilities were first introduced to deal with statistical data in which it seemed difficult to define objective probabilities. For example, the objective probability of drawing the queen of hearts in a fair deck of cars is 1/52 since there are 52 cards in a deck. But the objective probability that it will be exactly 18.00000. . . degrees Celsius on a clear summer day in Paris is either zero or undefined. The reason is that there are an infinite number of possible exact thermometer readings between, say 17.5 and 18.5 degrees, and if the temperature is in that range, the probability that it is precisely 18 is one divided by infinity, which approaches zero or is undefined. The subjective probability of drawing the Queen of Hearts is unproblematic. It is the same as the objective probability. But the subjective probability of its reaching exactly 18.00000. . . degrees on a clear summer day in Paris cannot be zero because it measures degrees or strength of belief and some people have, or at least could have, the relevant belief to some degree of strength.

Bayesian subjective probability has a role in biology. For example, we could measure fitness in terms of subjective probabilities—the betting odds about how many offspring a particular organism, or set of organisms, will leave. Moreover, biologists will make subjective probability judgments about evolutionary outcomes. The process of evolution is extremely complicated and involves many causes operating together. Even if the laws governing the process are deterministic, the biologist's best guesses as to its outcome may be statements of subjective probability. However, few philosophers of biology think that the probabilities in the PNS are subjective. Evolution by natural selection is supposed to occur regardless of whether there are, or even could be, rational agents actually or possibly making bets about it. Many philosophers and biologists hold that Darwinian theory is not just probabilistic as a reflection of limitations on our ability to plot the course of evolution on this planet exactly. It will be statistical even in a deterministic world in which biologists know everything. It will be statistical even in the simplest ecology, or indeed, even in a Petri dish or test tube. The probability in the PNS must be objective. It must be what philosophers sometimes call "chance" or even "objective chance" for emphasis. If the probability in the consequent of the PNS is objective, then drift is an objective force, factor, or cause of evolutionary trajectories.

But if drift is a real force and the probability in the PNS is objective, then what is its source in the world, what facts about the world make its claims about probabilities (and therefore the magnitude of drift) true? There are three main kinds or sources of objective probability: "long-run relative frequencies" (exemplified by flipping coins or pulling red and black balls from urns), quantum indeterminism (manifested in radioactive decay), and the sort of probability reflected in the second law of thermodynamics (the entropy of a closed system will probably increase over time).

Most biologists and many philosophers would rule out quantum indeterminism as the basis for the PNS's statistical character. The reason is obvious. Quantum mechanics says that whether a uranium atom emits a gamma ray during a given 60 second interval or not has no cause in any prior state of the atom. According to quantum mechanics, it's just a brute fact of randomness at the basement level of physical processes. But few biologists believe that probabilities at the level of macroscopic objects are the result of probabilistic propensities of subatomic entities "percolating up" from the subatomic level. Of course sometimes such indeterministic events can result in macroscopic events that we detect, as in the clicking of a Geiger counter. And sometimes these events will cause point mutations in the genetic material and so have effects with potential evolutionary significance. But no one thinks that quantum indeterminism is by itself the source or even a major additional factor contributing to the statistical character of natural selection.

Many biologists believe that the statistical character of natural selection has the same source as such commonplace processes as coin flipping or pulling black and red balls out of urns without looking. This makes the view that evolutionary probability is long-run relative frequency an attractive one to these biologists. Take repeated coin flipping or, better yet, the flipping of a perfectly symmetrical coin-shaped disk by the usual thumb-and-forefinger technique (or some mechanical substitute). Some sequences of flips will produce more heads than tails (and vice versa). Some will produce many more, and a few will produce no tails at all (and a few will produce few heads). But, almost always, the more times the coin is flipped, the closer the total number of heads and the total number of tails will approach equality and remain in its vicinity. And on this basis we say that the probability of heads is 0.5.

Of course the long-run relative frequency must be understood as an infinitely long run. On this meaning, the probability of this coin coming up heads when thrown by this thumb and forefinger = 0.5 means in part that were there to be an infinitely large number of such flips, half of them would be heads. "If there were an infinite number of such flips, then 50 percent would be heads" is clearly a "counter-factual" claim for which evidence can be amassed (flip the coin many times). But notice, the infinitely many flips could come in batches of 1000 heads followed by 1000 tails. So, we need to add that in any finite subset of flips, the larger the set, the closer to 0.5 will be the proportion of heads. But, suppose in fact that for a very long run of flips, heads and tails are perfectly alternated. That would suggest that the chance of heads on the next flip will be close to 1 if the last flip came up tails. So we need to exclude from the long-run relative frequency definition a large number of finite and infinite sequences in which heads and tails both do come up 50 percent of the time but do so in some highly predictable order. It is not clear that we can do this in a noncircular way. Some philosophers (including influential philosophers of biology) have argued that an outcome's probability equals its long-run—i.e. infinite—or hypothetical relative frequency, provided that every subset in the series, that is chosen without the choice being made on the basis of some common cause or effect of the chosen set's members, comes up with exactly the same proportion of heads to tails as the whole series for its relative frequency. This proposal does identify at least a necessary qualification on the claim that long-run or hypothetical relative frequencies are equal to objective chances.

The idea that the objective probability of an outcome is its relative frequency in an infinitely repeated sequence of trials cannot of course be applied in evolutionary biology, for the outcomes of interest in evolutionary biology are almost never repeatable at all, even once, let alone with some specific frequency in an infinite sequence of trials. But even if we simply stipulated that long-run relative frequency is just what is meant by the concept of probability that figures in the consequent of the PNS, we would still want to know "where" that objective probability "came from," what particular set of facts about the fitness to the environment of those particular organisms at that particular time produced the particular value of the objective chance that one would leave more offspring than the other. Compare the simpler question about where the objective chance that a particular coin will come up heads when tossed "came from." In that case, the answer is to be found in an infinite series that never actually happens. The objective chance of a coin coming up heads will be 0.5, even in an entirely deterministic world! So, where did the objective chance of heads on that toss come from? What facts about the world—even a deterministic world—cause it? These same questions arise for the statement that the probability of x's descendants outnumbering y's descendants is greater than 0.5 (sometimes much greater and approaching 1). What the PNS claims is that there is an objective probability of this outcome. But just as in the case of the coin's objective probability of coming up heads, what we want to know is where it comes from.

Before going on to answer this question, let's remind ourselves what "drift" has to do with it. In the case of a fair coin, "drift" names a sequence of tosses that departs from 0.5 in its proportion of heads. The larger the departure, the greater the drift, and the larger the sequence of tosses of a fair coin, the less drift there will be. Similarly, in natural selection, "drift" names changes in proportion of actual descendants that depart from the most probable proportions determined by the PNS. These departures will be greater when the number of organisms in the population is small, and smaller when the population is large. So whatever the objective chance of an outcome in natural selection is, drift is the "flip side" and both have the same source. But what is that source?

In the case of coin flipping, one is tempted to say that the 0.5 objective chance of heads comes from the fact that, of all the sets of possible coin positions on the thumb and values for the momentum imparted by it to the coin, the number of combinations that result in heads is equal to the number of combinations that result in tails and each of these possible combinations is equally probable. The troubles with this claim are several. First, its assumption that every physical possibility is equally probable is itself ungrounded. We can still ask where the probability of each of the possible alternatives "came from" and why they should be equal. Second, since the set of possible combinations of position and momentum that results in heads is infinite, the probability of any one combination obtaining is zero, so the addition of their probabilities cannot add up to 0.5. Third, there is no uniquely correct way of comparing two infinite sets to see which one is larger. So this answer is highly problematical. The problems are even greater when we turn to the question of where objective chances come from in biology. If we say the chance is greater than 0.5 owing to the fact that the number of combinations of x's traits and possible environments that produce more descendants for x is "larger" than the set of combinations of y's traits and possible environments that produce more descendants for y, we need some sense of "larger" that we simply do not have.

Another way to see this problem is to compare physical (including biological) processes to ones familiar from card playing. What is the probability of drawing the queen of hearts from a fair deck? Answer: exactly 1/52 or 1.9230769230769. . . percent. We know this because there are exactly 52 cards in a fair deck, and each card has the same chance of being drawn. This probability is known as an a priori probability just because the design of playing card packs makes it certain. No experiments in which we shuffle and deal are required. But ecology is not divided into any particular finite set of equipossible outcomes, and so the probability of any one outcome cannot be calculated a priori. We have no basis for assigning equal probabilities to "basic" outcomes since we have no idea what these could be or how many there are. Thus the sort and the source of the probability—objective chance—that the PNS requires remain mysterious.

Central tendencies, subjective probabilities, and theism

If drift can act as a force or cause operating in the world—along with fitness differences to produce evolution—then we need to find its source in the world. If we cannot do this we may not be thinking about drift and selection the right way at all. Another reason to think we do not understand the relation between them correctly arises from the difficulty of actually telling apart cases of drift from cases of selection empirically!

This issue is important partly for historical reasons. For many years, two famous evolutionary biologists, R.A. Fisher and Sewall Wright disputed the role of drift in the actual course of evolution on Earth and its role in any biologically possible evolutionary change. Wright argued that evolution almost always requires a good deal of drift, that is it occurs as a result of interbreeding within small populations in which genes, genotypes, and phenotypes are unrepresentative of the larger general population. Wright argued for this view in part because he believed that fitness differences within large populations were rarely great enough to produce much evolution in the amount of time available for it. But in small populations, repeated chance events affecting births and deaths will tend to cause frequencies of particular traits to depart from the objective chances dictated by selection, just as a small number of coin tosses will tend to depart from 0.5 heads. Fisher by contrast held that differences in fitness are big enough so that drift is not usually required. So this appears to be an empirical dispute, one that the facts should be able to settle.

Alas, matters are not that simple. Following Beatty (1984), consider the following case, modeled on Kettlewell's famous study of the microevolution of the peppered moth. This species comes in light and dark variants, and as the soot produced by coal burning in the English Midlands during the industrial revolution darkened the trees on which they alight, the fitness differences between light and dark moths shifted to favor the dark ones. (And they presumably shifted back to favor the light ones when coal burning in the UK was reduced after World War II.) Suppose that 40 percent of the trees in a forest have light-colored bark, and 60 percent have dark-colored bark, and suppose further the trees of these two colors are evenly distributed throughout the forest. So dark moths are fitter in this environment. But it is consistent with this fact that in some seasons more dark moths are killed by predator birds than light moths, if for instance dark moths *chance* to land disproportionately on the forest's light colored trees. If this happens in a given season, then the proportion of dark-colored moths will decrease, even though by assumption they are fitter in a forest of 60 percent dark trees. A probabilistic PNS will tell us that this outcome is unlikely. But it will not rule it out altogether. As it is unlikely, we should label as drift and not selection the decline of dark moths in a forest of 60 percent dark trees.

But suppose that, during this same time period, exactly the same number of white moths landed on the forest's dark trees as dark months landed on the light trees, there to be detected and eaten by birds. Surely light moths being eaten because they landed on dark trees is a case of selection! Now, let us ask, what is the difference that makes the case of dark moths landing on light trees a matter of drift and the case of the white moths landing on dark trees a matter of selection? The demographic facts are the same. There was an equal decline in numbers of light and dark moths during the period in question.

Beatty writes that "the problem . . . is that of distinguishing between random drift and the *improbable results of natural selection* . . . ." In other words, how could we distinguish the two empirically? In our example of course we know that the change in population of dark moths is a matter of drift because their dark color solves a design problem—camouflage in a forest of 60 percent dark trees, which the light moths cannot solve so well. For the same reason we know that the equal decline in light-colored moths is a matter of their being selected against. But in most real cases of evolution by natural selection, we have no prior access to such neat design problems and their solutions to tease drift and selection apart. In fact, we reason in exactly the opposite direction, from demographic changes of populations to fitness differences between them. And the case we have just considered shows that it is empirically impossible to distinguish drift from selection on the basis of the demographic data alone.

It may be argued that all this shows is that we need to have a prior conception of the design problems that individual members of populations face, and how they are solved, in order to at least make (subjective) probability judgments about what demographic changes over time show. The trouble is that many biologists and philosophers will argue that the theory of natural selection is just not about such finely grained differences between individual competitors in particular environments. Rather, they will hold, the theory is about "central tendencies" in large populations. Both drift and selection are inseparable features of populations, not separable and distinct causes. Treating the theory of natural selection as a claim about central tendencies in the evolution of populations is a strategy that goes back to the nineteenth century philosopher C.S. Peirce, and to R.A. Fisher in the twentieth century, and their comparison of the PNS with the equally probabilistic second law of thermodynamics. The second law tells us that, probably, the entropy of a quantity of gas in a container will increase. But the facts about the world that make it true are not facts about the entropies of the gas molecules—individual gas molecules do not have entropies, they have only positions and momenta. And the high probability of entropy increase does not depend on any indeterminism about the movement of the individual gas particles in the container. The probability in the second law is a property of the whole ensemble or population of the gas particles as their disorganization increases (or, improbably, decreases). Similarly, drift is a feature of the whole population of organisms that is evolving, its magnitude depending on the size of the whole population. When the population is large, drift is small, and the central tendency in its evolution is a matter of selection. "Drift" and "selection" describes population-level evolutionary tendencies. Neither obtains at the level of individual organisms. At the level of individual organisms all there is are births, deaths, and reproduction (just as there is no entropy or probability at the level of gas particles, only position and momentum). These are the causes of population-level changes that we describe as some combination of selection and drift. As populations are never infinite in size, drift will always be with us, but not as a cause of anything, just a population size effect.

But we are still left with the question of where drift and objective probability at the population level come from. And invoking the second law of thermodynamics will not help as philosophers of physics and physicists do not agree about where the probability in thermodynamics comes from either, though they do agree that it is objective. The behavior of gas particles is supposed to be perfectly deterministic, yet it produces objective probabilities about entropies. If the central tendencies in large populations are the aggregation of a huge number of individual cases of comparative fitness differences in the actual environments where animals compete and, in these cases, everything—including differential reproduction—is determined, then the same question must arise: where does the drift that inevitably obtains at population levels come from?

As quantum indeterminism is largely irrelevant to biology, it seems safe to assume that, between some pair of creatures, the difference between their fitnesses is fully determined by their specific environments, even though we do not know all the organismal and environmental factors that determine that difference. Because our knowledge is incomplete, prediction and explanation of which one out-reproduces the other will be have to be probabilistic. But it is plain that this probability will be purely subjective, a reflection of the incompleteness of our knowledge. The apparent randomness of evolutionary processes will be a sort of "pseudo-randomness," which reflects our inevitable ignorance. As we aggregate pair-wise fitness differences into lineage, population, and species fitness differences, and predict/explain evolutionary trajectories, our ignorance about details increases, though the values of our subjective probability estimates improve. But if it is these subjective probabilities that are reflected in drift, then of course drift is by no means a separate "objective" evolutionary force that, together with selection, determines the evolutionary trajectory of populations. It is just a reflection of our ignorance of all the factors to which lineages are adapting over time.

Now, treating drift as a matter of subjective probability has the evident advantage that it provides a simple explanation of where "drift" comes from—our ignorance. But the claim faces many serious objections. To begin with, as a matter of subjective probability, drift can hardly be contrasted with adaptation and/or constraint or constitute a serious alternative biological process explaining evolution. Second, too many events and processes with significant evolutionary consequences really do look completely random in their effects on reproduction, sometimes sparing the less fit and extinguishing the reproductive opportunities of the more fit. Floods, lightning bolts, forest fires, earthquakes, continental drift, meteorite impacts like the one that ended the age of the dinosaurs, and so on do not discriminate between organisms on the basis of their fitness in normal circumstances. And they happen often enough that we must either add a *ceteris paribus* clause to the PNS, one that we can never cash in for a finite list of excluding conditions, or we need to recognize the inevitably probabilistic character of the process of natural selection. Irregularities in the impact of environmental processes need not be anything like as dramatic as a meteorite collision to have an impact on reproductive rates, and to do so without being parts of a design

problem that individual organisms ordinarily face. Indeed, meteorite col-
lisions have had such effects perhaps a handful of times in the history of
the Earth. And floods, lightning, forest fires, earthquakes, and so on make
the process of evolution objectively chancy, not just probabilistic as a matter
of our ignorance. Or at least so most biologists believe. The trouble, as we
have seen, is justifying this strongly held conviction that natural selection is
inevitably and objectively a probabilistic affair.

It is worth noting that important matters in the public debate about
Darwinism and its relation to theism turn on the latter two interpretations of probability and drift in the theory of natural selection. If objective
chance plays an indispensable role in natural selection, then Darwinism
is arguably irreconcilable with the theology of the Abrahamic religions:
Islam, Christianity, and Judaism. This is an important matter in light of the
persistence of creationist thinking about human origins and its latter-day
guise, "intelligent design." To be sure, the compatibility of Darwin's theory
and theism is not to be met with in the biological literature. But whether
Darwinism can be reconciled with theism is an important issue in the philosophy of biology, as well as in theology.

Most sects of the Western religions are theistic, as opposed to deistic, that
is, they are committed to the existence of a benevolent God who is omniscient, who intervenes in the course of human and natural history, and who
has the power to change or negate natural laws, limited only by the laws
of logic. (Of course, a God who could abrogate the laws of logic would be
one that neither we nor any intelligent creature could contemplate, let alone
argue about coherently, and the religions of the West certainly hold themselves to be logically coherent, internally consistent, and intelligible.) One
way devout biologists and others seek to reconcile Darwinian theory with
theism is by holding that God—contrary to most creationist and intelligent
design arguments—in his infinite wisdom had no need to change any natural
laws, that he could perfectly well have employed blind variation and natural
selection to create us (and all other things in nature that show adaptation),
and he could have taken his own sweet time about it—say 3.5 billion years (as
suggested by the fossil record).

But, as the counter-argument goes, this reconciliation overlooks the role
of objective chance in natural selection. Objective chance is the source of at
least a good deal of the randomness in mutation and other variations that
are then filtered by the environment to produce descent with modification,
i.e. evolution. But owing to the role of objective chance, the operation of the
"mechanism" or "algorithm" of natural selection on the very same initial conditions over and over again will not produce the same outcome every time.
Thus, in *Wonderful Life*, Stephen J. Gould noted that if the tape of life were
rewound to the time of the organisms found in the Burgess shale (a fossil
outcrop in Western Canada, dated at just after the origin of the major animal
groups, about 500 million years ago), and if the tape were replayed a number
of times, humans would evolve in only a few of the replays (Gould 1989). The

reason is of course the low objective chance of any one of a very large number of alternative endpoints from the same starting point, assuming a process that is in part random. This means of course that Darwinian processes constitute a highly unreliable recipe for making humans, who presumably were made to a specific design: God's image. This line of argument concedes that given the initial conditions at the Big Bang, after 10 billion years or so, high levels of adaptation, diversity, and complexity will be extremely probable. Even multicellular life and intelligence may be likely. What will not be *likely* is that the results look like us and other organisms on this particular planet at this particular time or in its past. Thus, truly random variation and environmental filtration could not be God's method of choice in arranging for the appearance of creatures "in his image." Of course it would be easy to reconcile theism with the appearance to us that the theory of natural selection was true, even though it is in fact false. Suppose an omnipotent, omniscient deity employed a method of producing *Homo sapiens* that was so fiendishly complicated and hard to discover by agents of our cognitive powers, that the closest we could come to the right theory is Darwinian natural selection. This of course is not a way of reconciling Darwin's theory and theism. It is a nice way of suggesting that though false, the theory is a good heuristic device for agents of our cognitive limitations.

Notice that there is no difficulty in reconciling Darwinian natural selection with deism—the thesis that the universe was created by a supreme being, who however did not intervene in its subsequent history. But deism is not the most common theology of the Abrahamic religions. In the end, the only way out of the dilemma that a commitment to theism and Darwinism pose to those who embrace both is to find another account of the probability in the PNS that does not interpret it as objective chance. It is hard to see what interpretation this could be.

Function, homology, and homoplasy

Adaptation is a term which, over the 150 years since the publication of *On the Origin of Species*, has been entirely co-opted by Darwinism. Biologists can hardly think of something as an adaptation without imposing a pattern of variation and selection on its history. Yet, this was not always so. As we make clear in Chapter 1, before Darwin, students of biology had recognized two sorts of adaptations in nature, and sought to explain them both by appeal to an all-powerful designer. First, there is the adaptation of the parts of a biological system to one another—the way they fit and work together so smoothly. And, second, there is the adaptation of biological systems to their environments—the features of a cactus that suit it to the desert and of a polar bear that suit it to the Arctic. The centrality of adaptation in biology is reflected in the vocabulary of the science, so many of the terms, labels, predicates (i.e. property names) being *functional*, at least in the modern discourse. That is to say, so much of biology is defined not in terms of structure but in terms of causes and effects and, more specifically, those effects that were selected for and that reflect adaptations. Thus, a wing is not defined in terms of its composition, say its feathers, because many wings do not have feathers, or its shape, for wings come in a wide variety of shapes, or even its movements in flight, for some wings work by providing lift, some by producing thrust, and others neither. Nor are wings defined anatomically. Among vertebrates, bat wings, pterodactyl wings, flying fish wings, and bird wings are quite different even in their basic construction. Rather, a wing is defined in terms of its effects.

Now a wing produces many effects: it adds weight, takes up space, usually makes an animal more visible, diffuses heat, and casts shadows (and so sometimes alerts prey and other times reduces the prey's view of the winged predator). But among all the effects of a wing, there is one or a small number that defines it: its ability to produce flight (or its homology with a structure that produced flight in an ancestor—think of penguins). So, wings are defined in terms of one of their effects on some organism that has wings. Which effect? The one that performs a function that some animal employs to deal with a design problem presented by the environment—transportation in most cases.

Many structural terms in biology take their meaning from the role that structure plays in an adaptive process. And this is true across levels, from the molecular level—e.g. codons, introns, transcription factors, genes, and enzymes—to the anatomical level—e.g. organelles and organs such as flagellum, vacuole, valve, vessel, heart—up to the ecological level—terms such as predator, parasite, reproduction, altruism, etc. These objects look like they serve purposes of the larger systems that contain them, and therefore the descriptive vocabulary sounds goal directed or teleological. But here is the problem. Goal directedness suggests a kind of backwards causality, one that moves from future to past, and modern scientific thought rejects this possibility. Consider William Harvey's discovery in the seventeenth century that the function of the heart is to pump blood. This discovery seems to explain why vertebrates have hearts—in order to pump blood. But how can the cause of having a heart be a property of hearts, the ability to pump blood. A property of a thing cannot predate the existence of the thing itself, and therefore cannot be causal. Talk of function becomes deeply problematic in a scientific world from which purposes, goals, ends, and other final causes have been banished. One in-principle answer is that biology must not only give up teleology but the functional vocabulary that goes with it. This is impossible, of course. The commitment to this vocabulary runs too deep. But even if the vocabulary could be changed, the problem remains: even the most mechanistic biological opponent of teleology nevertheless believes that hearts are present in order to pump blood, that the enzymes *do* serve the function of catalyzing reactions, that the function of eye spots on butterfly wings is to simulate owls, despite the apparent reversal of cause of effect.

One of the major preoccupations of the philosophy of science between the end of the 1940s and the early 1970s was the need to strip biology's functional terminology of any commitment to time-reversed causality, to future results producing present effects, to purposes in nature, while at the same time acknowledging a very real difference not only in terminology but in phenomenology between biology and the physical sciences. There just does not seem to be anything like "function" in physics and chemistry. For the most part, this was not an especially productive project. Philosophers of science spent a great deal of time crafting definitions of the functional concepts of biology in terms of feedback systems and servo-mechanisms, definitions that were usually tested against purported counter-examples drawn not from biology but from the fertile imaginations of other philosophers.

The problem was solved by the philosopher Larry Wright, who recognized the role Darwinian natural selection could play in providing teleology-free functional explanation. The key to understanding how functions explain the presence of the traits or behaviors is to recognize that a trait's having a function is a matter of its *etiology*, the historical circumstances of its emergence. Vertebrates have hearts in order to pump the blood, i.e. they have hearts as the result of an "etiology," a prior causal history in which ancestral hearts or heart-like organs were randomly varied and successively selected for by an environment in which blood circulation enhanced fitness. The pumping of blood is a *consequence* or effect of the presence of hearts that was *selected for* in the course of evolution. The terms in italics above are often employed in labels for this analysis of functional explanation: such explanations exploit *consequence etiologies* and identify *selected effects* (naturally or, in the case of human actions and artifacts, consciously or intentionally selected ones).

Once Wright made this point about functional explanation it was obvious that the analysis of how such explanations works could be extended to an account of the meaning of functional terms and concepts in biology. First we need to distinguish between tokens and types: the general category, kind, or type, "heart" is exemplified by a large number of particular organs in particular bodies of animals. Presently, for example, there are about 6 billion tokens of the type "human heart," and a larger number of tokens of the type, "mammalian heart." Now consider any particular heart, say Charles Darwin's heart. The function of this token heart is to pump blood because, (and here is the etiology) in the evolutionary past, organs of the *type* heart, which this token instantiates, were selected for owing to their ability to pump blood. There are several things to notice about this claim that a token has a function in virtue of its type having a natural selection etiology. First, as Wright emphasized, Darwinian natural selection is not the only sort of etiology that confers functions. Particular forks, knives, spoons, and other artifacts have their functions in virtue of an etiology of tableware that reflects a history of human intentions, desires, and designs. The very word "utensil" reflects this fact. Natural functions differ from artifactual functions owing to differences in their etiology. Second, a trait may have a label that reflects not its current function, but some function that its ancestors fulfilled. Such exaptations, as Gould and Vrba called them, are common. Indeed, the penguin's wings, which do not enable it to fly but to swim, reflect a Darwinian etiology that explains why penguins have these appendages. And of course some biological traits may have no present function, even though their names reflect some adaptive etiology, the so-called vestigial traits.

Furthermore, as Millikan has famously noted, many things are functionally characterized in spite of the fact that most fail to have the effects for which their etiologies prepared them. Consider white-oak acorns, most of which fail to germinate. This failure led Millikan (1984) and Neander to modify Wright's analysis, identifying what he called "proper" or "normal" functions. Most seeds fail to germinate, they fail to function, but they are still seeds in the proper or normal functional sense, because their existence is owing to the successful functioning of tokens like them historically, in their etiology.

Notice that "proper" or "normal" are evaluative or normative notions. What is "proper" for a given trait is not its actual structure in any particular organism or even the mean or typical structure of it in the species as a whole, but rather the structure of the trait that was selected for in the trait's etiology. This of course makes "normality" relative to a selective environment, a target that moves as environments change. This fact about normality has important consequences in bioethics. It is often important to distinguish between the repair of clearly dysfunctional traits, which we would call treatment, and the modification of traits that are basically functioning normally, which we call enhancement. Treatment is often viewed as morally required and enhancement as optional, depending in part on issues of scarcity. But the standard of normality must vary with environment—for example among environments with differing trait distributions—and with social values. For example, providing human growth hormone to a person of less than 140 cm in height and with a normally functioning pituitary gland will be considered enhancement under some circumstances but treatment otherwise. It depends on whether the lesser height is considered normal or not, and that is a function of the social environment in which the individual finds him- or herself.

The Wrightian etiological, or "selected effects" (SE) analysis of function has happy results for biology. First of all, it allows biology to interpret its functional terminology as literally accurate in a world without teleology of any kind. But as with most philosophical theories, Wright's SE analysis did not sweep the field, and at least one other account of functional concepts has competed with it over the last 30 years or so. This is the so-called causal role (CR) account of functions advanced originally by Robert Cummins (1975). This alternative was first advanced as a way of distinguishing functional from anatomical or structural terms in psychology and cognitive science but has secured advocates in the philosophy of biology. Some contrast it with the SE analysis, and others view CR and SE accounts as compatible theories, as identifying two different notions of function both at work in biology. According to Cummins's analysis of functional description and explanation, terms such as "heart" or "gene," for example, have no teleological content, implicit or explicit. Rather they refer to "nested capacities," that is, to components of larger systems to whose behavior (whether goal directed or not) they make a causal contribution. Cummins's analysis makes the attribution of a function F to x relative to an "analytical account" of how x's F-ing contributes to the "programmed manifestation" of some more complex capacity by a system that contains x. Thus, for example, consider the concept of a "gene." This would be a functional concept, according to Cummins, not because a nucleic acid sequence being a gene is a matter of its having some effects that were selected for. Rather, the sequence is a gene relative to an analytical account of how the sequence's capacity, to record and transcribe the primary sequence of a protein, contributes to development and hereditary capacities of the organism that contains it.

Cummins's account of function differs from Wright's in at least one radical way: the nested causal capacity in which being a function consists can be realized by any number of completely non-biological systems in which contained capacities contribute to the manifestation of containing capacities. Thus, for example, there is an analytical account of how the position and composition of boulders in a stream contributes to the capacities of the stream's rapids to capsize canoes or to power turbines or make it difficult for salmon to swim upstream, even though no one would suppose that it is the function of the boulders to do so. Defenders of the "causal role" account argue that so far from being an objection, this fact simply shows that there is a continuum from less interesting to more interesting functional attributions which largely reflects the complexity of contained and containing capacities. Moreover, they argue, biology requires such a teleology-free analysis of functional description.

Advocates of the CR analysis argue that there are subfields of biology, such as anatomy or paleontology, in which it is important to be able to accord functions to items with nested capacities without any commitment to their "selected effects" etiologies. On this view, simply to express alternative hypotheses about consequence etiologies and to test them, we need to describe the traits that these hypotheses are about in ways that are neutral with respect to those etiologies. Consider the question of whether traits in different organisms are homologies or homoplasies, in other words, the result of common descent or of independent convergence on similar solutions to a common "design problem." Wings, for example, have evolved 40 or more separate times. Accordingly, each of these instances has its own unique consequence etiology. In one instance, the wing may have been favored originally as an organ for heat dissipation. In another it may have evolved as a sexual signal, later co-opted as an exaptation for flight. Given this, how are we to pose the question of whether the wings in these two instances are homologous or convergent? The term "wing" is a functional term, which, according to the SE theorist, refers to its selective history, but that selective history may be unknown. So the CR theorist insists that we cannot even pose the question, we cannot ask whether the two species share wings by homology or convergence, because we cannot even be sure they both have wings in the same functional sense. To pose the question we must, according to the CR theorist, be able to identify common function in structures prior to knowing anything about their etiologies. There must be scope in biology for both SE and CR functions, they argue, and we need to be sensitive to the contexts in which biologists invoke one or the other. They may go on to make common cause with Gould and Lewontin, holding that a more self-consciously CR approach to functional attribution is a useful antidote to the temptations of extreme adaptationism embedded in the SE conception of function.

Some SE theorists will find this compromise unsatisfying. They will go on to argue that insofar as the CR analysis has any plausibility it actually presupposes the truth of the SE analysis of functions, or at least that every CR function in biology is in fact a selected effect, the result of a consequence etiology, and that the evolutionary biologist's distinction of homologies and homoplasies had better accommodate this fact.

Consider the claim that the homology/homoplasy distinction requires neutrality about whether an adaptational consequence etiology is presupposed by the kind of terms in which we describe a trait of evolutionary interest. The SE theorist will distinguish between more generic and more specific etiologies, and argue that homology/homoplasy disputes must always assume some common etiology. That is the point of Darwin's claim that every creature on the Earth is a twig on the tree of life. Thus, consider the eye, which has evolved apparently independently in the insect, the squid, and the vertebrate. The gross anatomical differences among them, the very different ways they carry out the CR function of seeing, suggests three quite separate consequence etiologies. But what the molecular genetics of the *PAX6* gene, and its role in the development of CR-functionally quite diverse eyes, strongly suggest is that underlying these definitive convergences, the various eyes also share an important consequence etiology if we go back far enough. The SE analysis of functions never commits the biologist to any particular etiology, only to the generic claim that each item in biological taxonomy has some etiology or other, that if we go back far enough all traits share parts of a shorter or longer consequence etiology. Thus, when we ask whether the wings of two phylogenetically distant species are homologous or homoplastic, the SE theorist claims that we are asking how much of their consequence etiologies overlap and how recently they overlapped. And this way of understanding the distinction between homologies and homoplasy requires no further notion of function beyond the SE notion.

Further, the SE theorist will raise questions about whether or not the CR analysis implicitly adopts the SE account, despite the claim that it is an incompatible alternative to the analysis of functions Wright inspired. Recall the role played in Cummins's original CR definition of function by the "analytical account" of the contribution of x's F-ing to s's G-ing. This analytical account is supposed to show how x's F-ing contributes to the "programmed manifestation" of G by s. In the case of artifacts—tools, utensils, machine parts—we understand that the programming is accomplished by human artifice, prior design, intentions, plans, etc. But prior to the appearance of cognitive agents capable of programming manifestations of the required kind, what could have provided for the CR function of the elephant's trunk or the panda's thumb? It is obvious that the only programmer biology will accept is Darwinian blind variation and environmental filtration. If this is correct then every (biologically) interesting CR function will have a consequence etiology, that is an SE function, and it will be a CR function owing to its being an SE function, but not vice versa. The reason for this asymmetry is of course the history of successive improvements embodied in a consequence etiology which takes a set of items not nested in the way a CR account requires and programs them into such a set by variation and selection.

On the other hand, the CR theorist could reply, by chance, parts of an organism can come together and play a role in some novel CR function, even before there has been any opportunity for selection to act, in other words, before any SE etiology exists. Indeed, the argument says, all SE functions are CR functions at the moment of their origin, before there is any history of selected effects. The first time a thermoregulatory appendage helped an organism to stay aloft, even briefly, it was functioning as a wing in the CR sense, but not (yet) the SE sense.

The debate about SE versus CR functions is by and large a philosopher's debate, but it has some ramifications for practitioners. From the perspective of the CR theorist, the CR view is important because it draws attention to the crucial role that constraints can play in evolution. If, for example, the Gould and Lewontin notion that brain size was driven by selection for body size is correct, then our brains may have little or no prehominid history of selection for large size, in other words, no SE functionality. And yet that constrained increase in brain size could have produced enormous CR functionality, leading to complex behavior and social organization. More generally, constraints can produce changes that are by chance functional in a CR sense, and can even maintain that functionality in the absence of selection favoring them. Speculating, this combination of constraint and CR functionality could be a major source of novelty in evolution.

From the perspective of an SE theorist, the vindication of the SE approach would have important consequences for the social and behavioral sciences. For these disciplines are themselves rife with functional explanation and functional language, and have no more license to invoke final causes to justify their invocation of functional explanation and employment of functional description than does biology. Accordingly, they will have to provide an efficient cause–consequence etiology for the functions they invoke. Notice that this does not commit the SE theorist to selective explanations at any particular level. Functional behavior could be the result not of selection in biological evolution but of some selective mechanism in the learning process. The point is that, for an SE theorist, to explain function in nature, Darwinism at some level is "the only game in town."

Summary

We began this chapter with a set of apparent challenges to Darwinism that set off one of the liveliest debates between biologists and among philosophers, social scientists, and biologists themselves since Darwin wrote *On the Origin of Species*. Once Darwin identified a causal mechanism for producing adaptations, it became tempting to find it everywhere. Gould and Lewontin's famous paper challenged this temptation and described how to be a responsible adaptationist, and when it might be useful to forego adaptationism altogether. All biologists need to understand the role of constraint in evolutionary explanations and to see that it will always limit and sometimes swamp adaptationism.

The well-informed biologist will also recognize the role of drift in the evolution of many traits, and that traits resulting from drift have no adaptive explanation at all. But accepting this and understanding what drift is, how drift works, what its relation to selection really is, turn out to be matters on which biologists may not agree and philosophers have a good deal to say. Little of what philosophers have to say about drift and its cognate concept, probability, answer any of these three questions. But they show how important they are to understanding the theory of natural selection.

The dangerous adaptationist tendency that Gould and Lewontin warn us about will be extremely hard to surrender in biology, because most of the vocabulary of the field is functional. And the philosophical analysis of the meaning of the functional terminology of biology advanced by Wright and others reinforces this adaptationist tendency. For it shows how to understand this functionality in Darwinian terms, as a consequence of selected effects. Still, there is an alternative, one that accommodates the possibly important role of spandrels in evolution, namely the causal role account of functions, which we explored at the end of this chapter.

Suggestions for further reading

Gould and Lewontin's "The spandrels of San Marco and the Panglossian paradigm" is a lively and accessible article, which deserves its widespread notoriety. It is widely reprinted and also available online at *http://www.aaas.org/spp/dser/03_Areas/evolution/perspectives/Gould_Lewontin_1979.shtml*, among other places. This paper occasioned many others, and indeed several books and anthologies, including Orzack and Sober's *Adaptationism and Optimality* and John Dupré's *The Latest on the Best*. One lively attack on both the rhetoric and the substance of Gould and Lewontin's paper can be found in chapter 10 of Daniel Dennett's *Darwin's Dangerous Idea*.

The debate about the role of drift in biology began between Sewall Wright and R.A. Fisher early in the twentieth century. A philosophically helpful introduction to this dispute is Anya Plutynski's paper "Parsimony and the Fisher–Wright debate." The nature of drift has been the subject of lively debate among philosophers of biology at least since Beatty's paper "Chance and natural selection." A good place to begin to survey this debate is a paper by Walsh et al., "The trials of life: natural selection and random drift," which surveys a number of views (including a subjective probability treatment of drift) and defends a "central tendencies" population-level approach to drift. Elliott Sober's *The Nature of Selection* treats drift as a force, a view that others have contested; see, for example, Robert Brandon's paper "The principle of drift: biology's first law."

The original papers of Larry Wright, "Functions" in *Philosophical Review* (1973) and "Explanation and teleology" (1972), and Robert Cummins's "Functional analysis" (1975), are widely anthologized. Two anthologies which between them include almost all the important papers in this dispute are Allen, Bekoff, and Lauder's *Nature's Purposes: Analyses of Function and Design in Biology*, and Ariew, Cummins, and Perlman's *Functions: New Essays in the Philosophy of Psychology and Biology*. The former reprints Amundsen and Lauder's important paper, "Functions without purpose: the uses of causal role function in evolutionary biology," originally published in *Biology and Philosophy* in 1994.

4 Reductionism about biology

Overview

This chapter begins by making explicit some of the theses reductionists endorse and antireductionists reject and distinguishing them from views both parties endorse. There is an important asymmetry in these positions and therefore in the arguments each side needs to mount. The reductionist argues for what is in effect a "negative existential" claim—that there are no irreducible biological properties, or perhaps that there are no irreducible biological explanations. Like the denial that there are any ghosts, these denials can never be conclusively established by evidence alone. After all, a search of the whole universe for ghosts would take forever. On the other hand, antireductionism needs only one positive case to prove its point—one irreducible property or explanation. Thus, even when the reductionist successfully disproves a case of alleged irreducibility, there is always the prospect that another counterexample will be found. Nevertheless, both parties to the dispute have tended to focus on the same cases. Indeed, antireductionists often begin their arguments with the analysis of explanations in molecular biology, just where one would think the strength of reductionism is to be found.

The philosophical foundations of the dispute revolve around two concepts, "supervenience" and "multiple realizability," that recur frequently in three sorts of disputes, those about reductionism in biology, about the identity of the mind and mental states with the brain and neural states in the philosophy of psychology, and about "methodological individualism" in the social sciences. These phrases in quotes will be explained in this chapter. In Chapter 7 we will see their relevance to these other areas of the philosophy of the so-called "special sciences," that is human behavior and the rest of the social sciences, and moral philosophy.

A reductionist holds that biological theories, generalizations, and the explanations that employ them ultimately need to be grounded in theories, generalizations, and explanations to be found in molecular biology and ultimately in physical science, that is chemistry and physics. A reductionist accepts that many, indeed most, biological theories, generalizations, and explanations are themselves well grounded in empirical evidence and play important roles in the conduct of biological research. But the reductionist holds that grounding such theories, generalizations, and explanations in the physical sciences will strengthen their evidential support, improve their accuracy and precision, and make them more general and predictively more powerful.

Ever since Watson and Crick's discovery of the molecular structure of the gene in 1953, some evolutionary biologists and indeed a few molecular biologists have argued for the autonomy of a great deal of biology, indeed even of some parts of genetics, from molecular biology. Their arguments against reduction have often turned on the role of natural selection at every level of organization in the biological realm, a role that they claim insulates each level from reduction to the one immediately below it. Antireductionists draw our attention to the fact that molecular biology is still biology and not organic chemistry, owing to the role that Darwinian theory plays in the former and its silence in the latter. They argue that reductionists are required to show how the process of natural selection can be reduced to physical science. And this, say the antireductionists, is something they cannot do. Other antireductionist arguments turn on what is called downward causation, the ability of the higher level biological properties to affect the lower level molecular units that constitute them. If causation can run downward, as the antireductionist says it does in organisms—and even more clearly in certain models of organismal function (such as Boolean networks)—then reduction of the biological to its lower level parts would seem to be impossible.

Reductionism, eliminativism, and physicalism

Reductionism and antireductionism label a number of views among biologists, philosophers, and other scientists about the appropriate research program for biology. Many of the disagreements between reductionists and antireductionists result from simple misunderstandings about what is in dispute between them. However, even when these misunderstandings are dissipated, a number of important issues for biology remain.

An antireductionist holds that at least some theories, laws, and explanations in biology need no such additional support or grounding. Indeed, antireductionists hold that physical science cannot provide either evidential or explanatory grounds for these biological results. Antireductionists hold that many biological explanations, and the theories and laws they employ, are wholly adequate to their explanatory tasks.

Notice that both of these competing theses are "epistemic," that is they make claims about the relationships between biological and physical *knowledge*, as embodied in current and prospective developments in biological and physical science.

Reductionism needs to be distinguished from "eliminativism." This is the thesis that biological theories and generalizations and the explanations that employ them should be eliminated in favor of physical theories, laws, and explanations because the biological ones are wrong, false, imprecise, exception ridden, evidentially unsupported, or without predictive power. Unlike reductionism, eliminativism denies that biological theories, laws, and explanations have any role in a fully developed science. Indeed, it views them as mistakes and impediments to such a science that we need to give up immediately. In contrast, reductionism accords biological science an important and permanent role: biology identifies what is to be explained, it provides explanations that are more or less correct and on the right track and that for many purposes are adequate. But, reductionism holds, these explanations require improvement or at least can be improved by further grounding in more basic scientific findings. The distinction between eliminativism and reductionism is very important for two reasons. First, some antireductionists wrongly assimilate reductionism to eliminativism and suppose that by refuting eliminativism they can refute reductionism. Second, other antireductionists try to show that reductionism must eventually collapse into eliminativism willy-nilly. If this argument—and ironically it would be a *reductio ad absurdum* argument—against reductionism is valid, it would force many reductionists to surrender the position.

One way to see the difference between eliminativism and reductionism, and also to see what difference the disagreement between reductionists and antireductionists makes for biology, is to consider the methodology or research programs that each endorses. Reductionism advocates an opportunistic methodology that includes both "top-down" and "bottom-up" research. That is to say, it is happy to begin with important biological discoveries, but demands that they be explained by appeal first to molecular biology and ultimately chemistry and physics. This is top-down research. It also expects that at least some research in physical science—say organic chemistry, for example—will be bottom up. Sometimes, perhaps often, organic chemistry will lead us to important biological phenomena and to their explanation. And it rejects the antireductionists' notion that at least sometimes top-down and bottom-up research cannot be linked up. Antireductionism holds that at least some, perhaps many, important biological findings, theories, and explanations cannot be linked up by further top-down research with more basic explanations in physics and chemistry. It also holds that some biological phenomena cannot be studied by any amount of bottom-up research. In contrast to reductionism, eliminativism excludes top-down research and demands that we engage in bottom-up research only, starting at physical and chemical principles and descriptions. In other words, an eliminativist wants to eliminate biology. It is pretty obvious that the research strategy of eliminativism is a nonstarter. That is why it should not be mistaken for reductionism, which at least seems to offer a reasonable research strategy. This is also why showing that reductionism in the end collapses into eliminativism would be a serious objection to reductionism.

Reductionism is an epistemic thesis, a claim about our explanatory knowledge. It needs to be distinguished from the metaphysical thesis of physicalism. A metaphysical thesis makes claims about reality, the world, as opposed to our knowledge of the world. Physicalism is the thesis that the basic facts about the world are all physical facts, and that the physical facts determine and/or make up all the other facts. In terms philosophers employ, the physical facts "fix" all the other facts. "Fact" is used here quite broadly to mean true statements about all the events, processes, states, trends, laws, entities, systems, and objects that occur or exist in the universe.

One picturesque way that philosophers sometimes express physicalism may sound outlandish, but it is not uncommon: physicalism is the thesis that given two distinct worlds, if all of their physical facts are the same, all of their biological facts must also be the same. Notice that the reverse need not be the case. Indeed, the character of evolution would lead us to expect that even in the same physical universe two quite different physical processes could underlie the same biological facts. That after all is what produces evolutionary homologies, as when two quite different physical structures, such as the panda's wrist bone and the chimp's first metatarsal, both perform the same function, that is serving as opposable thumbs for gripping.

Almost all parties to disputes about reductionism acknowledge allegiance to physicalism. For biology no longer countenances nonmaterial, nonphysical entities and forces that nineteenth century (and even twentieth century) scientists for example appealed to—vital forces, free-floating purposes or "entelechies," and "omega-points" that teleologically draw matter into increasingly complex, highly adapted, biological organization.

There are problems in articulating physicalism that should concern the biologist who embraces it (i.e. almost all modern biologists). For physicalism tells us that the only basic kinds of things, properties, and relationships that exist are those that figure in physics, and everything else is composed of these basic items. But physics is incomplete and subject to change, indeed some of its components such as quantum theory are not just incomplete but the subject of great interpretative debate. So no final and correct list of the basic kinds of physical things and properties can currently be given. The doctrine of physicalism therefore includes a certain amount of vagueness that enables one to endorse it without much constraint on what theory in other disciplines can appeal to. Thus, if it is believed that someday physics will have to accommodate vital forces to explain physical phenomena, one can appeal to vital forces in biological phenomena while still claiming to be a physicalist. If, on the other hand, we restrict physicalism to the sufficiency of entities and properties that physics now countenances, many physicists will demur from embracing the doctrine. By and large philosophers have dealt with this problem by treating physicalism as the claim that the basic facts are of "roughly the same sort" that chemistry and physics currently allow, from quarks to macromolecules to entities we can observe, with properties "like" size, shape, mass, velocity, charge, etc. The words in quotes are weasel words that accord physicalism an unavoidable vagueness.

Physicalism is also vexed by problems about what the "fixing" or determining of biological fact by physical facts actually means. Do the physical facts fix the biological facts by composing them? For example, are all biological things just complex combinations of physical things, the way that molecules and their properties are made up of atoms? Or do the physical facts fix the biological facts only in some weaker sense, say by causing them to obtain without composing them, so that the biological facts are distinct and different from the physical facts and any combination of them?

Reductionists hold that physics is more basic than biology, because the physical facts fix all the facts, including those physical facts that are also biological facts. This of course is part of the reductionist's explanation for why biology is more difficult than physics. Its facts are the result of the interaction of a large number of physical things, properties, and relations. It may be that physics is a "hard" science in the sense that we can identify, describe, and replicate physical facts with great precision. Its facts are "hard" by contrast with the "softer" facts of other sciences about which we can be less certain (not "hard" by contrast with "easy"). But reductionists agree that biology is more difficult than physics. They argue, if the physical facts fix the biological ones, then surely the science of biology must be grounded in the science of these more basic facts. Antireductionists will reject this inference, even while accepting physicalism. Some will do so at least in part because the physicalism they endorse denies that biological facts are just made up of physical facts, even while accepting that the physical facts fix them.

Arguments for reductionism

The metaphysical thesis of physicalism may seem to some to be enough or almost enough of a basis for confidence in reductionism as a research strategy in biology. After all, if the physical facts fix all the facts, then, unless there is some limitation on our ability to know about all these facts, the reduction of biological science to physical science should in principle be possible. The reductionist will grant that biology is harder, more difficult than physics, so the reduction will not be easy. Indeed, some reductionists may grant that the combination of biology's complexity and limitations on the cognitive and computational capacities of the human brain may make the in-principle-possible reduction in practice *unattainable by us*. Notice that this would vindicate a sort of epistemic antireductionism perfectly compatible with physicalism. Some biological antireductionists would be satisfied with so weak a version of their claim. But most would not. To begin with, it suggests that the science of biology is just an instrument we employ for getting around in a physical world as a result of our intellectual weakness; creatures much smarter than us would not need it. More importantly, as our own computational and cognitive capacities are enhanced by prostheses such as super-computers, automated gene sequencers, microarrays, etc., the irreducibility of the biological to the macromolecular and thence to the physical may itself be threatened. On the other hand, some antireductionists are not impressed by this technology, pointing out how rapid computation and the ability to extract large molecular datasets has so far only scratched the surface of biological complexity, as evidenced by the failure so far to deliver on key promised results, such as cures for genetic diseases.

In any case, most antireductionists decline to let their views stand or fall on the success or failure of molecular biology. They want a version of their thesis that makes it true even for creatures of cognitive and computational powers much greater than our current ones. But if physicalism is right—and it seems that antireductionists do have to endorse it—it may be difficult to find barriers to reduction that not even epistemic agents of unlimited powers could surmount.

Scientists generally will not have much patience with these philosophical matters. And the reductionists among them will advance a much less abstract argument. They will argue that reductionism as a research strategy has been vindicated by the course of scientific developments since the seventeenth century. For it shows that the history of science is the history of successive successful reductions. Consider first the history of physics. Kepler identified the roughly elliptical paths of the planets around the sun and Galileo followed by identifying the roughly constant acceleration of bodies in the vicinity of Earth. Newton's achievement consisted in *reducing* both of their discoveries to a single set of fundamental laws of motion. In doing so, Newton was able to increase the precision of predictions of the motion of bodies, both terrestrial and celestial, and to unify their disparate explanations of the behavior of planets and cannonballs as special cases of a single phenomenon. The subsequent two centuries saw a persistent increase in the explanatory range and predictive precision of Newtonian mechanics as it subsumed more and more physical phenomena—the tides, eclipses, buoyancy, aerodynamics, and so on—until by the end of the nineteenth century, even heat was shown to be a mechanical process and thermodynamics was absorbed into the Newtonian worldview.

The reduction of the theory of gases developed by Boyle, Charles, Guy-Lussac, and others to Newtonian theory is another classic model of how reduction advances our scientific understanding. The ideal gas law:

$$pV = nRT$$

relates pressure (p), volume (V), and temperature (T, measured in degrees Kelvin) to one another via two constants, n and R. The law holds across a range of values for these three variables but breaks down at high pressure and low volume. In the nineteenth century, of course, physicists found themselves able to explain why this law obtains just across this range of values, and why it fails at high pressures and low volumes. They were able to do so by assuming that gases are composed of particles that behave in accordance with Newton's laws, and by assuming that heat is nothing but the aggregation of the motion of these molecules, that is by assuming that we can identify temperature with the mean kinetic energy of the particles that compose the gas. Thus the ideal gas law was derived from Newton's laws by adding the identification of heat with mean kinetic energy. What is more, if we treat gases as composed of particles obeying Newton's laws, the failure of the ideal gas law to describe the relation of pressure, volume, and temperature at the extremes will follow pretty directly from the fact that these particles have mass, take up space, and are not perfectly elastic. Thus, we explain the behavior of gases by deriving the gas law from more fundamental physics in a way that explains why it obtains for some values and why it does not for other values of pressure and volume.

However, as measurement precision in thermodynamics and elsewhere increased through the nineteenth century, the predictive accuracy of Newton's theory declined so that at the beginning of the twentieth century it faced serious explanatory problems. These problems arose both in regard to very large-scale phenomena such as the orbit of Mercury, and very small-scale phenomena such as radiation. And difficulties arose in the attempt to bring together mechanics and electromagnetism into one theory. But the solutions to these predictive and explanatory problems daunting Newton's theory was a new wave of reductions, this time to the theory of relativity and quantum mechanics. They explained both the accuracy and the errors of Newton's theory by reducing it to special cases of each of them, while both absorbed different parts of electromagnetic theory. The resulting problem facing physics was that these two theories—quantum mechanics and the general theory of relativity—are incompatible with each other, and much twentieth and twenty-first century physical research has been devoted to attempts to reduce one of these two theories to the other. In particular physicists have sought to show that there is a single theory that explains how gravitational force, and the forces between subatomic particles are all variations on a single underlying process that manifests itself in a variety of ways.

Meanwhile, the history of chemistry has shown a quite similar trend over the last 200 years. Mendeleev formulated the Periodic Table of the Elements at the end of the nineteenth century. Then, starting early in the twentieth century, physicists and chemists began to show that the regularities of chemical synthesis could increasingly be explained and predicted by reducing them to regularities about atomic and subatomic bonding, which in turn were reduced to regularities of quantum mechanics. The result of all this reductive unification has been a synthesis of chemical and physical theories with an explanatory range and predictive precision that is reflected everywhere we turn in twenty-first century technology.

Until 1953 biology had not followed the reductionist trend shown by the physical sciences. In that year Watson and Crick's discovered the structure of the gene. In the next decades, they and others discovered the macromolecular mechanisms that determine its role in heredity and development. Of course if reduction and predictive precision are as closely related as physics suggests, then it has been no accident that after Watson's and Crick's reduction of genetics, biology became more predictive and productive of technological applications.

Before 1953 there were a number of widely accepted explanations
biological processes, and some of them, especially in physiology, ma
indispensable use of chemical and physical theory. They also used genera
biological theory—the theory of natural selection—as well as narrower
theory—for instance Mendel's laws of segregation and assortment of genes.
But general theories, laws, and quantitative regularities were few and far
between in biology. Reductionists will admit that prior to 1953, biological
theories lacked features characteristic of theory in physical science, including
direct evidential support, explanatory generality, predictive precision, or all
three. But on their view, these were defects to be corrected by a reduction-
istic research program. Consider Mendel's laws. Almost immediately after
their rediscovery in the early twentieth century, exceptions to them began
to pile up, including crossover, linkage, meiotic drive, and so on. If we could
reduce Mendel's laws to their macromolecular foundations, then presumably
both their range of application and the known exceptions to them would be
explained, and, for that matter, other exceptions might then also be predicted.
We could then employ Mendel's laws with confidence in areas in which we
knew their exceptions would not arise and avoid reliance on them in applications where they would be likely to play us false. Such precision would be of
considerable value in agriculture and medicine, just for a start.

So the history of the physical sciences over the last 300 years or so is a
history of reduction, and reduction in the physical sciences appears to have
been a matter of the derivation of narrower theories from broader theories, of
special cases from general cases, of faulty earlier theories from more-correct
later ones. Why should the same pattern not be exhibited in biology and with
the same pay-off for increased explanatory generality and predictive precision? This prospect will look particularly appealing on some interpretations
of physicalism. For, after all, if biological systems just are physical systems,
then we ought to be able to enhance our understanding of them by decom-
posing them into their parts and examining the way in which these parts are
physically related to one another. And the revolution in molecular genetics
looks like it vindicates this opportunistic top-down/bottom-up research
program.

Exploiting the analogy with the reduction of the ideal gas law $pV = nRT$,
we should expect to be able to derive regularities about genetics, such as
Mendel's laws of independent assortment and segregation, from regularities
about macromolecules. Just as all the reduction of the gas laws to mechanics
needed was the identification of temperature and mean kinetic energy, similarly all the reduction of Mendel's laws requires is the identity that Watson
and Crick discovered between the gene and DNA.

The recipe for reduction advanced by philosophers of physical science had
two requirements. First, the laws of the narrower, reduced theory had to be
logically derivable from the laws of the broader, more fundamental, reducing
theory. The requirement of logical derivability reflected the thesis that explanation consists in derivation from laws and the view that reduction provides

the explanation for the reduced theory. The second requirement is not really independent of the first requirement. It is the demand that the concepts, terms, kinds, and properties characteristic of the narrower theory be defined by way of terms that figure in the more fundamental reducing theory. Now, it is obvious that if we are to explain chemical reactions by reducing them to the theory of the electron bond, we will first have to define various elements and compounds in terms of the atomic structure of their molecules and atoms. Similarly, if we are to derive Mendel's laws from molecular biology, we will first have to define Mendelian genes in terms of stretches of DNA. Satisfying the requirement of logical derivation of one theory from another presupposes that we have already satisfied the requirement of connecting the terms of the two theories in definitions. In fact, providing the definitions will be the really hard work, for once they are hit upon presumably the derivation may be pretty obvious or, if very complex, it will be enough to satisfy reductionists if we can just sketch out how the broader theory reduces the narrower one. (Antireductionists will, of course, not be satisfied with a mere sketch.)

So, let us consider in a little detail how the reductionist's claimed derivation of Mendelian genetics from molecular genetics proceeds, bearing in mind that if the reduction can be effected, it will not be the end of the story but only the beginning. For, in the case at hand, the reduction is not to organic chemistry but to molecular biology, and thus leaves reduction to physical science still to be effected. From Chapter 2:

> *Mendel's law of segregation* In a parent, the two alleles for each character separate in the production of gametes, so that only one is transmitted to each individual in the next generation.

> *Mendel's law of independent assortment* The genes for each character are transmitted independently to the next generation, so that the appearance of one character in an offspring will not affect the appearance of another character.

Reductionists will hold that when these two generalizations are true, it will be owing to the operation of some facts about macromolecules, including nucleic acids, enzymes, and other molecules as well. Their confidence in this claim rests on the truth of physicalism. No antireductionist should withhold assent to this much. For the reduction of Mendel's laws, it should suffice to have Watson's and Crick's identification of "gene" in terms of nucleic acids. Once available, we could start to link up molecular biology to Mendelian genetics in a way that would explain the Mendelian laws.

It should be clear at the outset, however, that nothing like the reduction of the ideal gas law to the kinetic theory of gases as aggregates of Newtonian particles, or any of the other famous reductions in physical science, is in the cards for biology! Reduction as the derivation of laws in the narrower theory from laws in the broader theory cannot even get started in biology if there are no biological laws! And the absence of such laws is strongly suggested by the considerations we explored in Chapter 2! Mendel's "laws" are not laws, and that is for good biological reasons. They are statements about local arrangements on the Earth that resulted from the operation of natural selection on initial conditions. And the large numbers of exceptions to them are also the result of selection, of adaptation of organisms to a huge diversity of different and sometimes unique local circumstances. Accordingly, Mendel's laws could not be derived from some set of laws of molecular biology. Indeed, we would not want them to be derivable, for then these molecular "laws" would have to be as false, exception ridden, and local as Mendel's laws are. What is more, there are no laws in molecular biology anyway, and so no laws to which Mendel's "laws" could be reduced. And this is true for the same reason that Mendel's "laws" are not laws. Consider the "law" that all genes are made of DNA. This one was falsified by the discovery of viruses whose genes are made of RNA. So we could revise the "law" to say that "All genes are composed of nucleic acids." But the discovery of prions suggests that this weaker claim is still no law. Worse for the reductionist, if we could find a generalization that is true now, of all organisms on Earth, nature's never-ending search for adaptive advantage will eventually falsify it. There are no laws in biology, and therefore no reduction is possible, conclude the antireductionists.

But reductionists will rightly complain that this argument proves too much. Go back to $pV = nRT$. This generalization is false, and what its reduction did was to explain both why it held across some range of values and why it failed across others. Reducing Mendel's "laws" does not require that they be true laws of biology, it is enough that they be rough generalizations, with known exceptions, so long as we can derive them and their exceptions and limitations from more fundamental "laws" in molecular biology.

To do this, however, requires that the concepts of Mendelian genetics, and especially the concept of "gene" be appropriately characterized in the concepts of molecular biology. But was this not just what Watson and Crick in fact did? And is this not a very powerful reason to endorse reductionism?

Antireductionist arguments from molecular biology

A little reflection on developments in molecular biology since 1953 suggests to antireductionists, however, that—far from providing the definition of the Mendelian gene in terms of DNA needed by reductionism—what Watson and Crick's discovery did was to begin the process of vindicating antireductionism! For what their work and that of others showed was that the concept of the gene at work in Mendelian genetics, population biology, and evolution generally cannot be systematically linked up with what the molecular biologist calls a "gene." This means that there is no scope for *deriving* Mendelian or evolutionary genetics from molecular genetics. In fact the two theories use the same word "gene" to describe quite different things that cannot be linked in any definition that will identify one in terms of the other. The unavoidable conclusion is either eliminativism—the concept of the gene in nonmolecular biology (i.e. Mendelian and evolutionary genetics) is to be banished from science—or antireductionism, with the consequence that the gene of non-molecular genetics, along with the theory in which that gene figures, is autonomous from molecular biology. Moreover, the concept of gene that figures in molecular biology makes the derivation of nonmolecular genetics impossible. Either way, reductionism is refuted.

Let us explore this argument in a little detail. Reducing nonmolecular genetics to molecular biology requires that we find a molecular way of iden-tifying the very same genes that nonmolecular biology picks out in terms of one of their most significant selected effects, i.e. their functions. What we want is to match function with structure, to identify the DNA sequence that "realizes," "implements," "instantiates," or constitutes the thing that performs the selected effect. The function of the gene is roughly to code for a phenotype. Now, what counts as a phenotype will differ across the range of applications in biology, from the shape of the hemoglobin molecule all the way up to eye color, for example. But to make the task easier for reduction, let us assume that the relevant phenotypes are molecular products, proteins, that have a role in development and physiology. Thus, we need to be able at least in principle to identify and locate the stretch of DNA nucleotides that make up a particular *type* of gene, say "the hemoglobin gene" or, more narrowly, the "alpha-hemoglobin gene" or, even more specifically, the "fetal alpha-hemoglobin gene."

The first problem for this identificatory project is raised by the degeneracy of the genetic code and the functional neutrality of many nucleotide substitu-tions. Genes code for proteins, proteins are composed of any of 20 amino acids, each amino acid is coded by a triplet of nucleic acids, a codon, and there are four different nucleic acids, so there are 64 different ways of coding for these 20 amino acids. The degeneracy means that different codon triplets can carry information about the same amino acid, and many, many differ-ent nucleic acid sequences can code for exactly the same protein structure. Because many different amino acid sequences can perform the same physi-ological function, these different sequences of amino acids will count as the same kind of protein. Thus, if a gene is what produces a given protein, there is an enormous number of different nucleic acid sequences that constitute, make up, realize, or implement the same gene. And if a gene is something that codes not just for a protein, but for something that nonmolecular biologists count as a phenotype—for example eye color—then the number of nucleic acid sequences, any one of which could be that gene, will be still greater. Defining even a very specific gene, such as the "fetal alpha-hemoglobin gene" in terms of its molecular structure is certainly beyond our unaided computa-tional and cognitive powers.

But the problem facing the reduction of the gene is actually far worse. There are at least two types of genes: regulatory and structural. The regulatory genes produce proteins (transcription factors) that switch on and off the structural genes. The structural genes code for proteins that build and operate the body's cells, such as hemoglobin or insulin. Besides regulatory and structural genes, there are genes that do not code for proteins at all, but for various kinds of RNA—transfer (tRNA), ribosomal (rRNA) and microRNA (miRNA)—essential to gene function. Of course if regulatory proteins and various RNAs are necessary for the synthesis of a structural gene, then do we not have to count the DNA sequences that make up the regulatory and RNA gene as also part of the structural gene itself? If they are no less indispensable to the production of the protein than the nucleotides of what we want to call the structural gene for hemoglobin itself, then these regulatory and rRNA-, tRNA-, miRNA-producing sequences will have to be counted as parts of the gene. Recall that the hemoglobin gene of nonmolecular biology is going to be the nucleotide sequence that was selected for producing the hemoglobin protein. As these regulatory sequences were certainly selected for, owing to their contributions to building this protein, it looks arbitrary not to count them as part of the hemoglobin gene.

Now one might argue at this point that it is reasonable to exclude from the gene for any one protein those sequences that play the same role in the production of more than one protein, even if they are casually required for the synthesis of that protein. If a regulatory sequence or a sequence that codes for a tRNA or an rRNA, needed in the synthesis of many proteins, was favored owing to its role in the synthesis of proteins in general, and not just the hemoglobin protein, then it might seem reasonable not to count the sequence as part of the hemoglobin gene. But there is a slippery slope here. There will be sequences that were selected for owing to the contribution they make to the synthesis of just two or three proteins. And we can count such a sequence as parts of two genes, if we want, but what about a sequence that contributes to five or six, or a dozen protein-synthesis pathways? The point of course is that the individuations of genes—the divisions into genes made by drawing lines between nucleotide sequences—just will not line up with the divisions that natural selection makes when it individuates genes by their functions in protein synthesis.

And there are still more problems for the attempt to line up nucleic acid sequences with evolutionary genes. First of all, there is the problem for individuating genes raised by the discovery of introns and exons. Introns are long sequences of DNA, lying between exons and having no coding function. Their transcribed RNA products simply get snipped out of the messenger RNA before it is shipped off to the ribosome to produce the relevant protein. We have already encountered the idea that the molecular gene might not be a single continuous sequence of nucleotides but one separated by other unrelated sequences, so the existence of exons is not an entirely new problem for counting genes. But the existence of introns certainly does not add to the physical integrity of the gene. More important are the further complications in the causal chain from the DNA to the protein that make it even harder to line up any particular nucleotide sequence with one gene when that gene is understood to be responsible for the protein it encodes. Translation into the protein requires the self-splicing role of mRNA to remove introns and, more importantly, the post-transcriptional modification of mRNAs prior to their translation into protein. Here too a variety of other molecular genes producing the machinery for post-transcriptional modification are required. These will presumably be genes for enzymes that catalyze the modification of mRNAs, thus necessary for the ultimate protein, though perhaps not part of the nucleic acid sequence that was favored because it codes for that protein. Then there is post-translational modification of inactive proteins into active ones and the silencing of some genes by miRNAs digesting their mRNA. Again, the nucleic acid machinery necessary for this modification cannot be counted as the part of the gene for the active enzyme, even though it is indispensable to the production of the protein that individuates the gene.

An even more serious problem, for individuating genes molecularly, arose with the discovery that the genetic material contains start codons (ATG) and three stop codons (TGA, TAG, and TAA). You might think that start and stop codons simplify the problem of counting genes molecularly. Why not just read the genes off the nucleic acid sequence? Begin anywhere, when you encounter a start codon a new gene begins, and it ends when a stop codon is encountered, what is called an open reading frame. For any nucleotide sequence, there will be several possible open reading frames. It is often assumed that the longest open reading frame in a sequence is a gene, and sometimes it turns out this way.

If only matters were so simple. To begin with, 95 percent of the genome in humans, for instance, is widely supposed to be junk DNA of either no function or unknown function. It certainly does not code for proteins (though some of it now appears to code for miRNA, which has important roles in development and evolution). Finding start and stop codons in this junk DNA will not individuate genes. So, it appears that we still need to approach matters from the prior identification of proteins and other gene products that nucleic acid sequences are selected for producing. If we know the amino acid sequence of the protein, we can read back the alternative nucleic acid sequences that code for them. Alas, given the code's degeneracy there will be a staggeringly large number of nucleic acid sequences for any protein, and several different nucleic acid sequences can be expected actually to have been realized in the germline and somatic cell nuclei of different individuals, even in the same small population, let alone different individuals in a species, order, family, or higher taxon.

Combine the multiplicity of reading frames with the existence of introns and another whole dimension of problems for gene individuation emerges. Within an open reading frame there can often be a dozen or more introns. It is easy to deny membership in the relevant gene to these introns, as their sequences are not represented in the gene product, but what are we to say when alternative excision of introns and splicing of exons produces two or more quite different mRNAs, and consequently two or more distinct protein products from the same open reading frame, i.e. the same nucleic acid sequence. In other words, there are ways in which the same nucleotide sequence can produce a number of different products, a process that is called alternative splicing. Further, a sequence beginning with one start codon may have a second start codon before the first stop codon, and so encode two different products. And the same sequence, read in different reading frames, will contain different start and stop codons and so can code for different products.

It is obvious that individuating genes by function just does not line up with any obvious way of individuating them by nucleic acid structure. As nonmolecular biological theory individuates by function, that is by effects selected through Darwinian mechanisms, its individuations cannot be reduced to ones that proceed by identifying molecular structure. This means that the theories, generalizations, and explanations of nonmolecular biology in even the most favored case of genetics just cannot be shown to be derived from molecular biology. The alternatives seem to be either eliminativism or the autonomy of biology from more basic sciences. As no one is going to take eliminativism seriously, antireductionism appears to be vindicated in the very region of biology where top-down research has come closest to meeting bottom-up research. Everywhere else in biology, reduction by derivation will be even less viable an option.

The antireductionist is confident about this conclusion, for it turns out to rest on the best of biological bases: the theory of natural selection. All biological structures from the gene, or for that matter the codon triplet, on up to cells, tissues, organs, etc., are selected for owing to their effects on survival and reproduction. But because nature "selects" only by effects, it will be blind to differences in structure when they do not make a difference in the effects it is selecting for. The "design problems" that nature sets are, even at the level of the macromolecule, sufficiently general that there is almost always more than just one solution to them available. Thus, humans can survive an ice age by moving south or wearing warmer clothes, animals can escape predation by fleeing or camouflage, vertebrates can thermoregulate by endothermy or exothermy. This pattern of multiple solutions and nature's frequent indifference to just how they are accomplished goes all the way down to the level of the macromolecular, indeed at the macromolecular there is probably the greatest range of alternative structures that have effects indistinguishable at higher levels of organization. When nature selects for an oxygen-transport molecule, the result may be myoglobin in some creatures and hemoglobin in others, and of course nature will be blind to differences in the hemoglobin protein's amino acid sequence that do not make a difference to its oxygen-carrying function. For this reason of course there will be differences in the amino acid sequence for hemoglobin between different mammalian species, and differences within these species too. Of course, nature will also be blind to certain differences in the nucleotide sequence for hemoglobin. As long as two sequences produce a molecule with the same function, they could persist world without end. Given the degeneracy of the genetic code, we should expect that the molecular sequences underlying any adaptation will be enormously variable. What this means is that starting with any biologically significant function at all, from the level of organisms all the way down to the level of genes, the blindness of selection to structure, combined with the persistent variation that Darwin first recognized as characteristic of life, will make for multiple structures fulfilling the same function.

This multiplicity of structure corresponding to the same function is what a large part of the impossibility of any kind of derivation of the less basic from the more basic in biology is supposed to rest on. Because, as we have seen, the very vocabulary of biology is mostly functional, and because functions are those effects that nature has selected for, there will always be a range of underlying structures for each of the functional types that the theories, generalizations, and explanations of biology provide. The impossibility of deriving the biological theories, generalizations, and explanations from theories about this diversity of structures does not just rest on the huge number of possible structures we will have to catalog in order to effect the derivations. Even when the number of alternative structures that realize a given function is not huge, there will always be alternative structures that could, as a matter of physical law, provide the same function. And, the antireductionist points out, the only thing these actual and possible physical structures will all have in common is that, as a matter of fact, they all fill the same function. A heterogeneous "motley" of diverse physical structures which, as a matter of fact, have nothing else in common cannot explain entities, systems, processes, and organizations that came into existence because they fulfilled the same function, that were selected for solving the same design problem. As Dobzhansky said, "Nothing makes sense in biology except in the light of evolution." It is no surprise that what physical science can tell us about structures will not make sense in biology. So much for reductionism!

The antireductionist will go on to note that this argument for the autonomy of the biological from the physical sciences is perfectly compatible with physicalism, the fixing of all the facts, including the biological ones, by the physical facts. Antireductionists admit that every particular biological fact is the product of a particular set of physical facts. But, as we have seen, the set of physical facts that make up a biological type, kind, or category—like being a wing, a Golgi body, or a gene, or like camouflage, parthenogenesis, or digestion—will be too physically heterogeneous to have any scientific role. The antireductionist accepts the statement that no two physically identical worlds can differ in their biologies. But, natural selection shows how two physically different worlds could have the same biology. And if the physical differences need not make biological differences, then they are irrelevant to biology, both actual and possible.

Reductionist rejoinders

The reductionist must concur with the above description of the facts about how molecular and nonmolecular biology fail to line up. But contemporary reductionists will still go on to advocate the reductionist's research program throughout the science of biology. They will do so first by arguing that the antireductionist has at most shown that the epistemological obstacles to reduction are temporary, when what they need to show is that they are permanent and reflect metaphysical obstacles, i.e. obstacles in principle. Second, they will argue that these epistemological obstacles are inconveniences that human biological ingenuity will overcome, and, third, that historically both the traditional reductionists (inspired by reduction in physical science) and the antireductionists have misconfigured the debate. Once we see what is at stake, modern reductionists argue, the complexities of the relationship between bottom-up and top-down research will not prove a barrier to reduction.

Let us consider the last and most serious philosophical issue first and then the first two. The reductionist admits that the model of reduction drawn from the history of the physical sciences is quite unsuitable to describe relations among theories, generalizations, and explanations at different levels in biology. The reason is simple: as we suggested in Chapter 2, it is difficult to identify laws at any level of organization in biology, whether macromolecular or nonmolecular. Accordingly, there is no scope for the derivation of less basic laws from more basic ones in this discipline. Yet reductionists and antireductionists have both assumed that there are such laws in biology, with the former arguing for derivation and the latter arguing against. As we have seen, outside of the laws of the theory of natural selection, there is a good case for the claim that the generalizations of the discipline at most record "local" truths, generalizations that are true for some time, often perhaps for many millions of years, but which are frequently subject to exceptions, and are eventually overtaken by adaptive evolution. Thus, Mendel's "laws" are not laws, nor even idealizations like $pV = nRT$. One tip-off to the difference between Mendel's laws and the ideal gas law is that, once geneticists began to record exceptions to them, due to linkage, crossover, meiotic drive, etc., no attempt was made to restate Mendel's laws to improve their generality, nor was there any search for successor laws that were more general and less riven by exceptions. Compare $pV = nRT$, which is the first of a sequence of proposed generalizations, advanced over the course of a century, about all gases. The quantum theory of gases is the culmination of a process of adding new variables, each with the expectation that the result would be truly general. Why does this matter? Well, it reflects the fact that Mendel's "laws" are not treated as hypotheses about natural laws, but as descriptions of a large number of particular facts, almost all the cases of sexual reproduction since the appearance of eukaryotic organisms. As this large set of processes emerged owing to a process of selection for their (common) effect, which was blind to the physical structures that produced the effect, it was pretty inevitable that a large variety of such physical structures would emerge, and that many of them would be subject to selection on their other diverse effects, with the result that a large number of exceptions to Mendelian segregation and assortment would emerge. The only way that all cases of Mendelian segregation and assortment could be "derived" from molecular biology is *one at a time* from the distribution of molecules that compose the genes and the "laws" of molecular biology. But there are no laws of molecular biology any more than there are laws of Mendelian genetics! And even if there were, there would be no point to this *one-by-one* derivation of slightly different Mendelian processes from slightly different macromolecular ones! It is no surprise therefore that molecular biologists are nowhere engaged in any program of research that looks like the sort of reduction to be found in physical science. But it is also true that there is apparently no obstacle to *one-by-one* explanations of cases of Mendelian assortment and segregation by appeal to the molecular details of each of these processes. So there is no basis for an antireductionist argument here either.

The conclusion that the reductionist draws is that we must completely reconfigure the specific debate about whether Mendelian genetics can be derived from molecular biology. And we must also reconfigure the more general debate about whether biological theories and laws can be derived from more basic laws in the physical sciences. The debate between reductionists and antireductionists cannot be about *derivation of laws*. What should it be about? One proposal that retains a great deal of the heart of the issue between parties to the dispute is to treat it as a disagreement about explanations. The reductionist holds that all biological processes, events, systems, and so on will ultimately be explained by appeal to physical laws and physical properties, whereas the antireductionist holds that most or at least many of these biological processes, events, and systems are adequately or correctly explained biologically, and these explanations cannot be grounded in more basic physical processes. Both parties can agree that in biology there are no laws to be explained by derivation from more basic laws, and that in biology the explananda are always particular events, states, processes that occur on this planet. And yet they can disagree about where the research program of seeking their explanations should stop.

Once the debate is reconfigured as one about explanation, reductionists will turn to the second part of their rejoinder. The limitations on molecular and ultimately physical explanation of biological explananda are all epistemic and may turn out to be temporary. Of course, the reductionist will admit, many macromolecular explanations of biological processes will be unattainable owing to the absence of information about molecular initial conditions, and others will be uninteresting because they show us nothing new beyond the molecular details. More important, many will involve details and complications as yet unknown to molecular biology. Most important, for many of these biological processes the full and complete macromolecular explanations will be beyond the cognitive and computational abilities of human agents to understand, keep in mind, and draw information from for further explanation and prediction. But notice, these are all epistemic limitations on reductive explanation in biology. And they are limitations that in many cases may be overcome by increases in imaging technology, computerized calculation of chemical interactions, and computational bioinformatics, over the near and more distant future. As the antireductionist has to identify more than epistemic obstacles to refute reductionism, all the complications about linking nucleotide sequences to evolutionary genes identified in the previous section are insufficient to establish the existence of such nonepistemic obstacles. But how do we know that the epistemological obstacles to knowing all the "gory details" of every particular biological process, state, or event, are in fact temporary inconveniences that human biological ingenuity can overcome? More important, asks the antireductionist, why would we or agents of any cognitive and computational powers want or need to overcome these epistemological limits?

That the limits on macromolecular explanations of the biological can be overcome is vouchsafed to the reductionist by physicalism. Even the antireductionist grants that the physical facts fix all the facts, and presumably allows that we can know all the physical facts relevant to a biological fact. So, if the biological fact just is a complex physical one fixed by the simpler physical facts, and not metaphysically different from them (how could it be otherwise? asks the reductionist), obstacles to knowing all this will not be impossible to remove, given enough ingenuity and research effort. As for why we should invest the effort, well, the reductionist accepts that in many, indeed proportionately most, cases, there is no reason to do so. After all, if all biological explanation turns out to be explanation of particular events, or vast but finite sets of them, occurring over long periods in many places on the Earth, then there is nothing much to learn biologically from piling up explanations of closely similar events, and no point in doing so. But where there is a pay-off to reduction, in terms of increased predictive precision, and consequent opportunities to control or improve on nature, as in agriculture or medicine, there is every reason to learn all the gory details, and no obstacle to doing so.

Biologists and others without a philosophical "agenda" may find this rejoinder unconvincing. After all, explanations that we cannot understand because they are too detailed, and the alleged long-term prospects of our eventually being able to understand and apply them, hardly provide much motivation to surrender the orthodox research program of biology and start doing bottom-up research. Of course, some reductionists demand no such surrender. Reductionism need only advocate a kind of "opportunism" in research, that is to say pursuing both bottom-up and top-down research. And where the prospects for their meeting do not seem great for the moment, there is no methodological obligation to try to force them to meet.

The antireductionist insists, however, that all this misses the point. For there are real nonepistemic barriers to reduction, real biological facts, and their explanations, that cannot be grounded in the macromolecular details that "realize" them and cognitive agents should accept as autonomous from physics, no matter what these agents' cognitive powers. Whether these facts and explanations are metaphysically different from the physical facts that fix them, and how the physical facts fix them, does not much concern most antireductionists. But they are certainly committed to the existence of such nonphysical facts independent of us and our beliefs. What is more, these irreducible biological facts are to be found at least at the level of molecular biology. So even if the rest of biology can be grounded in molecular biology, there will still be an unbridgeable gap between it and physical science, one that must reflect itself in the methods of biology. Let us examine the antireductionist's argument for this striking conclusion.

Multiple realizability, supervenience, and antireductionism

Recall the fact that natural selection for functions (selected effects, SE) is blind to structure. This means that almost all biological properties—those of being a fetal alpha-hemoglobin gene, being any alpha-beta-hemoglobin molecule, being a dominant phenotype, being a wing, or being a *Canis familiaris* (domesticated canine), will be "multiply realized." That is to say, almost every biological property, kind, or type, will be exemplified, instantiated, or "realized" by a disjunction (a or b or c or . . .) of different physical structures. To use the example discussed earlier, a hemoglobin gene can have a large number of different nucleic acid sequences, and the number of alternative amino acid sequences that can function just as well as a hemoglobin molecule is also very large. Of course, if two sequences have exactly the same nucleic acid structure, they will both be hemoglobin genes (this follows from physicalism). But they do not have to have the same structure in order to both be hemoglobin genes. What makes two physically different sequences instances of the same gene is their functional role. And the same goes for the hemoglobin protein, for the constituents of organelles, cells, tissues, organs, and even whole organisms! Philosophers describe this dependence of biological kinds on disjunctions of physical kinds as "supervenience." An example from ordinary life may help elucidate the notion of "supervenience." Take the kind term "chair." There are indefinitely many different ways something can be a chair—there are chairs of different sizes, shapes, materials, colors, cushions, and numbers of legs. There are electric chairs, and high chairs, barber's chairs and kitchen chairs. There may be nothing physical that is necessary and sufficient for being a chair because there are an indefinite number of different ways in which physical matter can be arranged to be a chair. But just because we cannot give a complete description of chair in terms of a list of its physical properties does not mean that a chair is not a physical object. Similarly, even if filling some functional role, like being a cell or a gene, is something that can be "realized" in many physically different ways, so that no complete physical description of all cells or genes can be given, it does not follow that cells or genes are something more than, above and beyond, purely physical things. Being a cell or a gene or any other functionally defined item supervenes on a set of physical properties.

The upshot of supervenience, according to the antireductionist, is that what makes something an instance of a biological kind, in particular an adaptation, is not its physical structure, as adaptations do not have a single common structure. What makes something an example of an adaptation is, of course, Darwinian evolution—natural selection for the function it performs! Reducing any particular biological process, event, or state to the particular physical structure that realizes it will hide, obscure, lose what that structure has in common with all the other physically possible structures that have the same selected effects! And that very selected effect that the physical description loses is what biology is all about. Reductionism thus misses the very facts that a biological explanation must include. And this problem for reductionism has nothing to do with limitations on our epistemic powers. Even an omniscient biologist will be interested in the biological kinds shaped by selection, and complete reductive "explanation" from which the kinds selection has shaped drop out will just fail to be biological. This fact about how the biology drops out will obtain even at the level of molecular biology. An example will make the point clearly.

Consider the biologist's question of why DNA contains thymine whereas RNA contains uracil. The answer is not given by describing the organic chemistry of thymine synthesis out of uracil. It is given by showing how thymine contributes the function of DNA and uracil to the function of RNA, and then hypothesizing that they were selected for making these contributions.

The function of DNA is high-fidelity information storage and transmission. Accordingly, there will be selection against DNA sequences that fail to maintain high fidelity, and selection for mechanisms that maintain high fidelity, in storage and transmission. Cytosine, one of the four nucleic acids in DNA, randomly and spontaneously "deaminates"—i.e. loses an amine group—and becomes uracil. In replication of a daughter sequence of DNA, a uracil in the sequence resulting from deamination of a cytosine will base-pair with an adenine, whereas the cytosine would have base-paired with thymine. The result is a point mutation in daughter sequence. The pressure to solve this "design problem" had to be very great, as point mutations are usually maladaptive and in this case frequent. This point mutation is prevented from occurring by the operation of a DNA repair mechanism that moves along the DNA sequence before base-pairing duplication and removes a uracil molecule whenever it encounters one. But if uracil were one of the normal nucleic acid bases out of which DNA sequences are composed, then this repair mechanism would have an extremely difficult task: it would have to distinguish those uracils that are parts of the normal sequence from those that result from the deamination of cytosine. Whether in the fullness of time nature could have solved this specific problem, in fact what happened is that it found a "quick and dirty" but expensive alternative. Thymine is exactly like uracil in its ability to bond with adenine, but it has a methyl group (CH_3) sticking out of the sequence. Thus thymine can do the same structural and coding job that uracil does. And its methyl group sticking out of the sequence prevents the DNA repair mechanism from latching on to the rest of the molecule (which has the same structure as uracil), removing it, and substituting a cytosine molecule. So, the DNA repair mechanism does not have to discriminate uracils that are the result of deamination of cytosine from ones that are in the right place (because there are none, or should be none, in the molecule).

By contrast, since each gene produces many mRNAs, and each nucleus contains many ribosomes, there will be selection for some combination of low cost and high fidelity in RNA's function of information transmission and protein synthesis. If one out of a hundred RNAs comes to have a uracil molecule where a cytosine molecule "should be," the result will simply be one malfunctioning protein molecule out of a hundred, or at worst one malfunctioning ribosome out of many, something an organism can live with. And as thymine is a more expensive molecule to build than uracil, the savings in building uracil molecules instead of thymine molecules more than compensates for the cost of an occasional malfunctioning RNA molecule. Ergo, nature will select for uracil in RNA and thymine in DNA.

The point of the story for purposes of the reductionism/antireductionism dispute is that it shows that even in molecular biology, what the biologist, even an omniscient one, wants explained cannot be explained by the details that organic chemistry provides about how DNA and RNA are synthesized. It can only be explained by considerations from the theory of natural selection. It was the well known biologist Ernst Mayr who made this point most forcefully in his own arguments against reductionism. Mayr distinguished proximate and ultimate explanations: proximate explanations provide the causal details of how a particular event, state, process, capacity, or disposition is brought about. For example, we can explain how the mammalian eye focuses so sharply by showing how the lens bends light rays. Here our explanation will make indispensable appeal to geometrical optics and, Mayr admitted, may well be reducible to more basic nonbiological processes. But it is ultimate explanations that provide the considerations explaining how these proximate causal mechanisms arose, and such explanations are almost always given in terms of the adaptational etiology of such mechanisms. Thus, biology interests itself in the question why did the sharply focusing mammalian eye emerge, and to this question the only explanatory answers will be ones that go back *ultimately* to adaptive considerations. What is more, ultimate explanations work without having to trace out the actual etiological path from incipient structures to highly evolved ones; most of the time they cannot, as the details have been lost in the mists of time. In most cases, there was more than one causal pathway from the incipient structure to the evolved structure, sometimes many pathways, owing to the supervenience of adaptations on disjunctions of structures that multiply realize them. Which pathway was taken just does not matter for purposes of ultimate explanation. The fact that we do not know exactly by what route DNA came to be made of thymine and RNA of uracil does not detract from the adequacy of the ultimate explanation of their difference. And knowing the route would not necessarily add to, or improve, the explanation either.

Of course this feature of biology, that it seeks ultimate explanations that cannot be provided by considerations from physical science, is built into the entire vocabulary of the discipline. For most of the concepts, kinds, and properties of biology are functional ones, that is they have an evolutionary etiology. Antireductionists exploit this further fact about biology to advance two more arguments against reduction. First of all, many apparently reductive explanations will require appeal to unreduced or irreducible things, pro-cesses, properties, and events. Thus, consider how a developmental molecular biologist explains the development of the anterior/posterior (front/back) differences in the growth of the fruit fly embryo, in terms of the interaction of certain sets of genes and the varying concentrations of the bicoid protein laid down in the unfertilized egg by the mother. Even if the genes could be identified in terms of the disjunction of all the nucleic acid sequences that multiply realize them, the explanation will have to help itself to notions such as "maternal" and "ovum," for those genes in embryos that are switched on by the presence of the bicoid protein laid down in the ovum by the mother. And concepts such as ovum and mother are obviously laden with ultimate evolutionary content. Reductionism in developmental molecular biology requires that these concepts all be defined, characterized, identified with macromolecular ones. And even if this could be done, the macromolecular properties will still make implicit appeal to ultimate explanations in their meanings and so obstruct the required reduction to proximate explanations, which are the only sort physical science can provide.

Reductionists hold that all the ultimate causal relationships reported in biology will turn out to supervene on the causal relationship between more basic events, states, and processes of physical things reported in chemistry and physics. Their confidence in this assertion stems from the commitment to physicalism that they insist even antireductionists embrace. But some antireductionists argue that the direction of causality sometimes runs the other way, from the biological *downward* towards the physical. Some bio-logical things and their properties have molecular effects, and the source of these effects cannot be traced back to the merely physical constituents that compose the biological things and fix their properties. Thus, for example, developmental biology has revealed that during development, cells have "positional information," that is they can detect the activities of surrounding cells and this information will cause such cells to produce certain enzymes and molecules, usually in order to develop in the same way as the surrounding cells. Here it is the position of the whole cell that determines macromolecular effects, and not the position of each of its component molecules with respect to one another and with respect to the molecules composing the membranes of the surrounding cells.

Both these antireductionist claims—about indispensable higher levels and downward causation—are subject to a serious counter-argument, however, serious at least for any antireductionist who accepts physicalism. Figure 4.1 will help to explain the problem using a biological example, meiosis: in the figure, the Bs are the well-known optically observable stages of meiosis—say metaphase, prophase, anaphase—whereas the Ms label the macromolecular processes that realize these optically observable stages, and the Ps label the particular physiochemical processes that realize these macromolecular ones. Physicalism tells us that each B_1 is physically, materially identical to each corresponding M_1 and P_1. Reductionism tell us that the causal pathways at the level of the Ps compose the causal pathways at the level of the Bs and Ms. Antireductionism holds that there are sometimes cases of causal influence from higher levels, the Bs, to lower ones—the Ms or the Ps. The figure records the direction of fixing of the macromolecular and ultimately the biological by the physical in the double lines between levels and the direction of causal determination by the horizontal and the oblique arrows. Events may fix events directly above them in the diagram either by constituting them or by some other way (if there is any other way that physical facts can fix nonphysical ones, something reductionists doubt). Now, consider macromolecular event M_2, to which arrows of causation and double lines of constitution both point. Suppose we ask why M_2 occurred. There appear to be two causal routes to M_2 which explain its occurrence: (i) P_1 occurred, caused P_2, which is identical to M_2, therefore M_2 occurred, or (ii) B_1 occurred and downwardly caused M_2

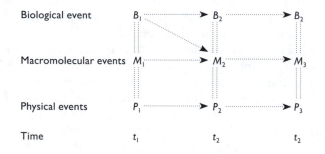

Figure 4.1 A reductionist challenge to antireductionism. Bs represent biological events, which are realized by (double vertical lines represent this realization) the macromolecular events beneath them, Ms, which in turn are realized by (double vertical lines) the physiochemical process underneath them, Ps. Horizontal arrows give the direction of physical causation; double vertical lines express physical identity, and the oblique arrow gives the direction of putative downward causation. (See text for further explanation.)

to occur. The antireductionist's downward causation claim commits them to the second route. But the antireductionist's acceptance of physicalism commits them to the first as well. So, how are the two explanations, (i) and (ii), related to one another?

There appear to be only two possibilities, both of them unattractive to the antireductionist. First, (i) and (ii) could be competitors, alternative explanations of how M_2 came about, only one of which is correct. The trouble with this view is that, as competitors, one or both must be wrong. If (ii) is correct, then it is hard to see how the antireductionist can continue to embrace physicalism. For physicalism says that the physical facts at P_1 and P_2 fix all the facts, including presumably M_2. The alternative to holding (i) and (ii) to be incompatible explanations of M_2 is to hold that they are both correct. But in that case M_2 is "overdetermined" by two mutually redundant processes. That is to say its occurrence is assured two different ways, rather like a pair of pants being held up by a belt and suspenders. But surely no antireductionist believes that all events above the physical level are "overdetermined" in this sense. Indeed, true overdetermination is uncommon in nature and really obtains only at the molecular level as far as any biologist knows. One might well expect nature to select for some overdetermination of processes essential to survival and reproduction. But the amount of redundancy that antireductionism requires to reconcile upward physical constitution and downward biological causation is beyond the range of plausibility. This problem leaves the antireductionist with the prospect of having to surrender physicalism as the cost of any commitment to downward causation and the indispensability of higher-level biological processes to lower-level macromolecular ones.

Self-organization and reductionism

The antireductionist has a rejoinder to the argument accompanying Figure 4.1. It is that in the figure, the reductionist seems to be playing fast and loose with the notion of what constitutes the physical facts. The physical facts at the bottom level could refer to the properties of all of the parts, presumably the atoms that constitute the macromolecules at the second level, taken individually. But macromolecules have properties that depend on the relationships among those atoms. For example, the shape of a protein that is so critical to its functioning is a result not just of the atoms that compose it but their spatial relations, and these spatial relations are the result of properties of interactions among *all* of the atoms in the molecule, not their properties taken individually. Consider some carbon atom in the protein. It matters very little where it is located in space, its x-, y-, and z-coordinates in the reference frame of the solar system, for example. What matters is its location relative to the other atoms in the molecule. It is these relational properties of the atoms that determine the properties of the molecule as a whole. In other words, the properties of every atom in a protein molecule, taken individually, do not explain the whole. The reductionist wants to explain a macromolecular whole in terms of its parts, but it turns out that the relationships among the parts are causal as well. Further, in the case of protein folding, there may be alternative folding configurations for the same amino acid sequence, and which configuration a molecule takes on could be the result of environmental influences, meaning interactions outside the set of atoms that constitutes the protein. In other words, a protein's folded shape can depend on the effect of other macromolecules.

The reductionist may reply that the physical facts to which we want to reduce a macromolecule include *all* of the physical facts, and these include all of the myriad physical relational facts and facts about physical interactions among the various atoms that constitute the molecule—their pair-wise or two-place interactions, their three-place interactions, their n-place interactions. Further, the reductionist will say, the physical facts also include the interactions between atoms in the environment and those that constitute the macromolecule, again the pair-wise combinations, the triples, the quadruples, and so on. But, the antireductionist argues, this concession is tantamount to surrendering reductionism. If reductionism means anything, it means explaining the whole as a consequence of the properties of its physical parts. But if the notion of physical parts is taken to include the parts and also all of their relational properties—their relationships and interactions—in all possible combinations, then, in effect, units larger than the parts—combinations of parts—are being accorded their own distinctive properties with autonomous causal efficacy. And that is holism, not reductionism.

Antireductionists sometimes illustrate their argument with an extended example attributed to the work of Stuart Kauffman (1995) on the emergence of complex systems. Kauffman has shown that starting with a small number of molecules with relatively simple chemical properties, there is a high probability of a network with certain life-like characteristics emerging spontaneously, that is to say, *self-organizing*. In particular, such networks spontaneously show stability, homeostasis, and evolvability, which are key features of life and—the antireductionist argues—properties that are not present in any of the components, considered individually.

What Kauffman did was to design a computer model of a set of molecular regulatory interactions that could be run repeatedly under a variety of different assumptions about the number of different molecules and the relationships among the molecules in the set. The model's critical inputs are n, the number of molecules in the system, and k, the number of molecules that control the production of each molecule in the set. If $k = 2$, then the production of each molecule is controlled by two other molecules in the set. Heuristically, it is helpful to think of the network as an array of lightbulbs, each representing a molecule. A lightbulb that is on represents a molecular type that is being produced. If a bulb turns off, it means that molecular type is no longer being produced. And each bulb is wired to k other lightbulbs that control it. Then, the model generates a rule table that determines how each bulb responds to all possible combinations of inputs from other bulbs. Thus, if $k = 2$, the rule table will decide for each bulb, which may be on or off at some time t, whether it will be on or off in the next time step, $t + 1$, based on the state of its two input bulbs at time t. For example, the rule table for bulb number 879 might dictate that if its first input bulb, say bulb number 34, is on at time t and the second, say bulb number 1128, is off at time t, then bulb number 879 will turn on at time $t + 1$. Or if number 34 is off and number 1128 is on, then 879 will turn off. Or if both input bulbs are off, 879 will also turn off. And the final entry in the rule table might dictate that if both inputs are on, then 879 will turn on. Each bulb has its own rule table, each table with four entries when $k = 2$, so that all possible combinations of inputs are covered. (If $k = 3$, the rule table would have eight entries.) Given such a set-up, with fixed rule tables and some starting condition—on or off—for all bulbs, a "run" of the system will produce some completely deterministic pattern of bulbs being lit or not, a pattern of blinking lights, some regular and some irregular (and indeed some sitting stably on or off, not blinking at all). Systems like this are called Boolean NK networks—Boolean from the language of computer science to reflect the fact that the system is binary, with each bulb either on or off, never partly on.

We can translate back from the language of blinking bulbs to molecular biology. In a molecular system, the presence of some molecules can control the presence of others by catalyzing or inhibiting their production. For example, in what is called "cis-regulation," the product of some gene, a protein, controls the rate at which another gene is transcribed, and therefore the rate of production of that gene's product, another enzyme. Thus a genetic regulatory system may realize a Boolean NK network, in which each of n genes is regulated by k other genes. But of course, Boolean NK systems are far more generally realized than by gene networks. Any system in which sets of entities control the production of other members of the set in binary fashion will be a Boolean NK network.

Returning to the lightbulb model, suppose that the number of bulbs is large, and the pattern of connections among bulbs is chosen at random. In other words, the "wiring diagram" that maps which bulbs control which others is random. And, further, suppose that the rule tables governing the behavior of each bulb are filled in at random. That is to say for each bulb, the "results" column in its rule table—the consequence for each combination of possible inputs—is decided at random by the flip of a virtual coin. Now it turns out that, despite all this randomness, if $k = 2$, the network will exhibit some remarkable features. For one thing, it shows stability. That is to say, the pattern of illumination of n bulbs goes through short predictable cycles, returning to the starting pattern after a small number of steps. Notice that this is exactly what cells do, they cycle stably in this way on a variety of scales. Cell division is a stable cycle, an excursion through a series of chemical states leading up to cell division, then with a return to a starting point to begin another similar cycle. Virtually all multicellular, indeed multiorgan, physiological processes, from digestion to walking, cycle stably in this sense.

Now it also turns out that the value of k is crucial here, not the value of n and not the rule tables, nor even the wiring diagram. Consider what happens when $k = 1$, so that each bulb receives input from only one other. In such a network, there are cycles, but they tend to be unrealistically short. In a $k = 1$ network, with a random wiring diagram and set of rule tables, the result is a mainly dead, frozen order, in which most bulbs are stuck permanently on or off, or in an equally unlifelike pattern of bulbs simply blinking alternately on and off. If k is set at 3 or higher, again with a randomly chosen wiring diagram and rule tables, the result is typically chaos, with bulbs blinking in an apparently random or disordered way. Of course such arrays do cycle but typically on huge timescales, often many universe lifetimes long. In other words, on biological timescales, they do not cycle at all.

Besides stability, in Kauffman's model, networks in which $k = 2$ also exhibit homeostasis, the tendency of a system to restore itself—as organisms do—after being perturbed. Wounds heal. One foot slips on a patch of ice, but I right myself before I fall. Still a third feature of such systems, typically absent when $k = 3$ or more, is evolvability, the tendency for small changes in the rule tables (which can be thought of as a model of genetic variation) to produce a new system very much like the old one. In other words, a random change in the rule tables tends to produce a pattern of blinking lights that is similar to but not identical to the old one, prior to the change. Such a property is crucial to the ability of replicators of any kind—molecules, single-celled organisms, metazoans—to evolve. A small mutation in a replicator should produce only a small change in its interactor's traits. For, if small genetic changes tended to produce large phenotypic changes, the odds of random variation producing long-term adaptive improvement would be essentially zero, rather than merely small, as we observe them to be. The reason recalls a point made in Chapter 1. Natural selection is cumulative, not random, because earlier adaptations constrain later ones. A large variation in phenotype has a much greater chance than a small one of interfering with an already established adaptation.

Thus once any set of relatively simple interacting molecules satisfying Kauffman's weak assumptions comes into existence, if $k = 2$, the system will tend to self-organize, that is it will tend to show stability, homeostasis, and evolvability. We get these properties, we get these biologically essential features of organisms automatically, spontaneously, without any special design engineering by natural selection. In Kauffman's terms, we get "order for free."

The antireductionist wants to make two points here. One is that these are properties of $k = 2$ systems that are not to be found in any of the components, considered individually. In other words, stability, homeostasis, and evolvability are not properties that can be found in any individual molecule in the network, nor are these properties inferable or derivable from of the properties of any molecule. Rather, they are properties that arise—spontaneously, as it happens—from the interactions of many molecules. They are higher-level properties of the network as a whole. The second point is that $k = 2$ is also a higher-level property, and it is partly responsible not only for the behavior of the system as a whole but also for its components considered individually. In other words, the higher-level property of k being equal to 2 in part determines the behavior of the lower-level components, the molecules in the network. Thus, in the terms of Figure 4.1, the antireductionist claim is that it is true that the physical facts at P_1 and P_2 fix all of the facts, but that the flow of causation from P_1 to P_2 is divided, and it goes only partly by the direct horizontal route. Causality also goes partly through the higher levels from M_1 and B_1 across to M_2 and B_2 and downward too by various diagonal routes. P_2 is therefore caused directly by P_1 but also indirectly via the higher-level properties associated with P_1.

Central to the antireductionist argument here is the claim that the reductionist is not allowed to include the relational properties of the components in the account of causes, or, more precisely, cannot do so and still be a reductionist. The reductionist cannot, in particular, acknowledge that $k = 2$, because $k = 2$ is a relational property, the pattern of connectivity among the components and not a property of any molecule in the system. However, it is $k = 2$, a relational property of the system, that does the explanatory work here. Each molecule has properties, of course, such as the (randomly chosen) rule table assigned to it, but this individual-level property does not explain the stability, homeostasis, and evolvability of the system, nor does it fully explain the pattern of behavior of that particular molecule. It does not explain, for example, why that molecule cycles stably (or if it doesn't, why it doesn't). Explanation, without the relational properties, will be incomplete.

Reductionists will consider some parts of this argument more threatening than others. For instance, the reductionist will grant that many physically important properties are relational, and will insist that a reduction of the biological to the physical can perfectly well help itself to such relationships and interactions; what it cannot do is appeal to nonphysical relationships among physical things. Spatial relationships, such as "x is between y and z," or "x has z times the positive charge of y," or other such relations are, so far as the reductionist is concerned, perfectly physical properties. It is nonphysical properties, whether "mondatic" (nonrelational) or "n-adic" (relational) that reductionism forbids. And this is where the challenge to reductionism lies; for the reductionist will have to show in general that properties such as stability, homeostasis and evolvability are purely physical ones. How can it do this?

In part, the reductionist will say, Kauffman's models have already done a substantial amount of the job. By showing that these three features can arise among a set of molecules among which there are only relations of chemical synthesis and regulation, he in effect reveals the purely physical character of these properties. It remains to identify explicitly the physically necessary and sufficient conditions for stability, homeostasis, and evolvability in order to show that the three terms name three purely physical properties—albeit relational ones. This will by no means be an easy task, as the last section of this chapter makes clear. For, even in the simplest of Kauffman's sets of molecules, these three properties will be realized by a multitude of differing relational properties expressed in distinct rule tables. Since Kauffman's model can be realized by many different kinds of molecules related by many different rule tables, reducing these three concepts will be another case of reducing multiply realized, or supervenient ones.

Natural selection and reduction

Reductionists will have to accept the multiple realizability of the biological and its supervenience on disjunctions of physical and indeed macromolecular properties and relations. For the existence of these disjunctions, indeed their ubiquity, is guaranteed by the process of natural selection itself. The reductionist may of course claim to have no difficulty in accepting the consequence that the physical processes to which biological processes are reduced will be vast in number, heterogeneous in kind, and hard to organize into very general explanations of classes of biological processes. But, the reductionist will insist, this is "merely" an epistemic limitation on reduction, one whose force will vary among biological subfields and over time as research techniques improve and research interests change.

More worrying to the reductionist is the proximate/ultimate distinction, and the role of the theory of natural selection in the antireductionist's argument. Recall Mayr's argument that biology seeks ultimate explanations and the further fact that most of its descriptive vocabulary makes sense only in light of adaptive explanations that flow from the theory of natural selection. Of course the reductionist must recognize the indispensability of the theory of natural selection to biology. Anything else would turn reductionism into an untenable eliminativism. Accordingly, in order to reduce the force of arguments against reduction that turn on the role of the process of natural selection, reductionists need to show how the theory of natural selection can itself be reduced to physical science.

We can express the challenge by appeal to the notion of "derivation" as that term figured in the original conception of reduction drawn from physical science. Let us assume that the theory of natural selection can be expressed as one or more general laws, say, the principle of natural selection (PNS) or the version of the theory advanced by Lewontin: Whenever there is hereditary variation and fitness differences consequent on them, there will be differential reproduction. Then the challenge to reductionism will be to show how such a law can be derived from more basic laws of physics or chemistry, the way that $pV = nRT$ can be derived from Newton's laws applied to gas molecules. This looks like a difficult challenge. Consider the properties and relations of "x is fitter than y," "heredity," and "variation" that figure in any version of the theory of natural selection. All of these properties and relations will themselves be multiply realized, and it will therefore be impossible to link them in physical science to anything less than vast disjunctions of sets of properties and relations of physical entities. But such linkage is exactly what is required for derivation. Notice that $pV = nRT$ can be derived from Newton's laws only because we can link temperature and mean kinetic energy in the equation $\text{Temp}_{\text{Kelvin}} = \frac{1}{2}mv^2$ where v is the mean velocity of the molecules composing the gas. If fitness, variation, heredity, and other key notions of Darwinian theory supervene on vast disjunctions of macromolecular and ultimately physical properties and relations, there is no hope of actually effecting the reduction of the law or laws of natural selection to those of physics and chemistry! Unless this problem can be resolved, reductionism will at best come to an end at the level of molecular biology. For it will leave unreduced the laws of natural selection, which figure at the level of the macromolecule as much as they do at higher levels of biological organization.

Denying that there is a law or laws of natural selection to derive from physical laws does not seem to be an available strategy for the reductionist. Suggesting that Darwinian theory is a mathematical model, an algorithm widely realized by physical processes, merely postpones the question of whether its widespread realization reflects the operation of a fundamental law or laws. Holding it thus to be a useful biological instrument, rather than a law, and holding that there are basic physical processes that work together on initial conditions to produce descent with modification, will seem to many reductionists more like a version of eliminativism than a defense of reductionism about natural selection. If reductionists cannot find some way of accommodating the theory of natural selection to physical science, then, ironically, it appears that they face a dilemma of surrendering physicalism or embracing eliminativism (or surrendering reductionism). For natural selection certainly appears to be a biological process and the failure to show how it could even in principle be fixed by physical facts leads to the surrender of physicalism.

Summary

Almost all biologists are physicalists, accepting that the processes they study are all of them physical, material, nonspiritual, and nonteleological ones. Yet no biologist nor many philosophers suppose that biology will be replaced by physical science. "Eliminativism" about biology is a view no one holds seriously. Though often mistaken for eliminativism, reductionism does not want to do away with biology but does claim that it needs systematic and complete grounding in the physical. Molecular biologists argue for this claim from their own successes ever since 1953. Philosophical reductionists argue for the same claim from metaphysics. Antireductionists assert themselves to be the equal of reductionists in their commitment to a physicalist metaphysics. But they deny that such a metaphysical worldview requires a reductionist research program, and further deny that a reductionist research program is possible.

For the reductionist the problem is to defend the promise of a research program. For the antireductionist it is to reconcile the autonomy of biology with the completeness of a physical description of reality. These are both perforce philosophical projects. Each of them rests on complex arguments that draw on distinctions not to be found only in biology but are of great importance wherever the relationship between levels of causation and organization are to be met with in science. This issue arises most acutely in biology, psychology, and social science. In all of these disciplines, the explanatory kinds—genes, organelles, cells, tissues, organisms, minds, communities, societies, markets—are "multiply realized." That is to say the tokens of each of these kinds are various in the elements from which they are composed, and even varied in the relations among these elements. In the biological case, the source of multiple realizability is the blindness of natural selection for adaptation to differences among structures with identical effects. Thus, if natural selection is the source of multiple realizability in all the "special sciences" from psychology onward across all the human sciences, then the arguments about reduction that arise in biology are also to be faced in all these disciplines as well.

Suggestions for further reading

The classic reductionist texts by scientists include E.O. Wilson's *Consilience* and Richard Dawkins's *The Selfish Gene*, though neither book involves itself in the philosophically salient issues they raise. A robust philosophical defense of reductionism is to be found in Dennett's *Darwin's Dangerous Idea*, in which antireductionist "skyhooks" are rejected in favor of reductionist "cranes." Kenneth Schaffner made important contributions to the articulation and defense of reductionism over a long period, culminating in *Discovery and Explanation in Biology and Medicine*. Influential arguments for physicalist antireductionism have been advanced by Philip Kitcher in "1953 and all that" and "The hegemony of molecular biology." Elliott Sober's "The multiple realizability argument against reducibility" reflects a shift away from arguments such as Kitcher's against reductionism. Influential contributions to the debate have been made by C.K. Waters, in, for example "Why the antireductionist consensus won't survive," and Paul Griffiths, including "The many faces of the gene." Sahotra Sarkar reviews the philosophical literature in *Genetics and Reductionism*. Rosenberg's *Darwinian Reductionism* articulates the philosophical argument against physicalist antireductionism in detail.

A deep and philosophically sophisticated discussion of supervenience and multiple realizability with special relevance to psychology is J. Kim's *Supervenience and Mind*.

Kauffman's notion of self-organization to produce "order for free" is developed in a technical work *The Origins of Order* and a more accessible work *At Home in the Universe*.

5 Complexity, directionality, and progress in evolution

Overview

A human seems like a more advanced animal than our ancient fish-like ancestor. And that ancestor seems more advanced than its single-celled ancestor. The history of life seems to be a record of progress. But what does "progress" mean? What does "advanced" mean? The notion of an ordering among organisms dates at least to Aristotle, who arranged living forms on a linear scale based on degree of perfection, also called the *scala naturae* or Great Chain of Being. Humans are more perfect than other apes, apes more perfect than mice, mice than snakes, snakes than fish, fish than snails, snails than worms, and so on. The Great Chain can also be thought of as a ladder, a ladder of perfection, on which each rung is occupied by some beast, with humans at the top, or in some versions ranking just below angels and God. For more than 2000 years after Aristotle, the Great Chain was understood to be static, meaning that organisms and their rankings did not change over time (Lovejoy 1936). But in the early nineteenth century, Jean-Baptiste Lamarck added an evolutionary component, so that organisms moved up the chain, or progressed, as they evolved. In Lamarck's view, progress was increasing complexity, with the complexification driven by invisible fluids within organisms (not by adaptation, which he saw as acting mainly to deflect or retard the process; Lamarck 1809).

A half-century later, the Darwinian view challenged the ordering of the Great Chain. Darwin saw evolution as a process of branching and divergence rather than linear ascent. In the Darwinian view, modern humans are not higher than modern worms. Both occupy the tips of the youngest twigs on a branching evolutionary bush, both have been evolving for the same amount of time, and therefore in a sense both are equally advanced. But Darwin nevertheless recognized progress, the notion that the moderns are in some sense more advanced, on average, than their ancient ancestors. In a now-famous passage in *On The Origin of Species*, he wrote of "that vague yet ill-defined sentiment, felt by many paleontologists, that organization on the whole has progressed" (Darwin 1859: 345).

Modern biology is thoroughly Darwinian. The Great Chain and the notion of ladder-like ascent are now almost universally decried as historical errors. But the idea of progress—in some sense difficult to specify—persists. One reason is that, as Darwin saw, the fossil record seems to provide prima facie evidence for advancement in some hard-to-specify sense. But another is that Darwinian theory seems to many to predict advancement and therefore to virtually guarantee that there *should be* progress.

Still, it is also widely acknowledged that the notion of progress raises real problems for biology. In ordinary discourse, progress means directional change, and in evolution it means long-term directional change, a pattern of regular or episodic increase in some variable representing progress over the whole history of life. But that is not all. To most people it means change for the better. So what does "better" mean in biology? Is "better" even a scientific concept? If not, then maybe progress cannot be one either, and biologists should purge the term from their vocabularies. Also, Darwinian theory does not speak with one voice. Some argue that even if "better" can be rendered scientific, natural selection does not predict improvement, i.e. it does not predict progress. Indeed, it can be argued that selection does not predict long-term directional change of any sort. And then there is the question of whether or not long-term directional change has in fact occurred. It turns out that the answer to this question depends critically on two things, first, what variable or variables are thought to be changing directionally. In other words, if we retain the notion of progress, what does progress consist in? Is it rising intelligence, complexity, body size, or something else? All of the answers that have been proposed are troublesome in one way or another, even the most widely accepted answer, complexity. Second, the issue of whether there has been a trend turns on how we understand that term "trend." Is a trend just directional change, or does it have to be directional change that is powered or driven by some force?

We start with the scientific status of the idea of progress.

What is progress, and is it (or could it be) a scientific concept?

"Progress" contains an inescapable evaluative component. If a human is a more advanced animal than whatever ancient fish-like animal humans evolved from, then we must be "better" in some sense. And better is a value term. Now there are two ways in which an increase in some feature of organisms might be valuable. The feature could be valuable to us, to human beings. Or it could be valued by the evolutionary process, so to speak, valued in the sense of preserved or enhanced owing to its adaptive value, the contribution it makes to survival and reproduction. The more progressive organism could be the one that is better at surviving and reproducing, the one that is more fit, so that progress would be an increase in whatever features of organisms underlie increased fitness, over the history of life.

From a scientific standpoint, the first alternative—valuable to us—is problematic. (We will discuss the second later.) In science, there is general agreement that human values should not be relevant, at least not relevant to the findings of science or to the process of determining what is true. Science is not an attempt to find out how the world should be, to determine whether or not it is good, or to judge it. It is an attempt to discover how the world actually is, for better or worse. It is said that science is supposed to be "value neutral." But care is needed here. Value neutrality does not rule out all values. What are called "instrumental" values are allowed, indeed they are essential. The values that scientific neutrality rules out are the "noninstrumental" or what might be called the "moral" or "intrinsic" ones. As we shall see, much depends on whether the value component of progress is understood instrumentally or noninstrumentally.

Here is what is meant by instrumental and noninstrumental. If we say that *X* is better than *Y* in order to achieve purpose *Z*, the word "better" is being used instrumentally. An electron microscope is better than a light microscope for the purpose of seeing the very small details of certain objects. The key is the phrase "for the purpose of." The claim is not that an electron microscope is better, or more valuable, than a light microscope in any other sense. Using an electron microscope will not improve the moral character of the nation or bring justice to the world. Still less is using electron microscopes valuable in and for itself, that is to say, it is not intrinsically valuable. The "better" in an instrumental value statement refers to a stated or implicit goal or purpose, in this case the goal of seeing the very small details of an object. In contrast, the noninstrumental or intrinsic usage invokes no further goal or purpose. Thus, human life is often said to be valuable in and for itself, and not owing to some further end, goal, or purpose it serves. Such judgments of intrinsic value are almost always "normative." They are considered matters of moral or ethical value, often reflecting religious doctrines. The value neutrality of science consists in part in its not asserting or denying the existence of intrinsic values or identifying anything as having or not having intrinsic value. But this does not preclude science's identifying the instrumental value of things. It can tell us that a Phillips screwdriver is good for, i.e. instrumentally valuable for, driving Phillips screws into wood and that it is better, more instrumentally valuable, for doing so than a slot-head screwdriver. Notice that in making this claim, science takes no view on the intrinsic value of Phillips screws, as opposed to slot-head screws, or even on the value of driving screws into wood at all. Switching to a biological example, the theory of natural selection identifies the thick coat of the polar bear as instrumentally valuable for insulation, and insulation as instrumentally good for survival and reproduction. But science stops at this point. It does not identify some further good for which survival and reproduction are instrumentally valuable. Nor does it suggest that survival and reproduction are intrinsically good in themselves. It is silent on this matter owing to its value neutrality.

There is a straightforward argument to show that noninstrumental or intrinsic values have no place in science, or at least (as we shall see) in the practice of science. A statement of instrumental value, such as "*X* is better than *Y* for the purpose of doing Z," is one that is subject to empirical test, once we stipulate the criteria of goodness we have in mind—efficiency, speed, cost, etc. And we can also test noncomparative statements of instrumental value, such as "X is a good way of achieving Z," once we set a standard of goodness. By contrast, statements of noninstrumental value do not lend themselves to any test or experiment that would settle disputes about them. Consider this example. The animal welfare movement opposes painful experiments on animals, even if such experiments may ultimately benefit human health. Supporters of animal experimentation often defend such treatments on the grounds that human life is "better" than other kinds of animal life, that it has greater intrinsic value than the lives of these experimental animals, that human lives are more valuable on some absolute scale than those of rhesus monkeys, rabbits, or mice. The point here is that such claims about intrinsic value go beyond anything that science can show. Even discovering that some laboratory animals do not have the neural mechanisms to produce conscious- ness or understanding or some other mental capacity would not show these animals had less intrinsic value than those animals with these capacities, because no experiment can demonstrate that such mental capacities are the source of any intrinsic value. Nor can it be shown that they are not, of course. Intrinsic valuation is simply outside the domain of science. (We return to some of these issues in Chapter 7.)

Now, the statement that humans are a higher or better form of life than other animals could be rescued for science but only by adding something to make it instrumental. One might say instead that "humans are better than other primates at surviving and reproducing," meaning humans are more adept at doing these things, that they are better adapted. So understood, the statement now employs only instrumental value terms and therefore become at least potentially open to scientific assessment (keeping in mind that there is no implicit assumption here that survival and reproduction are valuable in any noninstrumental sense). It is this sense of instrumental valuation, from the point of view of natural selection, that we will consider shortly. And what we will find is that even though the statement that humans are better adapted is a scientifically permissible one, establishing its truth is far from straightforward. By most instrumental criteria, there is virtually no evidence that we are.

It must be added that although science can take no sides on matters of intrinsic value, it does not by any means follow that what most people think of as intrinsic or noninstrumental values have no role in guiding scientists' actions. Some scientists would say that intrinsic values underlie their motiva- tions for doing science in the first place (perhaps to make new discoveries that help people). Further, scientists may pick problems to study for reasons rooted in their intrinsic values (perhaps studying dolphins because of what is taken to be their intrinsic value). And some would say that noninstrumental values are involved in deciding what question to pose about a given problem, and about how to formulate that question (maybe choosing to study only those causes of global warming that are potentially reversible). More broadly, noninstrumental values are said to be involved in larger societal decisions about what sort of science is worth pursuing (e.g. whether the government should fund stem cell research) and about how and whether to use certain scientific results (e.g. whether the government should build nuclear weapons). And there is yet another way that noninstrumental values might be said to be involved in science, as the object of scientific study. As we shall see in Chapter 7, biologists and social scientists have been interested in the sources of our noninstrumental values, the ones expressed in our moral views, and they have sought evolutionary explanations for them. But none of these involvements of value with science violate value neutrality. In none of them do values intrude on the collection of data and the interpretation of results. In none do they intrude on the process of answering a question once it is posed, in other words, on the *practice* of science. At least, they should not intrude and will not as long as the scientist is acting purely as a scientist, honoring the limits of the discipline.

What does this mean for evolutionary progress? It means that when biologists use the term progress in the practice of biology, the value component had better be entirely instrumental, with no implication of improvement by some intrinsic or noninstrumental standard of value. It also means that if biologists adopt a purely instrumental standard for progress, such as propensity to survive and reproduce, then when they come to make comparisons, they had better stick to their instrumental guns. They must insist that a more progressive organism is not necessarily better in any intrinsic sense. It is not morally superior. It is simply better able to survive and reproduce. Period. More concretely, if biologists discover that humans are the best survivors and reproducers of all, they are permitted to conclude that humans are the most progressive. But as scientists that is as far as they can go. The further judgment, if they choose to make it, that a human is also a superior animal in some noninstrumental sense would be a judgment outside of science.

Words are our creations, in science if not in ordinary life. Science is full of neologisms—new words such as transposon—and old words redefined—such as gene. So nothing forbids biology from deciding that in its technical usage, the word progress will have no noninstrumental implications. But in reality things are not so simple. Official definitions banning noninstrumental implications are well and good, but colloquial meanings rich in noninstrumental implications tag along willy-nilly. And this makes an official scientific usage for "progress" more than a bit awkward, given how heavily laden with noninstrumental values the word is in conventional usage. One might wonder why such a word as "progress" ever entered biological discourse anyway, and why it persists. One suggestion has been that the word reflects a tendency to read into biology the optimism about technological and social advancement so pervasive in Enlightenment thought, particularly in the nineteenth century. If history reflects a trajectory of improvement, the implicit argument goes, why not evolution as well? Given this background, and the inevitable tag-along connotations of progress, some have endorsed jettisoning the word altogether, banning it from biology. Indeed, the historian and philosopher of biology Michael Ruse has argued that in the mid-twentieth century, biologists did start to avoid the word and the concept for the most part, at least in their professional writings (Ruse 1996). And Stephen J. Gould has seemed to advocate an official purge, calling progress a "noxious, culturally embedded, untestable, nonoperational, intractable idea" (Gould 1988: 319). But this seems to be just howling at the moon. Progress continues to appear in popular writings, even of professional evolutionists (including Gould himself). The word, and the idea, are not likely to disappear from popular conceptions (and misconceptions) of evolution any time soon.

What does theory predict?

Tag-along associations aside, adopting a purely instrumental understanding of the value component of progress would seem to cleanse the term enough for scientific use. Progress could be whatever is valued by the evolutionary process, that is to say valued in the sense of preserved or enhanced. And if one assumes that natural selection is the major force operating in evolution, the prediction would be that the process would preserve or enhance adaptedness or fitness. Given these understandings, it might seem that natural selection virtually guarantees progress. If improved descendants always beat less-improved ancestors in what Darwin called "the race for life," then seemingly later organisms should be better adapted than earlier ones.

Problems arise immediately. Recall from Chapter 1 that fitness is an organism–environment relationship, that the adaptedness of an organism is relative to the environment in which it finds itself. So if the environment changes, and if the organism adapts under the influence of natural selection to an environment that is changing over generations, the result might not be a better-adapted organism at all but only a *differently* adapted organism. Suppose that a modern horse of the genus *Equus* is well adapted to a modern grassland environment. Is there any reason to expect that it will be better adapted in a general way than *Eohippus*, its dog-sized ancestor in the Eocene epoch 50 million years ago? Arguably no, because *Eohippus* may have been equally well adapted to a very different environment, the forests of the Eocene.

The difficulty is actually more severe than it might seem at first glance, because of course the "environment" includes the biotic environment as well as the abiotic environment. It is not just that the climate of the present differs from that of the Eocene, it is also that the predators, competitors, parasites, and food resources all differ as well. *Eohippus* was presumably well adapted to the biota of the Eocene, while the modern horse is presumably well adapted to that of the present. And so, given the complexity of their respective ecologies, there is reason to think that they will be *very* differently adapted, and that makes it hard to see why one should be better in any sense. In general, no overall improvement is expected to the extent that environments change and adaptation merely tracks environments. Indeed, to the extent that environmental tracking occurs, it is not clear that the notion of improvement even has any nonrelational meaning. "Improvement relative to what environment?" the skeptic wants to know. If there is no meaningful answer to this question, the notion of progress would seem to be sunk.

Of course, if environments were constant, or if they fluctuated in some consistent way around fixed values, then improvement could have meaning. One can imagine that in a constant environment, the extent of an organism's adaptedness to that environment increases with the passage of time. Natural selection "fine tunes" its adaptations, so to speak, so that later organisms are better adjusted to that constant environment than earlier ones. Is constancy of environment plausible? It is when one recognizes that constancy is relative to some spatial and temporal scale. Environments might change locally or on short timescales, while remaining roughly constant on longer ones. Climate cools and warms, continents drift this way and that, diversity rises and falls, and predators, competitors, and parasites come and go. At some timescale, average values of these and all relevant variables may be fairly constant. For long timescales, for most variables, for most organisms, environmental change could be just fluctuation around a fixed value. This is not to say that it is, just that it could be, and to the extent that it is, fitnesses of ancestors and descendants can be meaningfully compared, and later organisms are expected to be fitter, on average.

There is yet another way that instrumental progress could be rescued. Progress might depend on the degree to which adaptations to past environments are retained. Recall from Chapter 1 that lineages of organisms are not perfectly plastic in their response to natural selection. Various factors constrain development and prevent instantaneous loss of adaptations to past environments. Our own appendix might be thought of as a retained adaptation to a past environment, one in which hominid diets were different. If so, then to the extent that our appendices are still functional, we modern humans might be at once well adapted to a modern diet and also to an earlier one. Because our ancestors' digestive capabilities were well adapted only to the earlier diet (presumably), modern humans could consider themselves adapted to a greater range of environments, and therefore better adapted overall. More generally, to the extent that later organisms retain adaptations to earlier environments, as well as develop new adaptations to later environments, they are more progressive. Progress could be the accumulation of adaptations. (Of course, adaptations to past environments tend to decay, unless somehow constrained, but we will get to this shortly.)

Another, and different, route to progress could be the accumulation of what are called general adaptations. For example, there is an untested conventional wisdom in evolutionary studies that more specialized species have more complex structures, more complex "tools," so to speak, while more generally adapted species are simpler. Thus a modern lobster with its diverse limb types specialized for different tasks—food processing, sensing the environment, defense, walking, and swimming—is probably more specialized than an ancient trilobite, an animal with multiple limbs like a lobster but all of them more or less the same. The thinking is that the lobster with its more specialized tools is more precisely adapted to a particular environment, whereas the trilobite with more generalized equipment might be more broadly adapted to a range of environments. Arguably, if environments change significantly, then selection on long timescales ought to favor organisms with more general adaptations, or ought to favor the accumulation of general adaptations. (However, interestingly, trilobites are now extinct, the last species having perished some 250 million years ago.) The point is that to the extent that general adaptations arise and are retained, later organisms are expected to be better adapted, on average. Better adapted to what environment, the skeptic asks. The answer is: to a range of environments.

Notice that the notion of progress being developed here seems to require a somewhat modified understanding of fitness. Consider the propensity understanding of fitness discussed in Chapter 2, "X is fitter than Y in environment E if X has a greater probabilistic propensity to survive and reproduce in E." What the discussion of general adaptation suggests is that such an environment-specific understanding of fitness will not help us make sense of progress. For progress to be meaningful, what is needed is an understanding of fitness that spans multiple environments (at least on the assumption that the environment is not stable). Such a notion is undoubtedly part of what lies behind the common idea that humans are the most progressive (even in just the instrumental sense). We are better adapted, we think, to survive and reproduce in *many* environments, more environments than other species are well adapted to survive and reproduce in.

Suppose we adopt some multienvironmental notion of fitness, say propensity to survive and reproduce over some specified range of environments. More concretely, let's specify the environmental range as the Earth's oceans over the past 500 million years, roughly the history of animal life. In that case, we might predict that a modern marine snail species, say, ought to be more fit than a snail species living 400 million years ago. The reason would be that the evolutionary lineage of the ancient snail species was subject to selection only over the first 100 million years of changing environments whereas the modern snail lineage experienced selection over that time span *plus* an additional 400 million years of environmental variation. Assuming environmental variation is substantial, the modern snail arguably should be adapted to a broader range of environments (perhaps on account of having accumulated more adaptations or more general adaptations or both), and therefore should have a higher propensity to survive and reproduce over that greater range. To make this vivid, consider a hypothetical transplant experiment in which a modern snail is transported in time to the ancient environment and an ancient one to a modern environment. Arguably, neither would be expected to do very well, but the more generally adapted modern transplant would be expected to outperform the ancient transplant, to survive and reproduce better (or at least, less poorly), under the alien conditions in which each (startlingly) finds itself.

Of course, this prediction could be wrong. The environment of the snail lineage after the time of the ancient snail might not have been sufficiently variable. Or perhaps the snail's genetic and developmental mechanisms were not able to retain and accumulate general adaptations on long timescales. Selection, unimpeded by constraints, might tend to produce adaptation to local short-timescale environments only, erasing more general long-timescale adaptations. Interestingly, one way of protecting general adaptations against such erasures is constraint. To the extent that general adaptations can be rendered *less* variable, to the extent that they are constrained, it will be more difficult for them to be erased by short-term selection. Similarly, the more specific adaptations discussed earlier will tend to decay less rapidly, allowing them to accumulate, when constraints are present. In other words, constraints offer a possible route to progress.

Yet more general notions of cross-environmental fitness can be imagined. It could be propensity to survive and reproduce over *all possible environments* rather than just some specified range. This move raises further difficulties, of course, such as whether we have to think about the fitness of Earthly organisms on Mars. (A snail would probably have zero fitness on Mars, but some Earthly microbes might not.) In any case, the point is that claims about cross-environmental fitness could be meaningful, even though they require us to compare very different organisms in very different environments. And if this sort of fitness is meaningful, then the environmental relativity of fitness is not fatal to progress.

Is there any way to test the prediction of progress? At the level of the individual, this can be done sometimes, even with fossils, for example, through a comparative analysis of functional design in ancient and modern organisms. If there has been progress, then where design problems overlap, the moderns should be better designed, perhaps by engineering criteria. In any case, broader tests can be done at a higher level—the level of species or genera or higher—using extinction probability, which is eminently measurable using the fossil record. The approach has its problems. For example, fitness is not just propensity to survive but to successfully reproduce as well. And a short-lived species could, at least in principle, be more fit than a longer-lived one if it produces more descendant species before it goes extinct. In other words, a shorter-lived species could nevertheless have a greater propensity than a longer-lived species to leave surviving "offspring" species millions of years later. The same goes for genera and higher taxonomic levels.

Interestingly, one data set on extinction probability—from the paleobiologist Leigh Van Valen (1984)—does not show the simple pattern one would have expected for progress. In marine animals, the probability of extinction did decline over the first 300 million years of the group's history, but the decline was then interrupted by a resetting, a rather abrupt rise in extinction probability at the time of a major mass extinction, followed again by a slow decline over the remaining 250 million years of animal history. If declining extinction probability is progress, then it seems that millions of years of progress can be undone.

Another data set commonly cited in connection with progress—a famous one—needs some mention here. Van Valen showed 30 years ago that over a huge range of disparate groups of organisms, including protists, invertebrates, and vertebrates, the probability of extinction is constant with age, that is to say, groups do not become more extinction resistant as they age (Van Valen 1973). (Notice that this finding does not contradict the finding above that overall extinction probability declines: the time variable here is *age* of a group, not absolute time.) Van Valen reasoned that, other things being equal, this should not happen. Natural selection predicts improvement relative to the environment and therefore a reduction in extinction probability with age. But if extinction probabilities in fact remain constant with age, this raises the possibility that the environment actually becomes more challenging, that it decays, at the same rate as the organism improves. For this to happen, it would probably have to be the biotic environment that is changing, decaying (simply because it is hard to see how the physical environment could be changing directionally, for all groups, irrespective of time). And what that would mean is that across groups, as each organism adapts and improves, its predators, competitors, and so on all adapt and improve at the same rate, on average, with the result that in relative terms, all remain equally fit. Van Valen called this the Red Queen's hypothesis, after a character in Lewis Carroll's *Through the Looking-Glass*, a tyrannical chess piece called the Red Queen, who remarks that in her world "it takes all the running you can do, to keep in the same place" (Carroll 1960: 210). Exiting the metaphor, it takes all the adapting an evolutionary lineage can do to maintain the same extinction probability.

Do the Red Queen data demonstrate progress? It might seem that overall adaptedness must be rising if environments are decaying and extinction probability is stable. The answer is no, because constant extinction probability could occur if all organisms merely tracked changing environments, acquiring no general adaptations. Another way to think about it is this: it could be that the environment of, say, a modern horse (i.e., its competitors, predators, parasites, etc.), is no more challenging to it than the environment of *Eohippus* was to that species. Both live in decaying environments, with constantly improving competitors, predators, etc., but over the 50 million years that separate them the decay could have been peripatetic, not consistently directional, so that later environments are not worse in general terms, just different.

So do the Red Queen data *falsify* progress? It might seem that they do because extinction probabilities remain constant, rather than declining. Again the answer is no. First, the data report constant probability of extinction with age, meaning that—for example—a modern horse genus has the same extinction probability as its Eocene relative, when the Eocene genus was the same age as the modern genus is now. How could that be consistent with progress? The modern horse genus could have more general adaptations than its Eocene ancestor, making the modern animal better adapted to a wider variety of environments. If so, then in a reciprocal transplant, the modern horse would do better (or less badly) in the Eocene than *Eohippus* would do in a modern environment. And yet at the same time, the modern horse could have the same probability of extinction in its present environment as *Eohippus* had in the Eocene, that is assuming the modern's predators, competitors, etc. have also acquired a number of general adaptations, leaving the modern horse with no relative advantage.

Consider an analogy with baseball. It turns out that in the endlessly replayed duel between hitter (trying to hit a pitched ball where the fielders cannot catch it, "hitting it where they ain't") and pitcher (trying to throw the ball so that hitters cannot hit it), modern hitters and pitchers perform no better in relative terms than players 100 years ago, early in the history of game. The frequency with which batters succeed in hitting the ball (their batting averages) and the frequency with which they fail (reflected in the statistics for pitchers) have remained about the same. But, arguably, over the years the absolute level of baseball-playing ability among the game's players has increased, in part as a result of the competition between batters and pitchers. The suggestion is that today's players are better in some general way, across a variety of baseball "environments." (For example, they might be more "athletic," in some sense.) If so, they would presumably defeat players from an earlier era in head-to-head competition most of the time. And such an increase in general ability is consistent with, and could easily be hiding behind, the more or less constant performance averages of all players over time. Likewise, it could be that organisms become better adapted in some more general, nonenvironment-specific way. In other words, increasing cross-environmental fitness is consistent with constant environment-specific fitness. Thus, the data supporting the Red Queen's hypothesis are consistent with progress but do not demonstrate it.

Finally, it is worth mentioning one more reason that the use of extinction probability as a measure of progress might be problematic. The problem arises in connection with certain so-called "living fossils," the cyanobacteria. The earliest fossils from rocks 3.5 billion years old appear similar in some ways to modern cyanobacteria, a group that today occupies a huge range of environments, including most of the upper surface of the world's oceans. If those early species were cyanobacteria, or even moderately close relatives, and if the longevity of their lineage is as great as it appears, this raises the possibility that the most progressive organisms on Earth were among the first organisms. Or at least, these bacteria have—by surviving little modified for 3.5 billion years—made the most of the opportunity afforded them to prove their propensity to survive. Of course, cyanobacteria present a problem only if one accepts lineage survival propensity as a measure of progressiveness and only if one is reluctant to allow these bacteria the honor of being the most progressive, or of course if one is simply determined to have humans come out on top.

Some more specific proposals and their problems

Using extinction probabilities would be unnecessary if some variable (or some small suite of variables) could be found that is causally connected with fitness. What we are looking for are features of adaptations that have trended systematically in evolution, reflecting an increase in propensity to survive and reproduce. In effect, what is sought here is one or more features of organisms that are consistently "valued" by the evolutionary process, something that the various routes to fitness have in common. Is there a kind of "common currency" in which propensity to survive and reproduce over a range of environments can be cashed out?

There is some reason to suspect ahead of time that there is no such currency. Recall from Chapter 2 that the context sensitivity of fitness and the arms-race character of selection were raised as possible reasons to reject the idea that natural selection could be a law. There seems to be no feature of a robin that natural selection can be expected to favor in all environments. In other words, as environment changes, we are completely unable to predict what changes in robins will be favored by natural selection. And we concluded that if natural selection is a law, it is not a predictive one. For progress, the situation is actually somewhat worse than context sensitivity alone would lead one to suspect. It is not just that different environments require different adaptive solutions. It is also that different organisms often have utterly different requirements and evolutionary potentials. An increase in horn length might be advantageous to a great horned beetle but disadvantageous to a gazelle. Also, the huge differences among organisms seem to preclude any commonality among features that are advantageous. Suppose that horn length were advantageous for every animal species on the planet, including animals that do not have horns, such as snails, but which could in principle "increase" their horn length by acquiring them. Horn length would still be problematic as a common currency for fitness. What shall we do with an organism with a radically different body plan, such as a lilac bush, which not only does not have horns but for which it is not clear that the notion of horns has any meaning? What sort of structure on a lilac bush would be a horn in the same sense as a horn on a gazelle? Where on a lilac bush would one place such a structure? It sounds wrong to think of a thorn, for example, as a kind of horn. And this is the problem. It is hard to imagine how there could be any common feature associated with fitness, at least not at the level of horns and thorns.

So if a common currency is going to be found, it will be in variables that are shared across radically different designs, variables such as complexity or energy usage. A number of these have been proposed. What follows is a partial list of candidates. Proponents of the listed features have not used the word progress for the most part. But it is clear that their interest is in adaptation at the largest evolutionary scale, in discovering what is preserved or enhanced by the evolutionary process as a whole.

1 *Dominance* The mid-twentieth century evolutionist Julian Huxley described progress in the history of life as a succession of "dominant types," or groups with the potential to diversify and survive in a wide range of ecological settings. In the animals, the trend is reflected in the early dominance of trilobites, followed later by the insects on land and fish in the sea, and then the amphibians, reptiles and higher insects, birds and mammals, and ultimately the most dominant mammal, humans.

2 One recurring candidate in discussions of progress is intelligence. Perhaps natural selection generally favors increases in ability to analyze the environment and respond appropriately. Related to this is a proposal by the evolutionist Francisco Ayala that what generally increases in evolution is the ability to sense the environment, presumably along with the intellectual ability to make use of information gathered. (The word "generally"—for which might be substituted "on average"—is crucial here, as it is for most other proposed long-term trends, because it is widely recognized that selection will often favor decreases as well. For organisms living in constant or predictable environments, for example, intelligence and extensive environmental sensing ability could actually be disadvantageous, a waste of scarce energy and other resources perhaps. We discuss this further in the next section of this chapter.)

3 A common proposal over the past half-century is that progress consists in the increase in complexity in evolution. In the 1960s, the evolutionary biologist Ledyard Stebbins suggested that the upward trajectory of complexity is manifest in the evolutionary sequence that took us from self-replicating chemical system to bacterium, to protist, to simple invertebrate, to invertebrate with differentiated tissues, to animal with well-developed limbs and nervous system, to endotherm (an organism with its own internal heat source, like a mammal), and finally to human (Stebbins 1969). Variants of this sequence are a recurring theme in discussions of progress. And in the 1990s, another one popped up in the literature, this one from the evolutionary biologist John Maynard Smith and the molecular biologist Eörs Szathmáry, who identified what they called the "major transitions" in evolution, defined by increases in complexity and changes in the way information is transmitted from one generation to the next (Maynard Smith and Szathmáry 1995). They identified eight such major transitions: (i) the shift from individual replicating molecules—say RNAs—to collections of such molecules in compartments bounded by membranes; (ii) the joining of individual replicating genes into suites of genes joined on chromosomes; (iii) the shift from RNA functioning as both replicator and interactor to a division of

labor between DNA, acting as replicator, and proteins, acting as inter-actors; (iv) the historic merger of a number of prokaryotic (bacterial) species to generate the first eukaryotic cell; (v) the emergence of sexual reproduction in eukaryotes; (vi) the transition from solitary eukaryotic cells to aggregated clones of cells, that is multicellular individuals, and the later differentiation of those cells to perform special functions within individuals; (vii) the aggregation of individual organisms into colonies or societies, as in ants, again with specialization among individuals for performing particular functions; and (viii) the evolution of human, language-using societies from nonlinguistic primates.

Complexity appears in other guises as well. The suggestion has often been made in recent decades that what increases is genetic complexity, perhaps measurable as the number of genes in an organism. More genes presumably means more information, in the sense of more instructions involved in development, physiology, and behavior. And more informa-tion means more advanced, some have argued.

4   The paleobiologist Geerat Vermeij (1987) has suggested that evolution generally is characterized by "escalation," by which he means an increase in the energy intensiveness of organisms, and of the conflicts with their enemies, which includes their competitors, predators, parasites, and so on. According to Vermeij's theory, a common theme in escalation is arms races, such as the increase in shell-crushing ability of crabs that occurred in evolutionary concert with an increase in thickness and defensive orna-mentation of the shells of their main prey, snails and clams. In Vermeij's scheme, escalation also includes increases in metabolic rate, mobility, and other features associated with competition and predation.

5   Van Valen (1989) proposed that a possible common currency for fit-ness is energy available for expansion, that is, available beyond what's needed for maintenance. Expansion can take the form of reproduction, as in conventional thinking on fitness, but it can also take the form of an increase in body size, or for clonal organisms, an increase in number of clonal units. So a mosquito is fit if it is able to produce many offspring, while a whale is fit if it is able to grow to large size, and an aspen tree is fit if it is able to send out roots that give rise to many trunks. The common theme is expansion, making more of oneself. And the different modes of expansion become comparable by converting them to the common currency of expansive energy. Reproducing sexually, reproducing asexu-ally (e.g. clonally), and growing large all require energy, as do producing the various structures, physiological processes, and behaviors that make reproduction and growth possible and likely to succeed. For a clam, expansive energy would include the energy needed to produce the shell that it makes to protect itself and to burrow with (insofar as these capaci-ties are used for reproduction and growth, rather than maintenance), as well as direct expenditures on reproduction and body-size increase. Notice that in this understanding, a mammal may be more fit than a

clam, but its greater fitness does not follow simply from the fact that the mammal has, say, a higher metabolic rate, and therefore uses more energy. For the mammal to be fitter, it must have more *excess* energy, so to speak, meaning more energy available for expansion.

This viewpoint leads to certain conclusions that are highly intuitive and yet run contrary to the standard view of fitness, especially in the evolution of groups and in evolution on long time scales. In particular, consider these examples from Van Valen (1989). He asks why a grass colonizing an empty field by expanding clonally—that is without reproducing at all, in the conventional sense of the word—is automatically considered less fit than one that is colonizing an equivalent field using seeds. The clonally expanding individual could be commanding more expansive energy. On a much longer timescale, he asks us to consider the historical supplanting of an ancient group of mammals, the multituberculates—whose heyday was in the Mesozoic epoch, along with the dinosaurs—by modern mammals, the placentals. The multituberculates lost that competition but continued to diversify, to increase their species numbers, even as they were losing, at least in the early stages of the competition. Thus the placentals were expanding in energetic terms while the multituberculates were contracting, but that trend is harder to see if the focus is on number of offspring, in this case offspring species. Notice that using a measure like energy here –and also in Vermeij's scheme—it becomes easy to think about fitness in nonrelative terms. We can measure the *absolute* fitness of an organism, not in terms of its reproductive success relative to some other organism, but in energetic terms, for example in calories.

6 *Body size* A very old notion is that body size tends to increase in evolution, on average, a principle that in contemporary discussions is called Cope's rule, after the nineteenth century paleontologist Edward Drinker Cope.

The list is not exhaustive, nor are the candidates mutually exclusive. Perhaps all increase over the history of life. Indeed, all sound promising in some way. But to philosophers and biologists, the problems are myriad. One of the most salient is what might be called "the people problem." For three of these proposals—Huxley's dominance sequence, the notion of increasing intelligence and ability to sense the environment, and the Stebbins and Maynard Smith–Szathmáry complexity sequences—look suspiciously like reincarnations of the Great Chain, like attempts to bring back the discredited notion of a ladder of perfection, with humans at the top. Huxley considered humans the most dominant, but he offered no clear objective criteria by which we are. Ayala pretty clearly picked as his central criterion a capability at which humans excel, sensing—and presumably interpreting—the environment. Stebbins used the word complexity but offered no objective understanding of it, and there seems to be no particular feature of organisms that is increasing in his list except evolutionary proximity to humans. And the Maynard Smith and Szathmáry list begins objectively enough but lapses at the end. Looking at the first seven major transitions, all seem to be increases in complexity in the sense of degree of nestedness, in number of levels of association of parts within wholes. Chromosomes are associations of genes, multicellular individuals are associations of cells, societies are associations of individuals, and so on. But the last transition—apes to humans—departs from this scheme. Human societies are not associations of ape societies. We both form societies. Perhaps human societies are more complex in some other unspecified sense, but not in the nestedness sense that the other major transitions are. Interpreted uncharitably, Maynard Smith and Szathmáry were simply determined to crown the list of major transitions with the evolution of humans, and to do so they were willing to ignore the criterion that justified the rest of the list, complexity in the sense of nestedness. (To be fair, complexity was not their only standard. They characterized the major transitions as changes in complexity *or* in the way information is transmitted from one generation to the next, so that human culture could be a major transition above ape sociality by this second standard, human culture representing a different way of transmitting information. But in that case the criticism is that the two-part standard itself seems chosen, and the scheme therefore rigged, to make humans come out on top.)

This notion of humans as the most dominant, intelligent, or complex seems to some biologists to be transparent anthropocentrism, an attempt to flatter ourselves, to feed human vanity, or to put a scientific gloss on the Christian notion of humans as central in the universe and, since Darwin, as central to the evolutionary process. In the words of Mark Twain, if the Eiffel Tower represents the history of the world, and the skin of paint atop the knob at the pinnacle is the portion of that history in which humans have existed, "anybody would perceive that that skin was what the tower was built for. . . . I reckon they would, I dunno" (1962: 226).

But there is a defense, one that—if valid—vindicates the human-centered approach. A criterion for progress that puts humans first is flawed only if it has a noninstrumental component, that is if humans are ranked as the most progressive partly on account of our supposed moral superiority, perfection by some divine standard, and so on. But suppose that some important feature of humans turns out to be precisely what the evolutionary process in fact preserves or favors. In that case, that feature could be a perfectly good criterion for *instrumental* progress. What the anthropocentrism critique overlooks is the possibility that the intuitions suggesting human progressiveness are right, that they are based partly on a direct perception of our own instrumental superiority. Granted, this could be a feature that we are temporarily unable to articulate in scientific terms. The perception could be "precognitive." But it could still accurately report a truth about biology. For example, the perception that in your absence something has been moved on your desk could be such a precognitive perception. And it could be right even if you are temporarily unable to say precisely what it is that has been moved. So if the perception of progress is one of this sort, the task of evolutionary biology is to discover precisely what feature of organisms our precognitive analytical abilities have identified. The task is to find a way to say clearly what we already seem to know vaguely. And the recurrence of Great Chain-like sequences in treatments of progress may reflect more than religious dogma or human vanity. Of course, pending discovery of the basis for that vague precognitive perception, considerable suspicion is justified.

A second problem with most of the candidates in the list above is that the term for the feature of organisms it identifies is not operational. A term is operational if its definition makes clear how to measure it. Consider intelligence. It might seem obvious that humans are the top intellects on the planet, but it is also reasonable to ask by what standard of intelligence. Intelligence measured how? After all, there is a kind of intelligence at work in the behavior of the parasite, say, that protects itself from an immune system by shutting down its metabolic machinery and secreting an inert cyst to hide within. The parasite does not do any reasoning here. There is no weighing of alternatives or conscious invention of effective strategies. In other words, it is not a human style of intelligence. But it could be construed as a kind of intelligence. Now for many, counting such a parasite as intelligent would somehow miss the point. Maybe it is intelligent but not in the intended sense. So what is needed here is clarity about precisely what sort of intelligence is supposed to be increasing, an operationalization of intelligence, or, in other words, a well-defined measure and a scale. Intelligence might be operationalized, for example as a function of brain size or as number of different behaviors, or—if the target is human-style intelligence—some other scale on which a human scores high and a fish scores low (and the parasite presumably scores zero). Notice that a consequence of choosing human-style intelligence as a standard is that progress can be said to begin only rather late in the history of life, about 500 million years ago, with the origin of animals, that is assuming protists, plants, and fungi do not have human-style intelligence to any degree. In any case, the point is that without an operational scale, judgments about intelligence, and therefore about progressiveness, are subjective. There is no objective way to decide whether, say, a beaver is more intelligent than an octopus, and no way to investigate a possible large-scale trend. Most of the other features in the list above share the same difficulty. In the current state of the art, only body size is completely operational.

Complexity is an especially troublesome case. Complexity is probably the answer that most biologists would give if asked what sort of trend characterizes evolution as a whole, or what characterizes progress. However, most would also agree that this assessment is mostly, if not entirely, impressionistic. The difficulty is that complexity—in the colloquial sense, at least—has no operational definition. The colloquial sense is wonderfully rich. We call a contract complex if we do not understand it. We call a recipe complex if it has many steps. We might call a car complex on account of its many parts, but we might also call a device with few parts such as a violin complex if its manufacture involves a lot of steps, or if its few parts are machined very precisely, or if those parts are made of some high-tech material. In biology, colloquial complexity connotes an uncertain mix of organismal features, such as number of part types, degree of hierarchical structure, adaptedness, sophistication, and so on. This richness makes the word useful in many contexts, but it also makes it difficult to apply in any precise way. Suppose we wanted to compare a human with our fish ancestors hundreds of millions of years ago. As the eminent paleontologist George Gaylord Simpson put it, "It would be a brave anatomist who would attempt to prove that Recent man is more complicated than a Devonian ostracoderm" (1967: 252). So if the claim is that progress is complexity, the skeptic reasonably wants to know: complexity in what sense, measured how? In the absence of a clear answer, the term complexity in discussions of progress looks like a code word for proximity to humans, and a devious way to make the ordering in the Great Chain of Being sound more scientific.

Various attempts have been made—mostly in theoretical physics—to devise measures that capture all or most of complexity in the colloquial sense. But none of these have proven useful in biology so far. In biology, the approach has been somewhat different. Instead of trying to find a measure that captures all of colloquial complexity, the tactic has been to carve complexity into conceptually smaller and more manageable pieces. In other words, multiple operationalizations of the term have been devised, no one of which captures all of the colloquial meaning but which together cover a great deal of it. For example, there is complexity in the sense of number of part types. The complexity of a multicellular organism might be measured as the number of cell types it has or, at a lower level, as the number of different genes it has. Notice that part types must be relative to some chosen level of counting parts. Complexity at the cell level for a human is the number of cell types we have—on the order of 250 or so—while at the gene level it is number of different types of genes—24,000 or so, according to present estimates. There is no contradiction. Complexity in the sense of part types is simply a level-relative concept. In addition to complexity as part types—what has been called "horizontal complexity"—there is complexity in the sense of parts within wholes, hierarchy or "vertical complexity," as in (most of) Maynard Smith and Szathmáry's list. And there is complexity in the sense of number of distinct physiological processes, number of different behaviors, number of stages in development, and so on.

A drawback of this approach, of course, is that it overlooks some key components of the colloquial meaning, such as functionality and sophistication. A smashed car might have many more part types than an intact one, and therefore by the standard of part types it would be more complex. And a can opener with few part types is simple, even if it is made out of a sophisticated alloy. But recall that the basic strategy adopted here is to dissect complexity into some of its component concepts and to operationalize them, abandoning colloquial complexity (at least for the time being). The approach has the virtue that it allows for objective measurement. It also allows for the possibility of surprising results. Humans, for example, may come out on top in some aspect of complexity, but in others we may not. Humans do have extreme numbers of cell types, among multicellular organisms possibly the most. But we are probably not the hierarchically deepest. The next higher level of organization above the multicellular level is the society, and by some standards—such as the existence of sterile castes of individuals whose lives are devoted entirely to the colony—sociality is more highly developed in certain social insects, and even in other mammal species such as naked mole rats, than in us.

This approach has so far yielded only scant results. For hierarchy, it is clear that there has been a large-scale trend in the maximum, in the highest level of hierarchy attained, evident in the rise from single-celled existence to multicellularity to sociality (McShea 2001). For part types, there seems to be a trend in the maximum number of cell types, in the animals, at least (Valentine et al. 1994). But for complexity in other technical senses, such as number of behaviors or complexity of development, virtually nothing is known. In recent years, biologists have been able to produce some good estimates of genetic complexity in the sense of gene number (horizontal complexity, measured at the scale of molecules and limited to genes). The human count (24,000 genes) is higher than that of the "lower" organisms for which we have counts, such as a yeast cell (6,000), and a fruit fly (14,000), and a tiny worm called a nematode (19,000). Still, these numbers raise new puzzles. Why is the human advantage in gene number so low? Impressionistically, human complexity should not just be higher, but *much* higher than flies and worms. And then, the fly may seem simple compared with us, but it looks like quite a sophisticated animal compared with a tiny nematode. Flies have more than twice as many cell types as nematodes, and many more organs and tissues. Why do they have *fewer* genes?

Various answers are possible. Some of them have to do with the way that genes interact with development, physiology, and behavior. For example, much of the information in these processes is nongenetic, coming from the environment (including the maternal environment), and many of the phenotypic complexity differences among organisms are produced by differences in the way the flow of information is regulated, rather than by differences in number of types of instruction, i.e. gene number. Also, it is arguable that there was never any good reason to expect a good correlation between genetic complexity and phenotypic complexity. The reason is simply that complexity of generating processes need not be well correlated with complexity of outcome. Structurally simple outcomes may have complex generating processes (e.g. mayonnaise, which in some cookbooks has a *very* long recipe, with many steps). And structurally complex outcomes may have simple generating processes (e.g. snowflakes). Much of the complexity of organisms may arise directly from principles of mathematics, chemistry, and physics, rather than genes.

Other answers are worth considering too. Maybe flies and worms are not "lower" at all. Maybe they *are* extraordinarily complex in the colloquial sense, perhaps with physiological or behavioral sophistication not yet discovered or appreciated. Perhaps the expectation that they would be simple is a residue of Great Chain thinking. And the Great Chain, of course, may have nothing to do with complexity, or any other objective feature of the biological world. (Our precognitive intuitions could be wrong.) Along the same lines, recall that complexity was raised here as a candidate for a variable that might underlie progress. Perhaps these gene-count data are telling us that it is a poor candidate. In other words, perhaps humans are in fact extraordinarily fit but not on account of our genetic complexity (which apparently is not extraordinarily great). Indeed, there is some reason to wonder why complexity would ever be considered a good candidate proxy for progress. At least in the world of machines, it is true that complex design is often associated with impressive capabilities, as in the case of cars and computers. But complex cars and computers break down all the time, whereas simple skateboards and abaci hardly ever do. Complexity could be, on average, a bad thing!

Beyond sorting out these issues, complexity presents the philosophy of biology with one huge challenge: finding a way to operationalize the trickier aspects of colloquial complexity, such as sophistication and functionality, and then, if possible, developing a composite measure to recapture all or most of the colloquial usage, or, to put it more skeptically, to discover whether or not the colloquial usage has any real meaning.

A third difficulty with the list of candidate features has to do with use of the word progress in its instrumental sense. Suppose that the common feature of organisms that promotes survival and reproduction over the history of life turns out to be body size. Suppose that over 3.5 billion years of evolutionary history, larger organisms have had greater fitness, on average, than smaller ones. (Again the "on average" clause turns out to be important, because obviously smaller organisms arise and persist sometimes.) And, further, suppose that large body size is the only common feature among the fitter organisms. In other words, suppose progress turns out to be nothing but increasing body size. This finding would be nice in that body size is already operational. Biologists have some very direct ways of measuring it, such as the length of an organism, its volume, or its mass, some of them even applicable to fossils. But it sounds odd nonetheless to call an organism progressive simply on account of its mass or length. It should not, of course, not if we are using the word progress strictly in its instrumental sense. But those tag-along associations intrude. If progress is body size, then a redwood tree is more progressive than a mouse, or a human for that matter. And that sounds wrong, and makes one start to wonder whether it was wise to keep the word progress. Worse, suppose biologists discovered that the major trend in evolution is an increase in, say, the rate at which an organism wastes energy, a rise in profligate use of energy. Or suppose that over the history of life, selection favors a tendency to ruthlessly and remorselessly murder members of one's own species. In other words, suppose progress in the instrumental sense turns out to be something we do not value, or even something we abhor. (Increasing wastage of energy is a live possibility, possibly entailed by increasing energy intensiveness.) It would sound very odd to call any such trend progress.

There is much work here for the philosophy of biology. A serious philosophical discussion—so far absent from the literature—is needed about how treatments of progress ought to proceed. Biology needs to be clear about what sort of standard of progress it is employing or, if the word progress is to be avoided, about precisely what feature of organisms selection is thought to favor over the history of life, and ideally to do so in operational terms. Finally, the relationship between progressive or directional sequences and the Great Chain needs to be made explicit. Otherwise, when criteria seem contrived to make humans come out on top, critics will rightly suspect a noninstrumental component.

Trends versus tendencies

Progress has to do with what are called large-scale trends, or directional change in some feature in a group of species over some substantial chunk of evolutionary time. So the increase in brain size in the evolution of *Homo sapiens* from *Homo erectus* does not count as a large-scale trend because it occurs in a single lineage, not in a group of species. But the general increase in average body size over the entire history of life, from the ancestor of all life to the huge diversity of modern organisms, is a large-scale trend. And, obviously, progress—in whatever feature of organisms is deemed to capture progress—would count also.

Historically, much of the confusion surrounding the notion of progress has arisen from the confounding of two very distinct aspects of large-scale trends, a distinction that has been cleanly made only in recent decades. The critical distinction is between trends and tendencies. First, trends: a trend is directional change in some group statistic, usually the mean, maximum, or minimum. For progress, a trend in the mean would be an increase in the mean degree of progressiveness, the average over all the species in existence at a given time. (In this section, we leave the precise sense of progress unspecified, using the term as if it were well understood, as well it might be some day.) Figure 5.1A shows a hypothetical large-scale trend. Life begins with a single species, a single lineage, at some low level of progressiveness (the first vertical line at the bottom left). There is only the one species in existence at this time so the mean across all species is the same as the value for that one species: low. As time passes, new species arise (horizontal lines), some species become extinct (the termination of vertical lines) but, on the whole, diversity, the number of species in existence, rises. Further, in this scenario, every origin of a new species is an increase, a jog to the right on the graph. Change is rare and concentrated at speciation events, i.e. species remain static at a constant level of progressiveness (all those vertical lines), but when

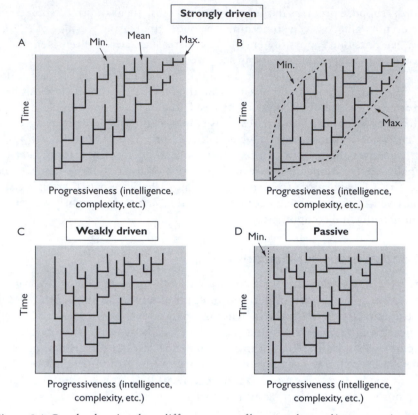

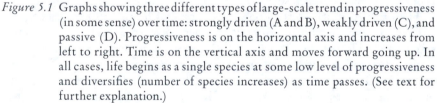

Figure 5.1 Graphs showing three different types of large-scale trend in progressiveness (in some sense) over time: strongly driven (A and B), weakly driven (C), and passive (D). Progressiveness is on the horizontal axis and increases from left to right. Time is on the vertical axis and moves forward going up. In all cases, life begins as a single species at some low level of progressiveness and diversifies (number of species increases) as time passes. (See text for further explanation.)

change occurs, it is always progressive (always to the right). It should be obvious that the average degree of progressiveness among all species present at a given time rises. At the start, the mean is low, lying far to the left. In the present, the top, the mean across all species in existence is quite high, lying to the right of the starting point (roughly the middle of the range of line segments ending at the top, as shown). In other words, there has been a trend in the mean.

Notice that there has also been a trend in the maximum. Figure 5.1B is the same as Figure 5.1A but annotated to show the trend in the maximum, the dashed line on the right. The maximum is the degree of progressiveness of the most progressive species in existence at a given time, in other words, a rise in the highest level of advancement achieved by life as a whole. This trend is of special interest in the discussion of progress, because it has been taken to represent the clearest evidence for progress, the rise from ancient bacterium 3.5 billion years ago to modern human, or, in Ruse's apt phrase, from "monad to man." The assumption, of course, is that humans are the most advanced, that we are the top right-most species on the graph. (We are leaving aside the problems with that assumption already discussed.)

A third group statistic is the minimum, the degree of advancement of the least-advanced species in existence at a given time. The left-hand dotted line in Figure 5.1B shows a trend in the minimum. Interestingly, current thinking is that in the actual history of life, the minimum has not risen like this. If the ancient bacteria were truly cyanobacteria, or even moderately close relatives of them, and if we accept the common intuition that they are the *least*-progressive organisms (contrary to what their seemingly low extinction probability might lead one to believe), then the minimum has remained roughly constant. In other words, the least progressive organism on the planet is now and has always been a cyanobacterium of some kind, and progress is not the rule. Evolution may have taken us from "monad to man," but it has also gone—at the other end of the advancement spectrum—from "monad to monad." And, if so, then the history of life does *not* look like Figure 5.1A and B. We will come back to this issue shortly.

That's trends. What about tendencies? A tendency is a bias in the direction of change among lineages, regardless of whether or not any trend results in the mean, maximum, or minimum for the group. If increases and decreases occur equally often, there is no bias, and therefore no tendency. If increases occur more often, there is a bias toward increase, and therefore an increasing tendency. Consider Figure 5.1A. There is—in addition to a trend in the mean, maximum, and minimum—a strong directional tendency, reflected in the fact that all changes are jogs to the right. They are all increases. Historically, trends and tendencies have been assumed to go hand in hand. Any trend must be the result of a directional tendency. But, in the modern discourse, it is clear that this is not so. To see this, consider an alternative scenario. Figure 5.1C is like Figure 5.1A in some ways. The mean and maximum both show a trend. However, now there are decreases in advancement as well as increases. This is realistic in the sense that we have reason to think such decreases do occur in evolution. Judged impressionistically, at least, many parasites seem less advanced than the free-living organisms they evolved from. In the Figure 5.1C scenario, such decreases occur, and often enough that even the least-advanced species are replaced from above, so to speak, whenever they become extinct. And therefore the minimum remains roughly constant. In the language of tendencies, the directional tendency is strong in Figure 5.1A but weak in Figure 5.1C. In the technical language that has grown up around trends, the trend in the mean in Figure 5.1A is said to be "strongly driven," that is to occur on account of a strong directional tendency, whereas the trend in Figure 5.1C is "weakly driven."

A third scenario is shown in Figure 5.1D. In this case, increases and decreases occur equally often, meaning that there is *no tendency to increase at all*. Notice, however, that there is a boundary, a lower limit on degree of advancement, or a kind of "left wall" that blocks the spread of the group on the left. This boundary can be thought of as the lowest level of progressiveness consistent with being alive. Suppose that the first organisms in existence fell somewhere near this lower limit. Given such a starting point, change initially could only have been in the direction of increase. In John Maynard Smith's words, there was simply "nowhere to go but up" (Maynard Smith 1970). But again, decreases are common, indeed in Figure 5.1D, they are just as common as increases (at least away from the left wall), so that the region near the wall remains populated with species. Thus, the minimum stays the same, as in the weakly driven scenario, while the mean and maximum increase. Such trends are said to be "passive," because they are the result of the passive spread, or diffusion, of species away from a lower boundary. (The word "diffusion" might suggest that passive trends depend on chance, and therefore that progress by this route is an improbable accident. But a moment's reflection dispels this notion. In a passive trend, the existence of a boundary makes the increase in the mean a completely predictable necessity. There is nowhere for the mean to go but up.)

It might seem odd that no mention has yet been made of natural selection or of "causes." The reason is that, in the modern discourse, cause is yet another distinct issue. "Trend" describes a pattern, directional change, in a group statistic. "Tendencies" describes the pattern at a lower level, among the species that make up the group. And "cause" is the explanation for the tendency. So, for example, for a strongly driven trend, one possible "cause" for a pervasive increasing tendency would be natural selection. Whenever change occurs, it is always an increase, because of the survival and reproduction advantages of progressiveness. But notice that selection is not the only possibility. A strong upward tendency could also arise from constraints of various kinds. For example, there could be some property of random variation that biases evolutionary change toward more advanced organisms. The same goes for a passive trend. A lower boundary could be caused by a constraint. Perhaps variants less advanced than a cyanobacterium do not arise for reasons having to do with limitations inherent in biochemistry or physics. But a boundary can also be caused by selection. Perhaps less-complex variants do arise but do not survive and reproduce as well.

In sum, for large-scale trends and progress, there are really three distinct issues:

1   *The existence of a trend*   Does the mean, minimum, maximum, or some other trend statistic increase over the history of life?
2   *Underlying tendencies*   If there is a trend, is there any tendency to increase, any bias in the direction of change among lineages?

3 *The cause* If there is a tendency, what is the cause (selection or constraint)? Or if there is no tendency (passive), what is the cause of the lower limit?

This way of thinking about trends has several consequences for the discussion of progress, consequences that have been understood and taken to heart by biologists only in the past couple of decades. The first is the emergence of a possibility that historically would not have been considered plausible, namely that progress—a trend in, say, the mean—is possible without there being any underlying tendency toward progress. In other words, progress could be passive. More generally, the existence of a trend in the mean—if one could be demonstrated—tells us nothing about underlying tendencies. Strongly driven, weakly driven, and passive all predict a trend in the mean. Thus, even if biologists could demonstrate an increase in the mean level of some variable over the history of life, that still would not demonstrate any increasing tendency. The same goes for the maximum. It too increases in all three scenarios. And therefore even if the trajectory from cyanobacterium to human is in fact a progressive one, in some sense, it does not demonstrate any tendency to increase in evolution. Monad to man tells us nothing about underlying tendencies, much less about causes!

What about the persistence of cyanobacteria, the apparent constancy of the minimum over the history of life? That *does* seem to tell us something about underlying tendencies, essentially ruling out a strongly driven scenario. It tells us that, if there has been a trend in the mean, it has not been driven by a strong increasing tendency. Of course, it does not help to distinguish between a weak driven trend and a passive one.

Finally, there is also much work to do on the theoretical end. Driven and passive are just paradigmatic cases (Wagner 1996). Many other sorts of mechanisms can produce trends. For example, a trend in the mean will result if more advanced species speciate more often, or if less advanced species have higher extinction probabilities. And even in the passive case, left walls may be only part of the story. The suggestion has been made that change is blocked frequently by occasional right walls along the progressiveness scale, by upper boundaries that are penetrable but only rarely or with difficulty. Such boundaries could arise from selection, perhaps from the risks or disadvantages that might accompany adaptive breakthroughs in their initial stages. Multicellularity might be advantageous in any number of ways but the first multicelled organism might not have been especially well adapted. Alternatively, right walls could arise from constraints. Whatever the cause, the failure of single-celled organisms to generate complex multicellularity—organisms with many cell types—over the first billion and a half years of their existence (from about 2 billion years ago to 600 million years ago) suggests an upper limit of some kind. Given right walls, the history of progress might have been quite episodic, characterized by long periods without progress and rare revolutions in which these walls were breached.

Complexity and intelligent design

In a discussion of complexity these days, some mention of the "intelligent design" controversy is obligatory. The phrase refers to an argument advanced in recent years by Michael Behe (1996), a biochemist who argues that the complexity of certain structures in organisms cannot be accounted for by natural selection. The argument targets complexity at the molecular level, at which the parts of a structure are molecular subunits and complexity is the number of different subunits in the structure. Certain organismal adaptations consist of quite a number of different subunits, i.e. they are complex, and the question is how Darwinism can account for this in cases where it is difficult to see how intermediates of lesser complexity could have been functional. In what has become a standard example in intelligent design arguments, the mechanism that powers the bacterial flagellum is said to consist of a large number of molecular parts, virtually all of them essential to the proper functioning of the device. If so, then seemingly any intermediates between some simpler ancestral molecular device and the modern complex flagellar motor would not have been functional, and therefore natural selection alone could not have been responsible for its evolution. In Behe's terms, the flagellar motor is "irreducibly complex." And therefore to bridge the gap between simplicity and complex functionality, an intervening intelligent designer is needed. (Essentially the same problem was raised by Darwin in the *Origin*. Darwin was concerned with the complexity of the vertebrate eye, which he tried to show could be linked to a presumably much simpler primitive eye by successive intermediates, all of them functional.)

The intelligent design argument has attracted many with a religious agenda—in particular a fundamentalist Christian agenda—who believe that the intelligent intervener must have been the Christian god. Often this agenda is explicitly denied for political reasons. By remaining officially agnostic about the nature of the designer, the intelligent design argument can be offered as a scientific claim, rather than a religious one, which could make it a viable alternative to Darwinism in American public school classrooms, i.e. an alternative that is acceptable to the courts. (However at the time of writing, intelligent design has failed its first serious legal challenge, in the Federal District Court in Pennsylvania, where the judge ruled that the idea was advanced with religious rather than scientific intent.)

But motivations aside, notice that nothing in the basic intelligent design argument *requires* a divine intervener, nor necessarily raises questions about the boundaries of science and religion. After all, the intelligent meddlers could be smart aliens, completely naturalistic creatures, perhaps with adaptations of a very different sort, that do not raise the same problem of functional intermediates. To put it another way, the intelligent design argument can be stated in such a way that it raises a well-posed scientific question: how to give a naturalistic account of the evolution of complex functional devices in cases where there are no obvious adaptive intermediates.

Still, caveats are required in light of the arguments advanced in this chapter. Just as progress has tag-along associations with noninstrumental values, so complexity has tag-along associations with progress. Thus while the public intelligent-design debate seems to be about complexity, one suspects it is also implicitly about the larger issues of progress and human superiority. Explaining the origin of complexity in evolution is especially important if one thinks that complexity underlies progress and that progress underlies human worth, in particular our intrinsic value relative to other species, our putative special standing in the eyes of God. What this chapter should have made clear, however, is that no connection has yet been established between progress and complexity (in any well-defined sense, such as number of part types), that complexity is just one candidate among many for what progress *might* consist in. (Indeed, as pointed out earlier, complexity might instead turn out to be a bad thing, in adaptive terms, complex devices being more prone to breakdown.) Nor is there any connection between progress, in any scientific sense, and intrinsic values, at least no connection that biology can comment on, intrinsic values being outside the domain of science. Thus, from a scientific standpoint, not progress, nor intrinsic values, nor the origin of human worth is at stake in the intelligent design argument. The intelligent design argument is about the evolution of complexity and, in particular, complexity in the sense of part types and nothing more.

So what might a scientific answer to the purely scientific problem posed by the intelligent design argument look like? Taking into account the larger view of evolutionary explanation offered in Chapter 3, which excludes certain question-begging explanations of adaptation, it should be clear that the problem of nonadaptive intermediates has more than one possible solution. The standard rejoinder—that Darwin himself used for the eye—is that intermediates could well have been adaptive. In the case of the flagellar motor, the biologist Kenneth Miller has pointed to the similarity between it and a much simpler device that bacteria use to inject toxin into cells that they are attacking, the so-called type III secretory apparatus. It turns out that the molecular parts of the apparatus are a subset of the parts of the flagellar motor, suggesting an evolutionary link between the two. This raises the possibility that the secretory apparatus, or some device very much like it, could have been an adaptive intermediate, a stepping stone from simplicity to complexity. If so, the flagellar motor is not irreducibly complex at all.

This tactic is fine, as far as it goes, but there is a larger array of evolutionary explanations available for complexity. Consider chance. Perhaps simple devices tend to neutrally accumulate new part types, simply by the introduction of neutral variation in existing part types. The suggestion is that complexity might increase spontaneously without affecting function. Intermediates, with intermediate complexity, need not be especially adaptive. They just need to not be maladaptive. Ultimately selection must be involved in sculpting neutrally complex structures into functional devices, assuming that for explaining function selection really is the only game in town. The point is that the gap from one level of complexity to another might be crossed on adaptively neutral stepping stones, by the chance accumulation of parts (later modified to become functionally interdependent).

Then too consider the possible role of self-organization, a notion we encountered in the discussion in Chapter 4 of Kauffman's NK networks. Contrary to intuition, it may be that complex systems do not need to be built up, step by step, with each step either adaptive, as the standard argument demands, or even neutral, as in the alternative scenario just offered. Maybe they need not be "built up" at all. Perhaps complexity arises spontaneously, suddenly, for free, in certain kinds of systems. The biologist Brian Goodwin (1996) has argued that organisms are not machines, in the sense that they are not like cars and computers, composed of largely inert parts. Rather they are what he calls "excitable media," in which components and their interactions are highly dynamic, leading spontaneously to complex novelty. One classic nonbiological example of an excitable medium is the so-called Belousov–Zhabotinsky cocktail, a mix of simple chemical components in which complex structures—spots, rings, and spiral waves—emerge spontaneously. If organisms too are excitable media, complex structures might emerge spontaneously from simplicity, following completely deterministic but presently poorly understood chemical and physical laws. Again, selection would be needed to render complexity functional, but self-organization obviates the problem of intermediates. There simply aren't any.

Summary

Consider this seemingly obvious, even banal-sounding, claim about the history of life: "Natural selection predicts a tendency toward greater fitness and therefore toward progress, evident in the rise in complexity from ancient bacterium to human." What this chapter should have made clear is that the truth of this statement is not obvious at all, indeed, it could well contain one or more non sequiturs. First, we need to make sure that our understanding of progress is purely instrumental, that it invokes not the subtlest hint of intrinsic value. If humans do turn out to be more fit than ancient bacteria, there can be no implication that our greater fitness makes us intrinsically better in any sense. Science simply has nothing to say about intrinsic values. Second, fitness in the standard senses is an environment-relative concept, so unless environments are assumed to remain stable (on some timescale), progress requires some notion of fitness that spans a range of environments. The standard environment-specific notion will not do. Third, it is not clear that selection predicts progress. In particular, it can predict increase only if general adaptations are able to accumulate. And it may be that selection on short timescales erases them.

Fourth, even if selection does predict an increasing *tendency* in complexity, as the statement claims, the rise in the maximum—from ancient bacterium to human—would not be evidence for it, because the maximum can rise without there being any upward tendency at all. For example, maxima rise in passive trends, in which there is no increasing tendency. Fifth, complexity is not the same as progress. It is merely one candidate among many for what progress in some instrumental sense *might* consist in. There are others, such as increasing energy available for expansion and increasing energy intensiveness. Sixth, there is more than one sense of complexity, and we need to specify which we are talking about. And seventh, even if progress is complexity in some sense, the data on complexity are for the most part pretty sparse. For most senses of complexity, we do not know that it actually does increase in a bacterium-to-human sequence.

Few would argue with the notion that if progress is to be a useful concept in biology, it must have a purely instrumental interpretation. However, while some promising proposals have been made, there is no general agreement on what progress in an instrumental sense actually is in evolution, on what it is that is increasing, much less on how to measure it. Given this situation, it is hardly surprising that there are no clear data demonstrating a trend in the mean or maximum. Further, in the absence of measures, we have to admit the possibility that the impression of our own superiority is largely a product of our own vanity. Finally, even if trends in the mean and maximum were granted, little is known about the existence of an underlying tendency, and even less about causes, about the roles of natural selection, constraint, and chance. What the modern discussion of progress reveals is how little biology knows about progress at this point and how much work—empirical, theoretical, and philosophical—there is to be done.

Suggestions for further reading

The distinction between instrumental and noninstrumental or intrinsic value goes back to Plato and Aristotle at the beginning of Western philosophy. A contemporary introduction to the distinction's role in ethics is Michael Zimmerman's *The Nature of Intrinsic Value*. Nicholas Agar's *Life's Intrinsic Value: Science, Ethics, and Nature* develops the distinction and argues for a highly unorthodox view that all forms of life have intrinsic value. It should be borne in mind that Agar's claim is not a scientific one but an ethical or normative judgment. We consider this idea again briefly in Chapter 7.

For a modern and skeptical discussion of progress and the predictions of theory, see Stephen J. Gould's *Full House: The Spread of Excellence from Plato to Darwin* and his earlier paper in a 1988 volume, edited by M. Nitecki, entitled *Evolutionary Progress*. Other papers in this volume are also quite useful, encompassing philosophical, theoretical, and empirical aspects of the problem. More technical discussion of the theoretical problems can be found in Dan Fisher's paper, "Progress in organismal design" in *Patterns and Processes in the History of Life*. See also a chapter on progress in G.G. Simpson's *The Meaning of Evolution*. Michael Ruse's *Monad to Man: The Concept of Progress in Evolutionary Biology* is a comprehensive historical treatment of the idea of progress. Leigh Van Valen's Red Queen's hypothesis, along with supporting data, were published in 1973 in the journal *Evolutionary Theory*.

Discussions of the various proposals for how progress can be "cashed out," for what feature(s) of organisms reveal progress, can be found in Simpson's chapter, and also Julian Huxley's *Evolution: The Modern Synthesis* (dominance), Francisco Ayala's paper in the Nitecki volume (ability to perceive the environment), John Maynard Smith and Eörs Szathmáry's *The Major Transitions in Evolution*, Van Valen's "Three paradigms of evolution" in *Evolutionary Theory* (energy available for expansion), and Geerat Vermeij's *Evolution and Escalation* (energy intensiveness). For broader reviews of the various proposals, see a paper by one of us (McShea) in the *Annual Review of Ecology and Systematics* and also a paper by Rosslenbroich in *Biology and Philosophy*. And for reviews of the problem of operationalizing complexity and of documenting a trend, see papers by McShea in *Biology and Philosophy* and *Evolution*. Trends and progress are discussed further in Gould's *Full House*. For a contrary view see A. Knoll and R. Bambach's paper in *Paleobiology*.

For the "intelligent design" argument, see Michael Behe's *Darwin's Black Box: The Biochemical Challenge to Evolution*. For alternative views of how complexity might arise, see McShea's "The evolution of complexity without natural selection, a possible large-scale trend of the fourth kind" and Brian Goodwin's discussion of excitable media and self-organization in *How the Leopard Changed its Spots*.

6 Genes, groups, teleosemantics, and the major transitions

Overview

Besides the global question of whether biology is reducible to physical science, there is a group of much more specific issues about evolutionary biology that divides biologists and philosophers of biology into reductionists and antireductionists, along with some eliminativists as well. These are specific issues of whether natural selection operates at many levels and on many different kinds of biological systems and, if so, whether its operation at "higher" levels is reducible to, fully explained by, its operation at lower levels or even perhaps whether natural selection operates at just one unique and basic level of biological organization. This latter view would in effect be an eliminativist doctrine, denying the need to invoke natural selection anywhere else in nature. Deciding on the global question of how biology is related to physical science in general will not—as a matter of logic—decide these questions, and vice versa. After all, global reductionists about biology do not have to claim that the natural selection of larger biological entities proceeds by natural selection of their lower-level components. And yet, it turns out that much of the global dispute about reduction in biology is motivated by the difficulties of deciding the apparently narrower and more biologically interesting question of whether the selection of larger biological systems is "nothing but" the selection of some or all of their lower-level components.

Are there many levels of selection? If so, can the higher levels be reduced to the lower levels? One response to this question, advanced by Richard Dawkins in a series of works since *The Selfish Gene* was published in 1976, is that there is only one level of selection, and it is the level of the gene. Appeal to any higher levels represents a misunderstanding of how natural selection works and is unnecessary, Dawkins argues. Others have argued that there may be multiple levels of selection but that they are reducible to selection at the level of the gene, or at least selection at any of these other levels can be adequately represented at the level of the gene. Still others have held the antireductionist view that there are higher levels of selection beyond the gene, and indeed beyond the individual organism. They hold that selection operates at the level of the group, population, species, and even higher levels, and it does so independently of how selection operates at some or all of the lower levels, all the way down to the gene. Even more radical opponents of

Dawkins's claim that all selection takes place at the level of the gene argue that his "genocentric" approach to evolutionary theory must be rejected because the gene has no special role in evolution at all. And some of these opponents of "genocentrism" think the view not only mistaken but morally and politically dangerous!

"Genocentrism" also names a doctrine embraced especially among molecular biologists, many of whom hold that what gives the genes their privileged role in heredity and development is the fact that they carry information, not just figuratively but literally, in a way that nothing else in the biological realm does. There are other biologists and philosophers who deny this thesis. One thing both proponents and opponents of genocentrism require in order to settle their dispute is an account of the nature of information they can agree on. Here the philosophy of biology finds a common problem with the philosophy of mind or philosophy of psychology. For these philosophers too are searching for an account of information to help cognitive science explain how information can be stored in the brain. A number of influential figures in the philosophy of psychology have sought such an account by exploiting the theory of natural selection. If they succeed, they may also provide an account of information that genocentrists could exploit, or that would at least enable them and those who deny a special informational role to the genes to agree on a concept of information relevant to their debate. Later in this chapter we will show the connection between these two issues and sketch the philosophers' account of information Darwinism has inspired.

In this chapter it becomes even clearer that many of the questions about which philosophers have found themselves arguing among themselves truly appear to be matters of substantive (though quite theoretical) biology. Moreover, a great deal of the thinking devoted by biologists and philosophers to the problems reported in the first four chapters of this book come into play in these controversies about levels and genes. The one thing philosophers can expect to be called upon to contribute to them is a clear analysis of the meaning of these controversial concepts.

Levels and units of selection

Recall the economical and general characterization of the conditions sufficient for evolution by natural selection stated in Chapter 1:

1   reproduction, with some inheritance of traits;
2   variation arising in inherited traits;
3   differences in fitness among variants.

And recall that any number of different kinds of things could satisfy these three conditions. Darwin's point in the *Origin* was that organisms do, but now we know that genes, for example, do also. They reproduce (meaning that they copy themselves), variation arises (due to mutation, especially), some of that variation is heritable, and that variation can give rise to fitness differences. The question therefore arises whether there are other things that also satisfy the three conditions and therefore can evolve by natural selection.

Darwin did not know about genes in the sense we know about them today, but he suspected that natural selection had to operate above the level of the individual organism, at the level of the group. For, otherwise, he saw, it would be difficult to explain the persistence over evolutionary time of self-sacrificing behaviors in human beings and other species. A willingness to sacrifice one's life in combat before reproduction, a common enough trait in young males, should have been eliminated from the human population long before the establishment of armies. Those individuals without a heritable predisposition toward self-sacrifice should have been favored by selection over those with such a disposition. Further, and by the same reasoning, social norms favoring the sharing of resources and cooperation should have been filtered out by natural selection owing to the reduced fitness of individuals honoring these norms. As this evidently did not happen, Darwin speculated that this sort of unselfish behavior persists owing to its adaptive advantage to the groups that contain self-sacrificing individuals. He wrote: "A tribe including many members who . . . were always ready to give aid to each other and sacrifice themselves for the common good, would be victorious over most other tribes; and this would be natural selection" (*Descent of Man*: 166). So in any given environment in which groups compete, the groups with the trait of being composed of cooperating members will be fitter than those lacking the trait or having it in lesser degree. Such cooperative groups, or groups with altruistic members, will persist longer and presumably give rise to more new groups (by splitting or spawning new colonies) than those characterized by less cooperation. Indeed groups of selfish individuals should be destined for extinction.

This line of thought has been described as showing that there is a level of selection above the individual organism on which selection operates. Here is the structure of the argument: it begins with indisputable data, such as the observation that people cooperate. It then appeals to higher-level entities with properties or traits that lower-level entities cannot have (in this case, human groups with the trait of being composed of both cooperative and selfish individuals). And it then offers an explanation that commits us to the existence of these higher-level entities (in this case, the selective advantage to groups containing self-sacrificing individuals). Finally, it suggests that if we cannot reductively explain the group's traits in terms of the traits of the individuals that compose it, then we have to accept groups as distinct and irreducible entities, undergoing selection at higher levels.

Notice that this argument works for other species and for other traits as well. Groups of vampire bats cooperate, sharing food nightly among those bats who happened to be successful and those that were unsuccessful in their forays. A vervet monkey will signal the presence of predators to other monkeys even when this attracts the predator's attention to her, increasing the likelihood that she will be the target of predation. The eusocial insects—including all ant species, some bees and wasps, and all termites—live in colonies with substantial division of labor, such as that among queen, soldiers, and sterile workers. The production of sterile offspring should be a selective disadvantage to a laying queen, because sterile offspring produce no grand-offspring. However, sterile workers could be advantageous at the group level. Colonies with sterile workers could be more successful, in the sense that they produce more daughter colonies, than those without. Still another apparent example of group selection, offered by Richard Lewontin (1970), is the evolution of virulence. A Myxoma virus was introduced in Australia to control a population explosion of rabbits. Apparently, over time, selection seems to have favored a reduction in the virulence of the virus. At the level of the individual virus particle, or virion, selection should have favored increased virulence. Presumably a more virulent virion will out-compete other virions in the same rabbit for the resources available from the rabbit. Of course, such virulence would also kill the rabbit faster, decreasing the likelihood that the offspring of such a virion will be transmitted to another rabbit. Thus, at the group level—that is to say the group of virions within any given rabbit—selection should have favored groups of virions that showed more restraint, that is those that are less virulent. Groups that killed their rabbit less quickly, or not at all, will be able to infect more rabbits and therefore would have greater reproductive success than groups that were quickly lethal.

However, these and other examples of group selection were all subject to an apparently devastating counter-argument. In each case, the group is composed of individuals whose behavior benefited the group, or all the other individual members of the group, at the cost of lowering their individual fit-nesses. Human warriors sacrifice their lives for others in their tribes, vervet monkeys draw predators' attention to themselves while warning others, and restrained virions leave more of their hosts' nutrients to more virulent viri-ons. Yet every one of these acts of self-sacrifice is an invitation to a mutant "free rider," or an immigrant one, who accepts the benefit provided by the rest of the group without paying any of the costs. Such free riders will be fitter, and if their disposition to free ride is heritable, then their descendants will swamp those of the group-benefiting individuals. Soon the entire group should be composed of selfish pacifists, silent monkeys, highly virulent viri-ons, or females laying fertile workers.

The conclusion of this argument is that biologists cannot explain the per-sistence of individual traits of altruism, cooperation, or other fitness-reducing dispositions by appeal to their aggregated effects on the fitness of the groups such individuals compose. In other words, natural selection cannot operate on units larger than reproducing individual organisms. If a group has a trait that no individual member of it can have, such as the trait of being composed of mostly altruists, or mostly less-virulent virions, then it is a trait the group will not have for long, a trait without evolutionary significance, and a trait Darwinism need not take seriously.

In the levels of selection debate, this argument against higher levels of selection actually went beyond the denial that natural selection requires us to postulate groups with traits irreducible to those of their individual members. The argument concluded that, from the Darwinian point of view, we really do not even need to take individual organisms seriously. For the only *real* level at which selection operates is the level of the gene. The gene is the only real subject of selection.

The argument for this view can be conveniently formulated using the distinction due to Dawkins (1982), and independently to the philosopher David Hull (1988), between replicators and interactors, introduced in Chapter 2. Recall that a replicator is a thing whose structure is copied in the next generation. Thus DNA sequences are paradigmatic replicators. An interactor, or in Dawkins's term, a vehicle, is a thing that interacts with the environment, well or poorly, for better or worse. A replicator may well be its own interactor, or the interactor may be the vehicle that "carries around" the replicator (hence Dawkins's term, vehicle). Evolution by natural selection can be economically expressed as the differential perpetuation of replicators owing to fitness differences among interactors. The claim Dawkins made in *The Selfish Gene* is in effect that so far as Darwinian evolution is considered, the only real replicators and interactors are the genes.

A great deal of the attractiveness of Dawkins's view is due to the fact that genes are far more faithfully copied across generations than phenotypes, or the traits of groups and individuals for which genes presumably code. Further, the genes seem to many to be the ultimate determinants of organismal form and function, and of group capacities. The genes are the cause of development, for both individuals and groups. And together these seem to some like a solid basis for holding that they are the ultimate beneficiaries and victims of natural selection, and therefore that they are the entities whose traits are ultimately selected for and against. In other words, the genes seem like real targets of selection, real interactors or vehicles. For these reasons, Dawkins argues that evolutionary theory should not take organismal interactors seriously. Compared with genes, which are passed more or less intact from generation to generation, organisms are ephemeral. They are born and they die. They come and go. But genes are forever, or at least their DNA sequences are almost perfectly copied over and over again, and they persist for very long periods. So we can think of organisms as mere extensions of the genes, as what he called "extended phenotypes." Dawkins's thesis is a species of qualified eliminativism. It is not that organelles, cells, tissues, organs, organisms, and groups do not exist. Rather, it is that they have no ultimate explanatory role in evolutionary biology. At most referring to them enables us to abbreviate our descriptions of evolutionary processes, which in fact all transpire only on the level of genes. All of the higher level entities, from cell to organisms to groups, along with their productions—bee hives, beaver dams, and spider webs—are built by the genes to ensure their own survival. When it looks like selection is operating at a higher level, selecting individual giraffes for neck length, it is really selecting genes the protein products of which contribute to neck length. In Dawkins's view, so far as evolution is concerned, there really are no interactors above and beyond the genetic replicators.

On this view, genes find themselves packaged together in "teams" on chromosomes, producing gene products that together make phenotypes, which in turn interact with the environment more or less directly. Sexual recombination of course breaks up these "teams" in every generation, so that genes combine with new genes to make new phenotypes. So the environment selects those genes that, on average, across all the teams of which their copies are members, build the most successful vehicles.

Dawkins's proposal was an attractive one to evolutionary biologists and population geneticists who were already used to describing evolution as "change in gene frequencies." But it outraged some biologists, philosophers, and social scientists. One objection was that it seemed to encourage "genetic determinism," to them a morally obnoxious view. Genetic determinism is roughly the thesis that socially significant traits, such as intelligence, a disposition to violence, alcoholism or schizophrenia, risk taking, and gender roles are somehow fixed by the genes, and cannot be modified much by changes in the social environment. We will return to this issue later in this chapter and again in the next.

One widely known argument against Dawkins's thesis that the gene is the sole level of selection, due originally to Sober and Lewontin (1982), is based on the well-known phenomenon of heterozygote superiority. An example is a "balanced polymorphism" in the hemoglobin gene, in which selective forces maintain two alleles of the gene, normal and sickle cell, in malarial environments such as West Africa. The sickle-cell allele has a point mutation that leads to a substitution of the amino acid valine for glutamic acid at position six in the hemoglobin molecule, and as a consequence to a tendency for a hemoglobin molecule to stick to other hemoglobin molecules. This in turn deforms the red blood cell containing the molecules into a sickle shape, which reduces oxygen levels in the blood and interferes with oxygen transport in the blood vessels. Now the blood cells of individuals with two normal alleles (i.e. normal homozygotes) are easy for the malaria parasite to invade, and therefore such individuals suffer reduced fitness in malarial regions. And those with two sickle-cell alleles (sickle-cell homozygotes) suffer reduced fitness from anemia. But in malaria-ridden environments, individuals with one of each (heterozygotes) are fitter than either of the homozygotes, because the resulting anemia is compensated by the resulting malaria resistance. And as a result, both the sickle-cell gene and the normal gene persist in the population in malarial regions in a balanced polymorphism. The fact that neither of these alleles is being eliminated from the population is, on this argument, due to the fact that the malarial environment is selecting for the *heterozygotic package*, not for either of the genes themselves. The protection against both malaria and anemia is a property of the package, a property of the combination, in other words a property not of a gene but of the *genotype*. So the persistence of the sickle-cell allele is the effect of selection at a higher level, if not the level of the whole organism then at least a higher level than the gene. If this "genotype" argument against Dawkins's genic selection thesis can be generalized, it would open the door to selection acting at any higher level, to the level of the group and higher, as we shall see.

Crucial to this argument is the assumption that the relevant selective environment in which the heterozygote genotype is advantageous is "the malarial environment." And the problem facing this argument is one we encountered in our discussion of drift in Chapter 3: What is *the* correct, appropriate, relevant, selective environment against which to compare traits for fitness? Exploiting a strategy proposed originally by C. Kenneth Waters, Sterelny and Kitcher (1988) have noted that a defender of genic selection might effectively argue that the relevant environment is the one in which the relevant gene finds itself, not the one in which the relevant genotype or individual organism finds itself. Thus, a single allele token for the sickle-cell trait will be fitter than an allele token for the normal hemoglobin if its chromosomal and cellular environment includes the normal allele and the malarial parasite in the vicinity. As the frequency of the sickle-cell allele increases in the population due to higher fitness, the frequency with which these copies find themselves combined with the normal allele declines. That is to say the sickle-cell allele's environment changes to one in which it is more frequently paired with other copies of the sickle-cell allele. And in this environment, of course, each such allele token's fitness will decline, as will the average across all sickle-cell alleles. So, on the view that the relevant environment includes the chromosomes on which paired allele tokens are found, along with the presence of the malarial parasite in the vicinity, selection does operate at the gene level, just as Dawkins supposes. Sober and Lewontin (1982) have simply not noticed that genotypic selection is really just a case of what is called frequency-dependent genic selection.

Which view of the matter is correct? Dawkins's "genocentric view" claims that the relevant environment is that faced by the individual gene token, and the relevant adaptive trait is that of producing a protein that prevents the malarial parasite from surviving in the red blood corpuscle. Sober and Lewontin's alternative holds that the relevant environment is that faced by the genotype token (in effect, the individual organism), and the relevant adaptive trait is preventing fatal malarial infection in the interactor or vehicle, the organism bearing the genotype. Which is the *real* selective environment, and which is the *real* adaptive trait? At least some parties to the dispute argue that there is no fact of the matter here, that both alternatives are equally good descriptions of the evolutionary process, and that we do not have to take sides. Sterelny and Kitcher have advanced this "pluralistic" view most forcefully, although in a way that appears to vindicate Dawkins:

Pluralistic genic selectionists recommend that practicing biologists take advantage of the full range of strategies for representing the workings of selection. The chief merit of Dawkinspeak [treating the gene as the level of selection] is its generality. Whereas the individualist perspective may sometimes break down, the gene's-eye view is apparently always available.

(Sterelny and Kitcher 1988: 360).

Notice the implications of "pluralistic" genic selectionism for even non-controversial cases of group selection, among the social insects, for example. In these cases, the persistence of groups is the result of their being composed of sterile individuals that do not maximize their own fitness but enhance that of others, the hive or colony queens, for example, and, through them, the group as a whole. These individuals and the group itself can be viewed as vehicles or interactors built up by gene tokens, each selected for in an environment consisting partly of the other gene tokens they work with, within an insect's body, and in other insect bodies. If there are no losses to viewing group selection in this way, some opponents of the gene's-eye point of view will suggest that pluralistic genic selectionism does not take group selection very seriously, even in the noncontroversial cases of ant colonies and bee hives. These groupings and their structures are just relatively long-lasting extended phenotypes of genes subjected individually to frequency-dependent selection. For this reason we have placed quotation marks around the word "pluralism" above. A stronger sort of pluralism would place the alternative views about the levels of selection on a par, and choose between them only on heuristic grounds.

Kin selection and selection within and between groups

For many, the gene's-eye view finds considerable support in the early work of W.D. Hamilton (1964), in which he first developed the notion of "kin selection." It was Hamilton who realized that in kin groups, giving resources to others could be fitness enhancing for the giver, because it enabled genes shared by recipient and giver to replicate. In particular, if the cost of providing resources to another organism is less than the benefit to the recipient multiplied by the degree of genetic relatedness, then providing such resources is a fitness-maximizing strategy. And kin groups composed of such altruistic individuals who can recognize their relatedness and act upon it will be fitter than groups of individuals who do not share resources among themselves. Hamilton's rule is expressed in the simple formula:

$C < r \times B$

which holds where kin selection obtains. C is cost to the individual convey-ing the resources, B is the benefit to the recipient, and r is the coefficient of their relatedness. If relatedness, r, is high enough, then individuals can sustain substantial costs from their altruistic behavior toward kin and their altruism can still be favored by selection.

From the gene's-eye view, the rationale underlying Hamilton's rule goes like this:

> A gene is favored not only if its effect tends to promote its own reproduc-tive success or that of the individual that carries it but also the success of all copies of it, wherever they occur, even in other individuals.

Consider an individual carrying a gene for altruism, and suppose that she will direct her altruistic behavior toward a sibling, a brother. In normal diploid species, the degree of relatedness between siblings is ½, meaning that if an individual has some gene, there is a 50 percent chance that her brother has it too. In the calculus Hamilton developed, the gene for altruism will be favored if the benefit to the brother is more than twice the cost to the altruist herself. Cousins are related by ⅛, so for the altruism gene to be favored, the benefit to a cousin would have to be more than eight times the cost to the altruist. Thus, in any group of kin, we might expect considerable altruistic behavior among its members. And this, according to the kin selection view, goes a long way toward explaining the high levels of altruism we see in kin groups, from social amoebae to social insects to social primates like us.

In the gene's-eye view, kin selection seems to contradict group selection. There is no differential survival and reproductive success of groups, just altruism genes "pursuing" their Darwinian self-interest. Indeed, phrased this way, the gene's-eye view seems to obviate the notion of altruism itself. An individual behaving "altruistically" toward family members is really just promoting the reproductive success of her own genes, which family members are likely to bear. In effect, she is favoring herself. And what's so altruistic about that?

But that was not the end of the matter. Based on Hamilton's insight, a more general argument was subsequently developed by George Price (1971), one that does not require that group members be related. Price's formula has been made salient among philosophers by Sober and Wilson (1998) as the framework for a general account of how group selection can persist. Below we offer an exposition of Price's equation and the implications that philosophers and biologists have accorded it in this debate so that readers can follow the issues as they are broached nowadays. (Those less inclined to think in mathematical terms may nevertheless be able to follow the discus-sion in qualitative terms.)

Price's equation expresses the change over time in group composition as a function of change in fitness due to selection acting directly on indi-viduals (within-group fitness), plus change in fitness that is due to selection acting on groups (between-group fitness). Group-directed altruism will be favored when the between-group fitness increases (due to the advantages of cooperation) are greater than the within-group fitness decreases (due to the disadvantages to individuals of cooperating). An example will make clear Price's equation and its consequences for group selection.

Suppose that in a large population some individuals carry a gene for altruism (or reduced virulence, female-biased sex ratio, etc.) and some do not. The frequency of this gene in the whole population is the number of carriers divided by the total number of individuals in the population. But if whole population is divided into groups, then this average for the whole population may be different from the group averages. Some groups will have many altruists, while others will have few. Groups starting with many more altruists than selfish members will initially be fitter (in the between-group sense) than those starting with fewer altruists, although the altruists in any group will be less fit (within-group sense) than their selfish fellow members. Also, the greater the number of altruists, the fitter any given selfish member will be, within that group, relative to selfish individuals in groups with fewer altruists, that is to say, the more the altruists there will be to take advantage of. In Price's equation, ΔP is the expected change in the proportion of an altruism allele, p, in the whole population over one generation. ΔP is equal to the within-group fitness (measured as the average fitness of an individual) plus the between-group fitness (standardized to the same units, average individual fitness):

$$\Delta P = \text{ave}_{n'}(\Delta p) + \text{cov}_n(s,p)/\text{ave}_n s$$

In this equation, the first term on the right side, $\text{ave}_{n'}(\Delta p)$, measures the average change in the frequency of the allele within groups, weighted by n', the size of the group after selection. If there are any selfish individuals in any group, then $\text{ave}_{n'}(\Delta p)$ must be negative and will tend to reduce ΔP. But this decline can be offset by the second term, $\text{cov}_n(s,p)/\text{ave}_n s$, the between-group contribution to change in the proportion of the altruism gene, p. Looking more closely at this term, the numerator $\text{cov}_n(s,p)$ is the covariance between s, the average fitness of a group's individual members, and p, the frequency of altruists (or the gene for altruism, p) in the group. If p and s change together, so that when p is high then s is also high and when p is low s is also low, then $\text{cov}_n(s,p)$ will be positive and large. In other words, $\text{cov}_n(s,p)$ measures the degree to which a group benefits by having more and more altruists among its members. Then, $\text{cov}_n(s,p)$ is divided by $\text{ave}_n s$ (the average group fitness) in order to be combinable in the same units with the first term, the within-group frequency change, $\text{ave}_{n'}(\Delta p)$. Adding the between-group and within-group components gives ΔP, the net population change in the frequency of the altruism allele. In sum, if the presence of altruists raises the average fitness of a group's members, altruists and nonaltruists alike, then $\text{cov}_n(s,p)$ will be positive, and if it raises that average a lot then the $\text{cov}_n(s,p)$ will also be large, potentially offsetting the negative first term, $ave_{n'}(\Delta p)$. And if it does offset this quantity, then the proportion of altruists in the population, ΔP, will increase, that is to say, selection will favor the evolution of altruism.

What the Price equation does is to break down the change in altruism gene frequency into two components. The first component represents the tendency of selfish individuals to out-reproduce altruistic ones within every group. If no other tendencies were present, the proportion of altruists within every group would decrease. And the average individual fitness of the group would decline from a high level at which all members secure the benefits of altruism to a lower level at which all the altruists have been lost. The second component of the equation captures the tendency for groups with a higher proportion of altruists to out-reproduce groups with a lower proportion, on account of the advantages arising from having many cooperating altruists. This will tend to increase the frequency of altruists in the population, and also raise average individual fitness. What the equation as a whole says is that if this second tendency is strong enough, if the magnitude of the second term is large enough, it will overwhelm the first, and altruism will persist in evolution.

Consider a simple example adapted from one offered by Sober and Wilson (1998). Suppose that there are two strains of parasites that reproduce in a host at differing rates, that is with different degrees of virulence (due to different rates of reproduction). One is extremely virulent, owing to a high rate of reproduction, and kills off its host rabbit quickly. Members of groups composed solely of high-virulence virions have little chance to hop to a new host. The second strain has reduced virulence, so host rabbits infected only by these virions live long enough to meet another host and transfer one or more members of the group living on the first host. In a group composed of both high- and low-virulence virions living on a single rabbit, let us say that the first strain will out-compete the second, on account of its higher reproductive rate. In that case, groups composed of exclusively low-virulence virions will eventually be invaded by high-virulence virions, which in turn will out-compete the low-virulence strain. Ultimately, all groups of virions on all rabbits will be composed of members of the high-virulence strain exclusively. Individual selection will have driven low-virulence virions to extinction. In terms of the Price equation, the system is dominated by the first term, within-group fitness effects.

But now suppose that a third strain of virus is identified, one that not only has reduced virulence like the second strain, but also secretes a birth-control chemical that reduces the virulence of other virions it encounters in the same host. In a group of virions within the same host rabbit composed of the first, high-virulence, strain and this third, virulence-reducing, strain, the high-virulence strain may still have a slight within-group advantage. Its native virulence is suppressed, but its members do not bear the cost of producing the birth-control chemical. However, from the perspective of the third strain, the cost of producing this chemical could be slight in comparison with the fitness disadvantage of not producing it. If a group of virions of this third, low-virulence, birth-controlling strain is invaded by a high-virulence strain, it will not be subverted from within at anything like the rate of subversion to which the first strain of low-virulence virions is subject. What is more, in competition between groups composed exclusively of high-virulence virions and groups composed of high-virulence virions plus the third strain, the mixed groups will have more opportunities to infect new rabbits (because their rabbit hosts live longer), thereby establishing more mixed groups than high-virulence groups will. If the rate of "colonization" of new rabbits is higher than the rate at which high-virulence virions increase their proportions of the mixed groups, these groups will persist. As Price's equation applied in this case would reveal, the result is due to the fact that between-group selection (mixed groups doing better than pure ones, i.e. $\text{cov}_n(s,p)$ is positive) swamps within-group selection (high-virulence virions doing better than low-virulence, birth-controlling virions, i.e. $\text{ave}_{n'}(\Delta p)$ is negative).

In the light of the Price equation, one can now take a fresh, group selectionist look at kin selection. The Price equation tells us that group selection is favored when bearers of the altruism gene find themselves in the same group as other bearers of the gene. The second term of the equation is most strongly positive when the frequency of the altruism gene is high within groups. In what sort of groups do we expect to find high frequencies of such a gene (or any gene)? One answer, says the group selectionist, is kin groups. The inheritance of the gene for altruism in an extended family group is one natural mechanism whereby groups with a high frequency of the gene can arise. In other words, kin selection is simply a species of group selection. The group selectionist then goes on to point out that there are other ways that altruist genes can end up in the same group, even if their bearers are unrelated, for example if altruists have ways of recognizing each other and are attracted to each other, that is if they assort together. Various routes to assortment can be imagined. And thus, the group selectionist claims, not only is kin selection just group selection but it is only one special case of group selection.

Philosophical pluralists contend that the gene's-eye view and group selection simply offer alternative descriptions of the same phenomenon. Monists like Dawkins insist that, description aside, the gene is in reality the only level at which selection acts. The Dawkinsian argument is inspired by the widely expressed slogan that evolution is change in gene frequencies, and this seems to be granted by using the Price equation, which measures group fitness in terms of the fitness of a hypothetical altruism allele. Moreover, it is obvious that in the absence of differential daughter colony production, group-level differences in traits such as virulence or sex ratio will be transitory. Eventually individually selfish strategies must invade each group and drive the group-benefiting traits to extinction. And even when colonies are propagated early and often, so that there are always some groups with group-benefiting individuals, doing better as a group than groups without such individuals, Dawkins would insist that this is no more than a manifestation of the success of the extended phenotype of a set of genes. Sober and Wilson argue that such a claim simply fails to distinguish between the outcome of natural selection and the process of natural selection. Counting genes and the changes in their frequencies over time cannot show the causal forces acting on the interactors or vehicles that carry around the replicators. It is the vehicles or interactors that "feel" the environmental forces, and whose traits are adaptations to them, which result in long-term changes in gene frequencies. The gene's-eye point of view that Dawkins advocates, on their view, commits an "averaging fallacy." By simply following the changes in the proportion of the various alleles averaged over all groups, one blinds oneself to the increase or decrease in numbers of groups and, more significantly, to the causes of these changes. Frequencies of alleles change, as do frequencies of individuals with corresponding phenotypes, but it is the changes in numbers of groups that cause these changes in frequency of the individuals and the alleles.

Dawkins (1994), however, has replied that his argument does not ignore vehicles but just denies that these groups really are the vehicles or interactors we need to count in evolutionary biology's "fundamental ontology," in the list of the kinds of things that actually exist and figure in the theories of the field. Adopting the "gene's-eye" point of view means taking into account the other genes with which any single gene is "packaged," and not just the other genes in the same cell nucleus or even in the same organism. For any individual gene, these other genes are parts of its environment, and therefore their behavior and evolution constitute the selective environment that will govern its evolution. The vehicle or interactor is nothing but a kind of convenient way of talking, a shorthand, for summing up the effects of many such environmental factors for a gene.

Macroevolution and the major trends: is group selection rare or frequent?

The debate about pluralism versus monism so far examined has focused on the dispute as it bears on genes versus genotypes (individual organisms) versus groups of individuals. But these cases do not exhaust the domain of the dispute. There are other important cases that reveal how this issue cuts across almost every area of biological science. In particular, there are data in macroevolution that seem to drive us inescapably toward monistic group selection, with no scope for equivalent redescription in terms of selection for genes or for individuals and their phenotypic traits, extended or not.

Consider a series of studies of fossil animals conducted in recent decades by the paleobiologist David Jablonski (2005). These studies concern what we have been calling group selection, but the groups of interest lie at a much higher level than organismal groups. They are groups of related species, that is groups consisting of species in the next higher-ranked taxon in the Linnean hierarchy, the genus (the plural of which is "genera"). Jablonski found that genera with the property of having large geographic ranges—meaning their species and individuals ranged over a large area—had a higher probability of surviving mass extinctions than genera with narrower ranges. His data were the geographic ranges of clams, chosen because their fossil record is especially good before and after a particular selective event, a great mass extinction 65 million years ago, the same one that destroyed the dinosaurs. That mass extinction is now widely recognized as having been caused by a meteorite impact and the ensuing planet-wide cataclysmic environmental change. In the wake of such a cataclysm, it is easy to see why genera that range widely would be more extinction resistant. The more widely a group ranges, the more likely that at least some of its members will find themselves in some protected pocket, some refugium.

Interestingly, as Jablonski discovered, species-level geographic range does not provide the same protection. Indeed extinction intensities in this mass extinction for both widely and narrowly distributed species were about the same. From one point of view this will seem odd, and perhaps even impossible. It seems sensible to assume that wide-ranging genera must be composed of wide-ranging species, and narrow-ranging genera composed of narrow-ranging species. If that were true, then the greater resistance to extinction of wide-ranging genera would have to be a direct result of the greater resistance of their component species, and the finding that these species are not more extinction resistant would make no sense. It turns out, however, that the sensible assumption is wrong. In fact, Jablonski found no correlation between the geographic range of a genus and the geographic range of the species that constitute it. Some wide-ranging genera were composed of a small number of wide-ranging species, but others were composed of a large number of narrow-ranging species, with many more having some intermediate composition. In other words, there are many different ways to be a widespread genus, and likewise there may be more than one way to be a low-range genus. And therefore we can say that species-level geographic range is just causally irrelevant to extinction resistance conferred on genera during mass extinction by their geographic ranges. Or, in selective terms, the selective forces acting on genera can "see" the genus-level property, and therefore can act causally on it. But they cannot see the species-level property.

If Jablonski's data are right, the advocate of the selfish gene, and indeed other opponents of monistic group selection, have a difficult case to deal with. Further, Jablonski's findings may be the tip of a macroevolutionary iceberg. In recent years, another troublesome set of cases for the gene's-eye view has been recognized, troublesome because the "groups" look a lot more like honest-to-goodness individuals than social insect colonies and more troublesome because they seem to suggest that group selection has not only occurred but has been quite common in the history of life. These cases are the so-called major transitions in evolution, in particular their treatment by John Maynard Smith and Eörs Szathmáry (1995), discussed in Chapter 5. Recalling that discussion, a common theme among most (but not all) of these transitions is hierarchy, or nestedness: the joining of lower-level units to form higher-level ones, as in the transition from solitary eukaryotic cell (or protist) to multicellular individual. Thus the emergence of hierarchy in evolution is, in essence, a group selection problem. Consider the protist–multicell transition. If the solitary protistan cell is an individual, then the multicellular organism is a kind of group—a group of altruistic or cooperating cells. Therefore the emergence and persistence of multicellular organisms, from sponges to insects to humans is a levels-of-selection puzzle, just like the emergence and persistence of altruism in social groups. The puzzle is why an emerging "social group" of cells is not destroyed by individual cells pursuing their own Darwinian self-interest, and further why multicellularity, even once established, is not continually undermined by mutant selfish cells.

One reply is that multicellularity *is* undermined, or at least attempts at undermining are constantly being made by lower-level individuals. Cancers are such attempts. For example, a cancerous skin cell is, from a levels-of-selection point of view, a cheater, a mutant lower-level individual that pursues its Darwinian self-interest at the expense of the whole. It is a cell that "declines" to act altruistically by curtailing its reproduction as most of the rest of the cell in a multicellular organism seem to do. Why don't cells do this all the time? One answer, of course, is that the attempt is short sighted and ignores the larger group, the individual. If a cancer succeeds, the individual perishes, killing off the cancer cell and all of its progeny along with it. Selection acting at the level of the group strongly opposes selection acting on the lower-level individual. In other words, the second term of the Price equation overwhelms the first. From the perspective of the group selectionist, what makes the cancer case so interesting is that it reveals the struggle between levels of selection. It shows the warring levels in action, so to speak.

The major transitions raise another issue, having to do with the notion of "individuality." Genic selectionists argue that we cannot treat groups as real, because groups are not individuals. A solitary lion is an individual, but a pride of lions is not. It is not an organism, or rather—taking into account the fact that it occupies a hierarchical level above the organism—it is not a "superorganism." For the group selectionist argument to succeed, the genic selection claims, it must show that groups are individuals, that they are superorganisms. So what are the biological criteria for organismic or superorganismic individuality? One might argue, for example, that an individual must be continuously bounded in space, perhaps by an outer membrane or skin. By this standard, a pride of lions would not be an individual. But then, by this standard, neither is an ant colony, which to many really does seem to be a superorganism. In any case, there is room for debate in these cases. But there is not room for debate, the group selectionist points out, in the major transition from solitary cell to multicellular organism. What this case offers is a nice, clean case of group selection and one in which the resulting group is unambiguously an individual, an organism. (And from the vantage point of the ancestral single-celled protist from which that multicellular individual evolved, the latter might seem to be a kind of "colony" or "superorganism.")

It may be debatable whether a pride of lions is an individual but not whether a single multicellular lion is one.

The group selectionist goes on to point out that individuality seems not to be an all-or-none phenomenon. Imagine a multicellular organism in which a mutant cell arises with the peculiar property of being able to insert itself into the organism's sex cells. Such a cell would enjoy a strong selective advantage over other cells in the body. It would be able, in effect, to take advantage of the reproductive capacities of the individual as a whole to further its own Darwinian interests. Clearly many cells adopting this strategy would tend to undermine the individuality of the organism. To the extent they do it, the organism is really an assemblage of competing cells, of protists, rather than a multicellular individual. So, why do cells not pursue this strategy? In some multicellular organisms they probably do! Sponges, for example, have a number of cell types, only one of which is specialized for reproduction while the others form the body of the animal, move water, collect food, and so on. These somatic cells would seem to have no evolutionary future. But all of the cells of a sponge at least have the potential to "dedifferentiate," and to transform themselves into other cells, including reproductive cells. In these organisms, the threat of selfish somatic cells dedifferentiating and inserting themselves into the germline is always present. This is true not just of sponges but of many other kinds of multicellular individuals. However, it is not true of our own group, the vertebrates, or of many others, such as insects, starfish, and snails. In these groups, the germ line is "sequestered," meaning that a group of cells that will give rise to the sex cells is set aside, so to speak, very early in the ontogeny of the organism, and insulated from intrusion by other cells. What is so interesting about this is that there seems to be a correlation between germline sequestration and the degree of "individuality" that the multicellular entity attains (Buss 1987). In the germline seques-terers, we see more specialization of cell types, and specialization is more irreversible, than in those with more open or porous germlines. Germline sequestration would seem to be one mechanism, presumably favored histori-cally by selection acting at the group level, to suppress the potentialities of the lower-level cells and to promote the individuality of the group. Again for the group selectionist what these intermediates show is the two levels of selection pitted against each other, revealing cases in which the group level— the multicellular individual—has "won," but also cases in which the battle with the lower level—the cell—is unresolved.

Finally, the group selectionist can use the list of major transitions to make a more general point, that group selection seems not only to be inescapable in certain cases but on the whole quite frequent over the history of life. The emergence of multicellularity (major transition number 6) and of sociality and coloniality (number 7) are just two of the major transitions. There has also been the joining of individual replicators into groups of replicators (number 1), the joining of genes to form chromosomes (number 3), and the association of bacterial cells to form the first eukaryotic cell (number 4).

For numbers 4, 6, and 7, the historical record offers some evidence of actual frequency, apparently revealing these transitions to have been quite common. The emergence of the eukaryotic cell happened only once, but multicellularity arose at least a couple dozen times, and sociality or coloniality arose many hundreds and perhaps thousands of times. Indeed, from this perspective, if there is any unifying theme to the history of life it is the repeated emergence of higher-level individuals from lower-level ones. Far from being a dubious process of limited significance, group selection is rampant in evolution. The history of life reveals group selection gone mad.

The gene selectionist has a rejoinder. Those thousands of cases of sociality and coloniality are dubious in that the "individuality" of the group is at best uncertain. But in any case, even if all were conceded, a few dozen instances, or a few hundred or even a few thousand, arguably do not amount to much over the 3.5 billion year history of life. The number of origins of new species is many orders of magnitude larger than thousands, surely in the tens of billions and perhaps much greater yet. At best only a tiny fraction have involved group selection. And therefore the gene selectionist can quite reasonably decline to be impressed with its prevalence.

The group selectionist reply might be that even if the numbers are judged to be few, these transitions seem to have an importance that far outweighs their infrequency. The origins of the eukaryotic cell and multicellularity are what are known as key innovations, inventions that led to the origin of new designs and to spectacular radiations of new species. Group selection underlies the major revolutions in the history of life, revolutions that permanently altered the ecological structure of life on Earth.

How are we to adjudicate this dispute? It is unlikely that empirical evidence will be able to answer questions such as when the evolution of individuality has gone to completion, when group selection has triumphed, so to speak. What is needed is a philosophical breakthrough, a way of thinking about, operationalizing, and perhaps quantifying degree of individuation, degree of "superorganismness." Similarly, it is hard to see how actual or possible empirical evidence could shed light on the question of whether there have been many major transitions or so few that we can count them as mere aberrations. As for deciding whether their importance would outweigh their infrequency, if indeed it were decided that they are rare, this question too is as much a matter for the philosophy of biology as for biology itself.

Genocentrism and genetic information

Dawkins and other opponents of group selection—whether macroevolutionary or microevolutionary—might be happy to describe themselves as "genocentrists," even though the term was originally coined as one of abuse. In fact, Dawkins and the anti-group selectionists have been more strongly motivated by genocentrism than almost any other perspective in biology. Genocentrism is the thesis that the genes have a special role in the explanation of both individual development and biological evolution. It is a thesis embraced by many people who have never heard the term "genocentrism," and did not know they were "genocentrists."

Genocentrists differ from one another about what makes the genes special and whether their special role suffices to vindicate a strong view such as Dawkins's, that only the long-term replicators (the genes) really count in evolution, and that all vehicles are merely their temporary expedients in the struggle for survival among replicators. Some genocentricists are not Dawkinsians. On the other hand, support for genocentrism would certainly offer comfort for Dawkins's selfish-gene viewpoint. Likewise, group selectionists are only a subset of the opponents of genocentrism. But the case for group selection would be strengthened if it were shown that groups or, for that matter, many things other than the gene can also be replicators, and, what is more, genes have no special advantage over these other things in their roles as replicators. Refuting genocentrism would go a long way towards denying the primacy of the gene's-eye view and vindicating group selection.

Other opponents of genocentrism have independent reasons for denying that genes have a privileged role in development and heredity. These biologists, philosophers, and others want to refute another controversial position, genetic determinism, roughly the thesis that socially significant human traits, such as intelligence, gender, criminality, or some mental illnesses, are fixed by the genes so that environmental intervention to change them is either pointless or harmful. Thus, the idea that intelligence is genetically based, that there exists a gene or genes for intelligence and that they are unevenly distributed in the population, is part of an argument for not extending educational resources equally to all people. After all, if this view is right, some will not profit from the expenditure, so the money and effort will be wasted. The idea that gender roles are controlled by genes on, say, the X and Y chromosomes suggests that attempting to spread childcare responsibilities more evenly across men and women will have a harmful effect on children by depriving them of the more beneficial maternal care that has been shaped by eons of evolution. Both attitudes reflect complacency about social differences that the opponents of genetic determinism wish to undermine. They believe that an effective way to do so is to refute the idea that, strictly speaking, there are "genes for" any trait of interest, biological or social. One way to do this is to show that for any biologically or socially important trait, the causal role of the genes in determining that trait is no different from the causal role of any of a number of environmental factors. If many other such factors have the same kind of causal role with respect to the embryological construction of trait T and the faithful storage of trait T over generations as does the "gene for T," then there will be many environmental conditions that also bring about T, in addition to the gene for it. This conclusion is sometimes called the "parity thesis" and occasionally "the causal democracy thesis," meaning that each causally necessary condition gets as much say as any other in development and heredity. Showing this would in fact refute genocentrism.

And, therefore, opponents of genetic determinism can make common cause with group selectionists in challenging genocentrism. Some philosophers and biologists (e.g. Griffiths and Gray 1994) who argue for the "parity" call their view "developmental systems theory" to indicate that the genes are merely part of a system that transmits information across generations and uses them, along with environmental factors, to bring about development.

The focus of the debate about whether the genes play a special role in development and evolution has revolved around their *informational role*. Genocentrists have argued that the notion of a gene coding for, or carrying information about, traits is not just a widespread belief among scientists and laypersons, it is reflected in much of the descriptive vocabulary of molecular biology, and in its theory as well. We have, on this view, the best of reasons to believe that the genes literally code for specific proteins and through them for traits that show up reliably in development. The genetic code described in every textbook of molecular biology tells us that, for example, the nucleotide triple, cytosine–adenine–thymine (CAT) codes for the amino acid histidine. This three-nucleotide "codon" is the way the gene signals to the ribosome to add a histidine amino-acid molecule to the growing end of a newly forming chain of amino acids that will, when complete, make a functioning protein. A point mutation in the DNA or a transcription error in the RNA copied from it is a kind of spelling mistake in the writing out of this message.

Opponents of genocentrism argue that serving as a signal is not enough to distinguish the gene from many other environmental factors necessary for a developmental outcome. There is nothing more to the gene's carrying information about the traits it is supposed to code for than there is in the statement that clouds carry information about rain. Now, there is a sense in which clouds do signal that rain is coming. We interpret clouds as signs or harbingers of rain just because, pretty regularly, clouds cause rain. In this sense, of course, no one denies that CAT is a sign or signal for histidine, but then everything in nature that is followed regularly by something else is a potential signal of it. So there is nothing special about genes signaling traits. Think of bird songs. In some species a male chick needs to hear the signature mating song of its species from an adult male at a critical time in early development in order to copy it, to attract females, and therefore to reproduce. The adult's song is a message to the chick conveying the song it needs to sing, information just as critical for building a reproductively fit bird as the information its DNA carries. One could say, in this case, that to the extent that the genes build the auditory equipment of the bird, the genes provide the channel through which this information is transmitted. In general, when two or more factors are both causally necessary for an outcome, each can be viewed from some perspective or other as the source of a signal or the channel through which the signal is sent. Since genes and environmental factors are both necessary for a developmental outcome, from two equally valid perspectives, each is both signal and channel. Genes are just as much channels for nongenetic signals as they are signals themselves.

Genocentrists reply that this argument misses the point. Genes are more than just signals or signs, they carry information the way *symbols* do. The genes are not just causes of developmental or of hereditary transmission, they contain the directions, the recipe or the program for creating these outcomes. A program or a recipe is a piece of software, abstract lines of code, which are symbolized in hardware, whether it is ink on paper, currents in a microchip, or nucleotide sequences on a gene. Consider the genetic code described in every molecular biology textbook. It has all the attributes of a symbolic system for recording information. To begin with, it seems to be "arbitrary" in just the way the Roman, Cyrillic, or Greek alphabet, or the 1s and 0s of a computer code, is arbitrary. The genetic code is apparently a "frozen accident," coding for all the proteins and enzymes that make every organism we know, using an alphabet of four letters (the four types of nucleotides) in combinations of three (per codon) to spell only 20 different words (amino acids), which can be combined in a huge number of different ways to generate long sentences (proteins). (As discussed, the four nucleotides could in principle generate $4^3 = 64$ amino acids, but there is some degeneracy, so that many words signal the same amino acid, reducing the number of actual words to 20.) Thus, the codon CAT (cytosine–adenine–thymine) *represents* the amino acid histidine. In fact, part of Dawkins's argument for the uniqueness of the gene as the sole real replicators in selection turns on the gene's allegedly unique digital character as an information carrier. He argues that only a digitized symbol system can store information with the fidelity required by evolution. This makes the genes not only carriers of information, but in the long term the only reliable carriers of the information available in nature to produce evolution by natural selection. It is the fact that genes carry information about proteins, enzymes, and the traits built out of them, the fact that they "code for these traits," that is reflected in the shorthand expression "the gene for" a trait *T*.

Here the philosophy of biology comes up against the same problem that two other subdisciplines of philosophy face. The problem is how symbols can have meaning, a problem that faces the philosophy of language, or how brain states can represent anything that faces the philosophy of mind. Consider the question in the philosophy of language of why, when we say "scat, cat!" the second syllable sound we make usually refers to a particular member of the species *Felis domesticus*. A partial answer is that "cat" means, signifies, or symbolizes cats, and knowing the meaning of the word enables us to establish its reference in these cases. But this raises the question of why and how the sound "cat" in English means what it does. Some philosophers of language are prepared to pass this question on to the philosophy of mind or psychology by explaining that the meaning of noises like "cat" is conferred upon them by the speaker and/or hearer's interpreting them as referring to cats. So "cat" refers to cats owing to the fact that there is some brain state in English speakers and readers that represents cats as the subjects of the thought "cat." But then the question naturally arises, how does the brain represent cats?

This is the same problem the philosophy of mind faces. Is there an inscription, written in the configuration of neurons and the neurotransmitters coursing between their synapses, that means "cat." If so, we are pretty well back where we started, only now asking how a set of brain cells means cat instead of how a set of noises means cat. This is a hard question to understand, and an even harder question to answer, but we are going to have to at least understand its significance if we are to properly assess the arguments for and against genocentrism in biology!

In fact, the philosophy of psychology's problem of how the brain represents, how the 10^{10} neurons in the brain encode and carry information, is really as much a problem for the philosophy of biology, quite independent of its overlap with the problem of how the 3 billion polynucleotides in the genome encode and carry information! For the brain is an organ, a biological system. If there is no biological explanation for how the brain thinks, for how the physical stuff out of which the brain is made can be the mental stuff that represents to itself the way the world is, and interprets things as symbols, then the way is open to Cartesian dualism. That is to say it is open to the notion that the mind is distinct from the body, that it is nonmaterial, and that it cannot be studied empirically (say, by studying the brain). Worse, the way is then open to "spooky" talk about other nonphysical things and forces.

Indeed, it is hard to see exactly how the brain or the genome could carry information, could represent things that, for example, do not yet exist or may never exist. Particular human brains seem to be able to represent unicorns or perpetual motion machines or tomorrow's lunch. And a particular nucleotide sequence in a particular sperm cell seems to be able to represent or carry information about development, even about developmental outcomes that are never realized, if, for example, that sperm never fertilizes an ovum, or if the fertilized embryo is crushed or frozen. How can they do this, how can they represent things that have not happened and may never happen? Consider how one physical thing can be a symbol for another physical thing or event, or for something that does not even exist. Everywhere in the world, red octagons standing by the side of an intersection mean "stop." These physical things symbolize, in part, the event of vehicles coming to a halt (and they also symbolize the command that they do so, "Stop!" but let us leave this part of their meaning aside). Why do these physical things, red octagons, symbolize vehicles coming to a halt? Well, obviously because creatures with brains *interpret* them as symbols. We treat a physical thing as symbolizing a type of event (vehicles halting), and this act of interpretation is what gives red octagons their meaning, their status as symbolic carriers of information about vehicles halting. So it must be the case that there is some configuration of neurons in a person's brain that stores the information that red octagons symbolize vehicles halting. Otherwise we could not remember and recognize the meaning of the red octagons by the roadside. The question arises, how do those brain cells symbolize red octagons? Are the cells red? Are they octagon shaped? Of course not! So, what is it about this set of cells, this piece of grey matter, this physical thing in the head, that makes it mean, symbolize, or represent stop signs?

One answer we need to rule out is that there is some other part of the brain that gets information from the stop sign information-storing cells and interprets the activity of these cells as meaning "stop sign." Therein lies a regress, for we will have to ask the same question about this second bit of grey matter: how do its neurons recognize the first set as being stop sign-symbolizing neurons? Another answer that must be ruled out is that there is a mind that is independent of the brain, and that this mind reads information off the configuration of grey matter in the brain. The reasons science rejects this alternative are obvious. First, if the mind is distinct from the brain, it could not be a spatial thing, nor could it have the usual physical properties such as mass, size, temperature, charge, distinct parts, and so on. Without these properties, we cannot study scientifically the way it works. Worse, we cannot even imagine how it *could* work, so we could not even frame hypotheses about how the mind learns, remembers, forgets, becomes happy or sad, in short how it behaves or changes state. How shall we understand a mind to be engaged in thought, as thought is a process, when the mind has no parts to change during the process? Finally, it is impossible to see how such a nonphysical mind could use or deploy or interact with a physical brain, how such a mind could to connect itself to the body to carry out the mind's plans, desires, or wishes. To do so, it would have to somehow affect the grey matter, its chemistry, its physical state. But as a nonphysical thing, this is just what the mind could not do. In short, neither science in general nor biology in particular can explain how brain states symbolize things by assuming that there are nonphysical minds that interpret the brain states.

In recent years, several influential philosophers of psychology have attempted to deal with the problem of how the brain represents by an ingenious application of the theory of natural selection. In retrospect, it should be no surprise that Darwinian theory should have great attractions to someone trying to solve the problem of how the brain represents, and to solve it in ways that are consistent with modern science's view of how the world works. As we saw in Chapter 1, the scope for explaining things by appeal to purposes has become narrower and narrower since the late seventeenth century. Darwin's theory of natural selection killed off goals, purposes, ends, etc. in the life sciences almost 150 years ago, by providing the causal mechanism that made them superfluous. Now the brain is the quintessential, paradigmatic, purposive, goal-directed system. Accordingly, a scientific account of the brain must find a purely causal account of its apparently purposive character. If, as we tentatively suggested in Chapter 1, blind variation and selective retention is the only way to displace purpose by causal mechanisms, then this mechanism must underlie apparent purposiveness in psychology as it does elsewhere in biology. In fact, the attractiveness, if not the inevitability, of Darwinism as an approach to understanding how the brain represents has made many philosophers of psychology into philosophers of biology! Needing the theory of natural selection to solve one of the most daunting problems in metaphysics, the mind/body problem, forced them to begin to pay attention to the problems that Darwin's theory faces in its home territory, biology! And of course it will also come as no surprise that some philosophers of biology and some biologists have adapted this notion of how the brain represents to explaining how the genome represents or carries information, and thus to vindicate genocentrism.

Teleosemantics: philosophy of biology meets the philosophy of psychology

The theory adapted from Darwinian natural selection to explain how physical systems like the brain can encode symbolic information has been called "teleosemantics" to indicate that the meaning, or semantic content of a brain state, is given by its function, where function is to be understood biologically, that is in terms of selected effects. The teleosemantic theory of neural content is best explained by an illustration.

Frogs can snatch flies out of the air with their tongues. Presumably their brains "tell" their tongues where to flick in order to catch flies. So if a frog flicks its tongue out to a point in space where a fly is located—call it x, y, z, t, for the 3 spatial coordinates plus the time at which the fly is located at that spot—presumably there is some set of cells in the frog's brain that contains the information "fly at x, y, z, t." One reason to think this is that selection has operated on frog neurobiology for millions of years, selecting for brain states that are adaptive, i.e. states that, among other things, solve the "design problem" of catching flies in the frog's vicinity. So, having the neural state "fly at x, y, z, t" is a capacity selected for, in the frog's phylogeny, and manifest ontogenetically in this particular frog's development. And this neural state is of a sort that usually causes fly flicking at the right place and time. In general, teleosematics holds that the content of a brain state is imparted by the appropriateness (ultimately for survival and reproduction, but more immediately for feeding, fleeing, fighting, sex, etc.) of the behaviors they produce in the environment where they find themselves. Selection acting on neural development in the evolution of this frog has shaped its brain cells to have the capacity to represent "fly at x, y, z, t," when flies are in fact at that location, and this particular frog's biography of neural development—including programmed development and perhaps environmental reinforcement of appropriate behaviors (perhaps the occasional fortuitous but successful trapping of flies)—endow the cells that now cause it to flick its tongue at a fly at x, y, z, t, with the meaning "fly at x, y, z, t." So the selective history of these cells is the source of this meaning. It explains where the meaning comes from. But what is the meaning itself? What is its content? It is just the appropriate behavior, fly catching, that is produced in and by those cells. Teleosemantics is the claim that the presence and appropriate behavior of these cells in the causal chain that leads from the fly at x, y, z, t to tongue flicking a moment later *constitutes* its fly-at-x-y-z-t content.

Thus the content of a brain state can be inferred directly from the naturally selected behavior it causes. Teleosemantics claims that content follows from the environmental appropriateness of the behavior. This makes it sound like behaviorism, the thesis once popular among experimental psychologists that we can neglect the causal role of internal brain states. Behaviorism holds that all we need to do to explain behavior is identify its environmental triggers and the results of the behavior. We can ignore the intervening mental variables. Teleosemantics is a far more sophisticated thesis. It accepts that our data are, at the outset, the same as the behaviorist's data. But it also seeks the internal brain states of organisms as crucial causes that we need to uncover in order to understand behavior. And it credits the causal role of those brain states to their content, which can be identified by their selected function. Teleosemantics recognizes that pending further advances in neuroscience, it will often be difficult to determine the exact content of brain states, given limited data about behavior and environmental stimuli, even for language users like us who claim to be able to describe the representational content of our minds or brains. But, teleosemantics holds that content consists in the effects the states of our brains were selected to cause, in the environment in which those states are appropriately stimulated. Of course, the selected effects that content consists in will differ from creature to creature depending on the evolutionary complexity of their neural architectures. Teleosemantic research will probably reveal that the brain's representing "fly at x, y, z, t" is not a matter of the frog's having a separate and distinct concept of time, or location, or fly, stored in the frog's brain, and somehow syntactically put together into the sentence "fly at x, y, z, t." The mental and behavioral repertoire of the frog is very limited and therefore explanation does not require us to attribute to its brain a "language of thought." On the other hand, some non-human primates undoubtedly do have concepts, say, of "self" versus "other," as revealed in a range of behaviors elicited in the presence of other primates, or in the presence of a mirror!

The philosopher of biology's interest in the research program of teleosemantics should be obvious. In addition to claiming to solve the long-standing philosopher's mind/body problem—by a deft application of the principle of random variation and selective retention—it also underwrites behavioral biology's increasing willingness to attribute a complex mental life to all sorts of infrahuman creatures. Teleosemantics' pay-off for genocentrism is direct as well. The codons that code for particular amino acids were selected for by the same mechanism that produces meaning, representation, and symbolizing in neurons. Therefore, the genes made from these codons must also be accorded the same status as representational systems, carrying symbolic information. In solving the mind/body problem, teleosemantics vindicates the informational status of the genome, and with it genocentrism's claim that the genes have a unique role in heredity and development.

Of course, like all such theories purporting to solve age-old problems in philosophy, teleosemantics has been subject to serious objections, both in its solution to the mind/body problem and its vindication of genocentrism. Opponents in psychology have argued that the discriminations as to content that it allows are much too coarse to explain the fine-grained character of human thought. Can we provide a teleosemantic account of the content of a composer's thoughts when creating a melody, or a mathematician's brain states the first moment when he or she realizes the validity of a proof? Even a dog's barking, salivating, straining at its leash, just out of reach of a prime cut of beef in plain sight seems to be a problem for teleosemantics. The behavior seems to offer reason enough to attribute content to some set of neurons in the dog's brain. But exactly what content? Surely not raw beef, or butchered animal parts, or high protein and fat content foodstuff, or anything else we could express in a human language. Dogs do not think in the concepts of English, Urdu, or Hausa. And there does not seem to be any set of experiments on a dog that we could undertake to narrow down the content of the dog's brain to that one particular thought about that particular piece of meat in front of it. Teleosemantics must either fail to provide us with the right analysis of what the exact content of the dog's brain state is, or it must deny that there is such a thing as its *exact* content. And the same may go for the human speaker of another language, or even for that matter another speaker of our language.

This is only one of the problems teleosemantics faces. Whether it has an answer is a matter for the philosophy of psychology. Meanwhile, its supposed vindication of genocentrism faces problems in the philosophy of biology. Recall the genocentrist's claim that the genetic code is symbolic because, like the alphabet, it is arbitrary. It may not be. There are currently several purely chemical theories that purport to show that the code emerges nonaccidentally from chemical relations between amino acids and nucleic acids. If one or more of these theories is correct, the code is no more arbitrary than the Periodic Table. On the other hand, suppose that the code is the result of natural selection. Then its (near) universality on Earth after 3.5 billion years of selective filtering, suggests either that it was so much better than any other code that it survived leaving (almost) no competitors, or that it is (almost) the only code evolutionarily possible here on Earth. Either way, it will not be arbitrary like Morse code, Greek letters, Arabic or Roman numerals, etc. One reason clouds literally do not mean rain, or symbolize it, but are at most its natural "signs," is that the relation is not an "arbitrary" one, which could be changed. (We could decide to use "+" to symbolize subtraction if we wanted to.) If the same fixity goes for the genetic code, then the codon CAT no more represents, means, signals, or carries information about the amino acid histidine than a raincloud represents, means, signals, or carries information about rain.

But there is an even more serious problem for a teleosemantic approach to genetic information. We want an account of why the codon CAT symbolizes histidine. What we get from teleosemantics is the insight that its symbolizing histidine has been selected for its adaptational appropriateness to the environment in which the connection emerged. We do not have much of an idea what that environment was like, but perhaps we don't need to know. It may be enough to know that competition among early chemical systems was intense, and that our present coding system was the victor. What is more, if we consider what contribution histidine makes to the proteins and enzymes it helps constitute, it might turn out that in all cases the job it does is to make the enzyme a polar molecule, or a hydrophobic one, or to add a hairpin turn in the molecular structure of the enzyme. Suppose it is the last of these. Well, then it will turn out that CAT is selected for providing an amino acid that helps make hairpin turns in enzymes. But then we will have to say that CAT means "make a hairpin turn" instead of histidine. Perhaps this is not a problem. But at a minimum it will imply that the genetic code relating codons to amino acids does not after all tell us what in fact a codon means.

Finally, genocentrism's reliance on teleosemantics raises a much more serious problem that opponents will seize upon. The whole point of genocentrism's argument that genes carry information is to show they have a special role in development and heredity as the sole carriers of real (as opposed to "clouds mean rain") information. On the teleosemantic view this informational role is conferred on them by natural selection. But if natural selection can confer an informational role on gene sequences, then it can and presumably does confer an informational role on a lot of other biological traits of organisms that are as much the products of natural selection as the order of polynucleotide bases in a genome! Thus, if CAT means histidine, then it will turn out that, for instance, the exoskeleton of an insect *means*—carries the information about, symbolizes—protection against dehydration. It will turn out that meanings are everywhere in the biosphere, for adaptations are everywhere in it! So much for the special role of the genes! More to the point, recall the genocentrist's counter-argument to the claim that the song of an adult male bird is just as causally necessary to the development of a male chick as the genes that code for its auditory equipment. The genocentrist's reply grants equal causal necessity but claims that the genes are special because they carry real semantic information about how this equipment is to be built in symbolic form, whereas the song is just a causally necessary environmental factor. For the chick will imitate whatever tune it hears at the right moment of development. But if the song was shaped by natural selection to attract females, and learning it will enhance the chick's attraction to females and therefore its fitness, then doesn't the song qualify as carrying symbolic information about the world, about say female song preferences? The song would seem to carry symbolic information about the world, to the same degree and for the same reason as the DNA that builds the auditory equipment.

Almost all molecular biologists are wedded to genocentrism, and even more strongly committed by their theory and their terminology to the conception of the genes, and their immediate molecular products, as literally, really, semantically informational in the way that nothing else is in biology.

And giving up this way of thinking and talking about the genes would doubt-less seem to them not just an inconvenience, but a serious impediment to research. But we have seen that they need to earn the right to such descriptions, or else just treat them as metaphors, heuristic devices, and therefore potentially misleading descriptions, such as "natural selection" (there is no real entity in nature that selects in the human sense) or "design problems" (the phrase is not intended to imply a real designer). Doing this, however, may erect real limits to biology's ability ultimately to explain how larger systems like brains can carry information, have content, and constitute the mind. Francis Crick began his career in biology with the expectation that learning how the genome solves the problem of the hereditary storage and transmission of information would help us understand how the brain stores and transmits information. Having to his satisfaction solved the former problem, he spent the last 45 years of his life on the latter one. In doing so, he left unsolved a problem that has vexed philosophers—and should have troubled biologists—ever since: the problem of whether and how the genome carries information. Until it is solved, genocentrism remains unsubstantiated.

Genocentrism and group selection both raise issues of reductionism. What is the relationship between the broad version of the reduction issue broached in Chapter 4—where the issue was whether higher-level biological properties and systems are "nothing but" lower-level ones—and the narrower one raised here—whether higher-level selection is "nothing but" lower-level selection? There is some reason to think that the two issues should be connected. If natural selection is *the* central process in evolutionary change, then most questions about reduction in biology will be questions about levels-of-selection reduction. However, at least in principle, the first question about reduction in general could be answered yes, while the second question about levels reduction is answered no. Higher-level selection may be reducible not to lower-level selection but to lower-level *non*-selective processes. That is, the units subject to higher levels of selection could have been built up out of lower-level units not by *selection*, but by some purely physical, non-Darwinian process instead, perhaps a self-organizing process. Thus the connection between these two issues—general reduction and levels-of-selection reduction—appears to be an empirical matter, and therefore one for scientists: how do higher levels of selection arise?

The problems of group selection, genocentrism, and how Darwinian theory can account for the major transitions in the history of life on Earth are among the most pressing on the current agenda of the philosophy of biology. It may be wondered what makes these problems philosophical at all, as opposed to just very general, theoretical, and abstract issues of biology. One answer is that philosophers have long concerned themselves with the most abstract, general, and theoretical questions of the sciences. Indeed, sometimes the disciplines have ignored their most general and abstract questions, and philosophers have been the only people to take these questions seriously. If this was ever the case among biologists, it is not the case today. But it must be said that, unlike physicists, at least in the last 100 years or so biologists have almost always invited philosophers of science to participate in their inquiries and taken the considerations of philosophers of science seriously.

On the other hand, it is pretty clear that answers to the questions broached in this chapter will turn at least in part on issues that were of interest to philosophers long before their post-Darwinian fascination with biology. For example, the dispute about group versus individual selection turns crucially on what counts as an individual, a spatiotemporally particular thing, a problem that philosophers have long been wrestling with. Should only obvious cases like solitary lions or social insect colonies count as individuals, or should family groups and species (and perhaps higher levels yet) also be treated this way? Can a gene properly be said to carry information, and does it therefore have a unique role in our understanding of natural selection and biology generally? This is a philosophically vexed question. Information is endemic to biological theory and description. But actually vindicating its actual presence in biology, its nonmetaphorical role in biological processes, has regenerated questions about the mind and body that were raised by Descartes in the seventeenth century. Thus, individuality, information theory, genocentrism, and group selection—these are hot topics in biology and the philosophy of biology these days, and many of the questions they raise are new. But they are also very old.

Summary

The claim that evolution can or does operate at levels of organization greater than the individual has repeatedly been advanced and repeatedly challenged since Darwin first suggested it in the *Origin* and in *The Descent of Man*. And since Dawkins's *Selfish Gene,* the apparently even more radical notion that selection does not even really operate at the level of the individual—only at the level of the gene—has also been debated in biology. And now there are even more alternatives, in particular, pluralism about the levels of selection, which has become a common view among philosophers and biologists, especially on account of recent macroevolutionary findings and recent interest in the origin of individuality in the so-called major evolutionary transitions. But there remain some who are unhappy with pluralism. Genocentrists reject pluralism, arguing that the level of the gene is special owing to the unique role the gene plays in heredity and development. And those who reject the perspective of the selfish gene argue that genes in general make no distinctive contribution to development and are not the sole agents of heredity. On their view there is nothing special about genes to single them out as particularly important replicators, in comparison with others, and there are any number of other causal factors in evolution that play an equally indispensable role in hereditary transmission and the generation of interactors.

Each of these opponents of pluralism faces special challenges. Genocentrism needs to give an account of how the major transitions of evolution from the macromolecule to the human social group are possible, given the ever-present threat of subversion by selfish genes from within. Exponents of developmental systems theory need to show that there really are other things under heaven or Earth that could control development as reliably and transmit heritable traits as faithfully as the genes.

Finally, genocentrism as a thesis about the special role of the genes, in particular their informational role, as so many molecular biologists insist they play, raises questions about information that intersect with questions about how matter carries meaning—whether in the genes or in the brain—that have concerned philosophers at least since the seventeenth century. These are problems which in recent years philosophers of mind have sought to solve with the resources of Darwin's theory. Whether they succeed or fail, the attempt shows the relevance of biology and its philosophy to the most central problems of philosophy.

Suggestions for further reading

Much of the most original work on group and individual selection and kin selection can be found in the papers of W.D. Hamilton, many collected in two volumes entitled *Narrow Roads of Gene Land*. Dawkins's arguments for the selfish gene hypothesis extend across several decades and a series of books from *The Selfish Gene* to *The Extended Phenotype* to *Rivers Out of Eden*. Among the earliest opponents of group selection was the distinguished biologist, G.C. Williams, who attacked previous writers' theories of group selection in *Adaptation and Natural Selection*. Elliott Sober, *The Nature of Selection*, evaluates Williams's arguments. Another resolute opponent of group selection is Robert Trivers, many of whose papers on the subject can be found in *Natural Selection and Social Theory*. Against the background of these works, Elliott Sober and David Sloan Wilson advanced a widely discussed model of group selection exploiting Price's equation in *Unto Others*. Samir Okasha's *The Levels of Selection Question: Philosophical Perspectives* is a sophisticated, authoritative treatment of the quantitative, methodological, and philosophical issues in this debate.

Species selection and the paleontological evidence for it is famously advanced by Stephen J. Gould in his magnum opus *The Structure of Evolutionary Theory*. Sterelny's *Dawkins vs. Gould: Survival of the Fittest* summarizes and assesses the argument between these biologists about genocentrism and species selection.

A pluralism with special place for the gene is defended famously in Kim Sterelny and Philip Kitcher's paper "The return of the gene," while Paul Griffiths and Russell Gray's paper "Developmental systems theory and evolutionary explanation" rejects any special role for the gene in evolution or development.

Exponents of a genocentric approach to evolution, John Maynard Smith and Eörs Szathmáry, explore its challenges in *The Major Transitions of*

Evolution. A more accessible work by the same authors is *The Origins of Life*.

Teleosemantics was expounded originally in Dennett's *Content and Consciousness*, and later defended by Ruth Millikan in *Language, Thought and Other Biological Categories* and, more briefly, in Fred Dretske's *Explaining Behavior*. Jerry Fodor, in *A Theory of Content*, challenges the relevance of Darwinian theory to meaning, either in the brain or in language. Its relevance to genocentrism is treated by one of us (Rosenberg) in *Darwinian Reductionism*.

7 Biology, human behavior, social science, and moral philosophy

Overview

One reason that the philosophy of biology became the focus of much interest, and even controversy, over the last quarter of the twentieth century is the bearing biology has increasingly been thought to have on the social and behavioral sciences. Not just biological and cultural anthropology, but sociology, psychology, even economics and politics, have felt the influence especially of Darwinism. This incursion of biology and the attraction of biologically inspired research programs in the social sciences can be dated from the publication of E.O. Wilson's *Sociobiology: The New Synthesis* (1975).

From the time Darwin wrote *The Descent of Man* (1871) until the publication of Wilson's book, much social and behavioral science successfully resisted Darwinian approaches, for three main reasons. First of all, it was difficult to see how a theory about random variation and natural selection of genetically inherited traits could shed much light on the learned behavior of humans or their social and cultural consequences. Second, and closely related, fieldwork by cultural anthropologists in the first part of the twentieth century suggested that there was a wide variation in human institutions, norms, and values around the world. The breadth of observed cultural variation suggested that the differences among people, and among peoples, had to have a different explanation from the similarities. Third, the conventional understanding of the Darwinian mechanism was that it operated over millions of years to produce organisms designed to maximize individual fitness. And this seemed to undermine even Darwin's own group selection account of cultural norms and social institutions. From the point of view of his own individual-level theory, human sociality, society, and political and economic institutions should all be impossible in the long run. For they all require cooperation, trust and promise keeping, unselfishness, and other fitness-reducing behaviors, preferences, habits, and dispositions that should condemn the lineages of people who act this way to long-term, and perhaps even short-term, extinction. Thus, as people cannot be just fitness maximizers, it must have been that when natural selection finally got around to producing *Homo sapiens*, it made a species smart enough to slip off the leash of the genes, to transcend Darwinian constraints on evolution. Accordingly, many social scientists considered that it was safe to disregard Darwinian theory in the projects of the social and behavioral sciences.

In this chapter we explore how, in one generation of research, Darwinian theory went from irrelevance to unavoidability in the examination of human behavior and social institutions.

Functionalism in social science

The notion that natural selection has no relevance for human affairs should have been dismissed long ago, for at least one important reason that is easy to recognize in the light of previous chapters of this book. At least since the nineteenth century, social scientists have identified various social institutions, practices, rules, and norms, adaptively important for the existence and flourishing of the societies in which they are found. Equally, they have argued that other societies have been harmed by the absence of these social traits. The founder of sociology, Emile Durkheim (1897) famously argued that social institutions, such as the family, the church, and the organization of work and trade, had functions, ones that were not recognized by members of the society whose behavior these institutions organized and regulated. And these functions existed *in order to* maintain the well-being of the society. A holist, Durkheim also held that there were facts about the institutions and norms in a society, "social facts," that were not reducible to facts about individuals and the causes of their behavior. And these social facts reflected the function of family, religious, and economic institutions in providing for the well-being of society as a whole. In *Suicide*, one of the most influential works in the history of social science, he employed empirical data to argue that the aggregate rate of suicide in a society was to be understood as a measure of its "health," analogous to the health of an individual. Further, it was the proper functioning of society's institutions that explain their persistence, character, structure, and role in societies, just as the heart's function explains its presence, character, structure, and role in the human body.

Following in Durkheim's footsteps, social scientists in many different disciplines and with many very different assumptions about what societies need to survive or to thrive, and about what their institutions do to further this end, pursued this "functionalist" methodology. Even those like Levi-Strauss (1949) who adopted the label "structuralist," to distinguish themselves from Durkheim's "functionalist" theory, nevertheless adopted the explanatory strategy of functionalism. Thus, having uncovered interesting regularities in cross-cousin marriage among many non-Western peoples, Levi-Strauss hypothesized that the explanation for such marriage and kinship rules is that they enhance social solidarity. Compare the explanation of why the heart beats: because in doing so it circulates the blood. Both explanations are implicitly teleological, and therefore functionalist. This approach evoked a number of different criticisms. In particular, it was objected that this approach treated social groups as "organisms" or even "superorganisms," which at best could be a metaphor for real societies. Further, invoking some need of society as the explanation for the presence of some feature of it is either untestable or even worse a throwback to Aristotelian teleology. These theories were also subject to two sorts of moral or normative criticisms. First, they either implicitly or explicitly made a society an object of moral concern, one of potentially greater importance than its individual members. Thus, the sacrifice of individual rights to social needs could rationalize a good deal of twentieth century totalitarianism. Second, functional theories seem implicitly to endorse the status quo, the current arrangements of society, as against reforms or revolutionary changes in it. For by identifying a function that current institutions serve, they seem to demonstrate the utility or even indispensability of these institutions to the society's survival. It is obvious that these normative issues made functionalism in social science a matter of great concern beyond merely methodological issues. We will return to these matters several times in this chapter.

Subsequent to Durkheim, functionalist social scientists introduced the distinction between manifest and latent functions. The manifest functions of an institution are those of its effects that human agents recognize and that they erected the institution to achieve. For example, the manifest function of the law courts is to administer justice. Latent functions are those adaptive effects of social structures that their participants do not recognize, never intended, but are nevertheless necessary for the survival and success of the society. To use an example that became famous among cultural anthropologists, Levi-Strauss argued that marriage rules permitting or forbidding unions among maternal versus paternal cousins function latently to ensure social solidarity between clans and families in a society. No participant in these societies may have noticed this fact about the marriage rules nor were they intentionally introduced by anyone with a view to having this beneficial effect. Latent functions do not require anyone's recognition of their goals or purposes or intention to attain them.

Now recall that Darwin's theory banished all "free-floating" goals, ends, purposes, along with God's designs, from nature. So how is functionalist social theory going to account for function, especially latent function? Without some purely causal theory to explain functions or adaptations that are "good for" societies or their institutions, the social sciences had no right to help themselves to explanatory notions such as function or adaptation! Of course, what functionalist social science needed is exactly what Darwinian theory provided for biology. As we saw in Chapter 1, once we demand a causal theory of adaptation or function, the only game in town, the only available theory, is natural selection, an account of functions (especially latent ones) in terms of blind variation and environmental filtration. So if social science invoked functions and also honors strictures on causal explanation, it would willy-nilly have to embrace the "selected effects" account of function, and with it Darwinism.

But the theory of natural selection was not well understood among social scientists during the period in which functionalism flourished among them. Even within biology, the theory was the subject of controversy during this period, and of repeated accusations that it is untestable or unfalsifiable. Moreover, social and behavioral scientists assumed that Darwinism required that social traits be genetically inherited, unlearned, innate. And the prevailing view among social scientists since the Enlightenment was that almost everything of interest in human behavior is learned, the result of nurture, not nature. Thus, it is not surprising that, as a research program that needed Darwinian mechanisms to vindicate its explanations, functionalism became increasingly unpopular, especially among empirical social scientists over the course of the twentieth century.

As we shall see in this chapter, applying the theory of natural selection in the social sciences does not commit us to a gene-based theory of the evolution or current character of societies. Recall that the theory of natural selection requires some theory of heredity or other but not any one in particular. When applied to the social or cultural evolution, the theory needs to identify fitness differences among social cultural variants and it needs it to be the case that these variants are transmitted from generation to generation. But it does not need the vehicle of transmission to be DNA, and it does not need the generations to be the neat and orderly ones that sexual reproduction has produced. Thus, a better grasp of Darwin's theory could have vindicated a good deal of twentieth century social science's identification of latent functions and dysfunctions, of social adaptations and maladaptations, without committing these disciplines to the innateness, inevitability, or permanent fixity of social structures, institutions, and behaviors. And when Darwinian evolutionary theories in the social sciences did finally emerge in recent decades, it should therefore have come as no surprise. Except for one big thing.

Human social institutions, norms, behaviors, are all characterized by a thorough-going cooperation, by altruistic exchanges, by the inculcation of moral norms enjoining or prizing unselfishness, and their enforcement. It was Darwin who first recognized the problem that these stubborn facts about human life made for the application to it of the theory of natural selection. As we saw in the last chapter, Darwin's group selection solution to the problem of rendering fitness maximization compatible with altruism or other forms of cooperation is highly problematic. Subversion from within becomes even more inevitable and even more rapid when members of a group can detect free riding and switch to it when they see it paying off! When combined with suspicions about the consequences of a theory that makes groups into distinct and substantial entities, perhaps even foci of moral interest or value, the group selection gambit was unlikely to attract social scientists to a Darwinian social science.

All this was changed by the work of W.D. Hamilton (1964). His theory of kin selection and inclusive fitness encouraged behavioral biologists to consider how altruism towards close kin can enhance the chances that a selfish gene will leave more copies of itself in the next generation. The point is now so well understood as to hardly bear elaboration: as discussed in Chapter 6, organisms are selected to behave altruistically toward relatives, because these relatives share the same genes. And of course if organisms generally live most or all their lives in small family groups, in which most individuals encountered are family, then any mechanism that generates such cooperative behaviors will be favored, including generalized and unqualified cooperation with everyone (again, since virtually everyone is likely to be at least somewhat related). Of course, once the interacting population expands beyond the family group, unconditional strategies of altruism will be subject to subversion from within, but not from within the kin group. If a group of interacting cooperators remains genetically linked over long periods, the institution of cooperation may persist, may accord advantages to the group as a whole and so vindicate Darwin's "group selection" account of the emergence and persistence of cooperation. And, of course, as these kin groups increase in size and fission or send out colonies, the mechanism captured by the Price equation—between-group selection for cooperation swamping within-group selection against it—takes effect. The trouble is that humans ceased to remain in genetically closely related kin groups at the end of the Holocene, when hunting and gathering ceased to be a viable adaptation. The persistence of cooperative institutions since then means that what Darwinism really needed to gain a foothold in the social sciences was an account of how altruism among genetically unrelated organisms can persist.

The need for an account of cooperation among unrelated organisms is one Darwinian behavioral biologists faced as well. One solution was "reciprocal altruism." For example, when vampire bats forage successfully, they share food with other genetically unrelated vampire bats who have not found food and would otherwise starve. But a bat does this preferentially with other bats who have themselves shared with him or her in the past, when he or she was unsuccessful! If vampire bats could do this, then presumably so could *Homo sapiens*. But for both, biology faced the task of explaining how such cooperation was even possible, consistent with Darwinism.

Evolutionary game theory and Darwinian dynamics

It is not just Darwinism that needs an account of how cooperation is possible, among humans and nonhumans. Economic theory too needs an explanation of why economically rational agents cooperate even when it appears not to be in their rational self-interest to do so. Here the theory of strategic interaction or, as it is more commonly called, game theory can make common cause with evolutionary theory.

To see the problem economics raises, consider the most well-known strategic interaction problem in game theory, the prisoner's dilemma (PD). Suppose you and I set out to rob a bank by night. However, we are caught with our safe-cracking tools even before we can break into the bank. We are separated and informed of our rights as criminal suspects and then offered the following "deals." If neither of us confesses, we shall be charged with possession of safe-cracking tools and imprisoned for two years each. If we both confess to attempted bank robbery, a more serious crime, we will each receive a five year sentence. If, however, only one confesses and the other remains silent, the confessor will receive a one year sentence in return for his confession, and the other will receive a ten year sentence for attempted bank robbery. The question each of us faces is whether to confess or not.

Only a little thought is required to see that this problem is easily solved. As a rational agent, I want to minimize my time in jail. So, if I think that you are going to confess, then to minimize my prison sentence I had better confess too. Otherwise, I will end up with ten years and you will get just one. But, come to think about it, if I confess and you don't, then I will get the one year sentence. Now it begins to dawn on me that whatever you do, I had better confess. If you keep quiet and I confess, I will get the shortest jail sentence possible. If you confess, then I would be crazy not to confess as well, because otherwise I would get the worst possible outcome, ten years. So, I conclude that the only rational thing for me to do is to confess (and implicate you).

Now, how about your reasoning process? Well, it is exactly the same as mine. If I confess, you would be a fool to do otherwise, and if I don't, you would still be a fool to do otherwise.

The result is we both confess and we both get five years in the slammer. Where is the dilemma? It is best seen in a diagram of the situation (Figure 7.1). The top of the box labels your choices: confess and don't confess. The left side labels mine: confess and don't confess. The numbers in the lower left of each square are the number of years I would serve under each combination

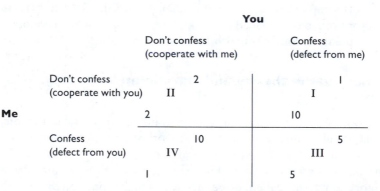

Figure 7.1 Pay-off matrix for the prisoner's dilemma. The four cells (roman numerals) show the results for the four possible turns of events (two people, you and me, each of us with two choices, cooperate or defect). In each cell, the number above the diagonal shows the jail sentence you receive, and the number below shows my jail sentence. (See text for details.)

of choices, and the numbers in the upper right of each square are the numbers you would serve. Each square is labeled in roman numerals for reference.

The rational strategy for you and the rational one for me lead us to square III, in which both of us confess. These are called the "dominant" strategies in game theory because, as the reasoning shows, they are the most rational ones for each of us, in the absence of certain knowledge about what the other person will do. They dominate all other strategies. But now, step back and consider the preference order in which each of us would place the four alternatives. My order is $I > II > III > IV$; in each successive square I get more years in jail. Your order is $IV > II > III > I$, for the same reason. We end up in square III. However, if we compare our orderings, we both prefer square II to square III, that is we prefer both getting two years to both getting five years in jail. Yet rationality, maximizing our utility, leads us to a "suboptimal" outcome, one less desirable than another that is "attainable." The dilemma is this: In the terms of the story, there is no way we can rationally get to square II, even though both of us rationally prefer it to square III. The reason is easy to see. Suppose before starting on the bank job, we both took oaths not to confess. If either of us believed that the other party would live up to the promise not to confess, confession would be even more tempting, for it would increase the chances of getting the lightest sentence by confessing. Suppose we backed up the promise by hiring a hit man to shoot whoever confesses and gets out of jail first. Then, of course, the rational thing is to make a further secret pay-off to the hit man not to carry out his job, and then to confess anyway. In short, there seems no way for rational agents to secure a more preferred alternative. This then is the dilemma: Given the pay-off rankings, the agents, by trying to maximize utility, are prevented from cooperating to attain a utility-maximizing alternative.

(It is worth mentioning that in political philosophy and political theory the prisoner's dilemma, PD for short, is often introduced to justify government coercion to enforce cooperation. Or, in this case, sticking to the storyline, we might introduce a mafia-like organization, of which both of us are members, that would enforce our prior deal not to confess. Once a government or mafia-like organization is introduced, of course, the pay-offs to cooperation and defection have changed, and the choice problem agents face is no longer a prisoner's dilemma. Note that changing the pay-offs is not a solution to the PD; it is the substitution of another game for the PD.)

What does the PD have to do with evolution? Well, a PD is any strategic interaction in which there are two choices for each agent, and the rankings of the pay-offs are in the same order as that given above ($I > II > III > IV$ and $IV > II > III > I$), but the dominant strategy takes both players into box III. And if the pay-offs are reproductive opportunities, then the prospect of animals of all kinds finding themselves in a PD are considerable. Consider the case of two scavenger birds who come upon a carcass. They could both fight to decide which will have the carcass to itself, during which time a third scavenger might steal it away, or either one could defer to the other, which would reduce its fitness and enhance that of the other scavenger, or they could both start consuming the carcass. The trouble with this last option is that a bird engrossed in eating a carcass is vulnerable to attack by the other bird, an attack that could be fatal and that could enhance the fitness of the attacker—by eliminating the competition, thereby allowing the attacker to secure the resource for itself. Now the birds cannot negotiate an agreement to share the carcass and, even if they could, there would be no reason for either to trust the other, so the scavengers face a PD. Accordingly, they will not share the food but both will warily stalk each other, neither eating nor fighting, until the carcass rots.

Fortunately for humans and other animals, nature rarely imposes single PDs on interacting organisms. Much more frequently it imposes repeated, or iterated PDs, in which each of many individuals finds themselves playing the game many times, either with the same or with different players. For example, only a little thought is needed to see that every purchase over the counter at a shop one frequents regularly, in which money is handed over for goods, is a single turn in an iterated PD.

Under fairly common circumstances, there is a far better strategy in the iterated PD than defecting—choosing strategy III—every time. As Robert Axelrod (1984) showed in a series of computer models of repeated PD games, the best strategy is almost always "tit for tat" (TFT). It works like this: cooperate in round one, and then do what your opponent did in the previous round. If in round 1, or in round n, the opponent defected—i.e. tried to take advantage of your cooperation—then on turn 2, or on $n + 1$, you should decline to cooperate, you should defect. Then, if on $n + 1$, the opponent switches to cooperate, on $n + 2$, you should go back to cooperation. The conditions under which Axelrod argued that TFT is the best strategy in the iterated PD include:

1   There is a nonzero probability of playing the game with this opponent again. If this round is known to be the last game, there is no point cooperating in order to encourage further cooperation.
2   The value of the pay-offs to cooperation in the next games is high enough to make it worthwhile taking a risk cooperating in this round in order to send a signal that you may cooperate again in the next round, if the other player cooperates in this one.

In both computer models and PD tournaments among real players, TFT almost always comes out on top. For example, suppose we set up an experiment in which a thousand undergraduates play PD for money 100 times with randomly chosen opponents in the group, in which the pay-off to mutual cooperation is, say, 5 or $5 or some other unit of currency large enough to buy, say, a beer, the pay-off to defecting when the other player cooperates is 10, the pay-off to cooperation when the other player defects is only 1 unit and the pay-off to mutual defection is 3 (Figure 7.2).

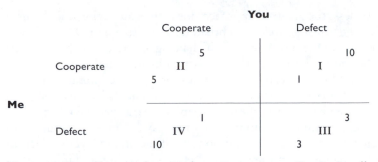

Figure 7.2 Pay-off matrix for a "tit for tat" experiment. Entries in cells show benefit received. (See text for details.)

Suppose that every 10 turns, we eliminate the players whose strategies tied for earning the smallest winnings and increase by the same number the number of players whose strategies secured the highest winnings. This simulates an environment that filters out the less fit and selects for the fitter PD strategies. We can expect the players to employ a variety of strategies, such as always cooperate, always defect, cooperate until first defection and defect thereafter, flip a coin and cooperate if heads, etc. When experiments of these kinds are run, TFT almost always emerges as the winning strategy. That is to say, in experimental circumstances with the sort of pay-offs experimenters can afford to provide, reasonably well-educated people in their late teens (i.e. university students) raised in different cultures all over the world generally find themselves cooperating in the iterated PD. Similarly, when we program computers to simulate such a "tournament" over a wide range of pay-offs, various distributions of alternative strategies, different number of turns in the game, and a diversity of weightings of future pay-offs to present pay-offs, the results come out the same. TFT, the conditional cooperative strategy, wins.

Axelrod explains this result by pointing to three features of this strategy: it is nice, that is it begins by cooperating. Also, it is retaliatory in that it cannot be treated badly more than once without punishing the defector. And it is clear, meaning that opponents do not have to play against it many times to figure it out and fall in with its strategy to their mutual advantage. Of course game theorists have recognized that TFT is not always the best strategy. For example, suppose every player makes mistakes a certain proportion of the time, for example pressing the defect button when they meant to press the cooperate button, simply by accident, once every 10 turns. In an environment that contains mistake-prone players, tit for two tats might do better, as it is slightly more forgiving, and so will not provoke as many mutual defections caused by sheer accident. Or again, suppose for example that the set of players contains some significant number of altruists, who always cooperate, no matter how their opponents have played against them in the past. Under these conditions, a "tat for tit" strategy, of defecting first and then switching to cooperation if the opponent switches to defection, may do better than

TFT. Nevertheless, the Axelrod approach does vindicate reciprocal altruism as likely to be the fittest strategy in a broad range of iterated PD situations.

Iterated PD is not the only game in which being nice to others has a higher pay-off to the individual player than looking out for number one in each game separately. Consider three other games, or strategic interaction problems that game theorists and experimental social scientists have explored. In one called "cut the cake," two anonymous players are each asked to select some portion of a significant amount of money, say $10 or 10 of some other significant currency unit, on the condition that if the other player's selection and theirs adds to more than 10 units, neither gets anything, and if it is equal to or less than 10 units, each receives what they selected. In this game, almost everyone pretty spontaneously asks for half the amount. Consider a second game called "ultimatum." In this game one player, the proposer, specifies how much of the 10 units the other player will receive and how much the proposer will keep. If the second player, the disposer, agrees, each party gets what the proposer decided. If the disposer declines, neither party gets anything. In this game, it would obviously be irrational ever to decline, even a quite unfair split, as even a small portion of the total is better than nothing. And yet, across a broad range of cultures (including non-Western, non-university students) in which even $1/10$ of the total to be divided in the experiment is a nonnegligible amount, parties to the ultimatum game almost always propose a fair split, and reject anything much less than a fair split.

What is interesting about these two experimental results is that the acting on preferences for fair and equal division that each of them reveals has been shown to be the winning strategy. In other words, these strategies have the highest pay-offs in iterated cut-the-cake and ultimatum computer models designed to simulate natural selection acting on self-interested agents or fitness maximizers. Of course, such results are significant for explaining human commitments to fairness or equality only on a number of important assumptions. The pay-offs in the model games must reflect real life alternatives, the interactions have to arise frequently enough in real life so that players' choices have effects on their future opportunities, and the players must be anonymous to one another (otherwise reputations for fairness or selfishness will complicate matters).

A third game could be of particular importance for understanding the emergence of teamwork and other multiple-agent cooperative social practices. It is called the stag hunt, after a thought of the eighteenth century philosopher Jean-Jacques Rousseau: Successfully hunting a deer requires a group to surround it, but each member may be tempted to leave the circle of stag hunters if the prospect of trapping a rabbit arises. So why would a rational agent even begin to hunt the stag if the prospect of at least one other hunter's defecting to trap a rabbit will make the whole stag hunt fail? The game is explained in Figure 7.3.

In this version, if we both go for hare trapping, the result is a smaller pay-off than if only one does, reflecting an assumption that there is some costly

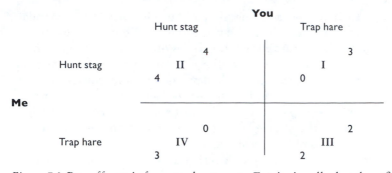

Figure 7.3 Pay-off matrix for a stag hunt game. Entries in cells show benefit received. (See text for details.)

interference between hare trappers. Here, as in the PD, we both prefer box II to box III, but unlike a PD each of us prefers it above all other outcomes. Another important difference from PD is that my best strategy is contingent on what you do. (Recall that in the PD my best strategy is to defect, no matter what you do.) In the iterated stag hunt, there are several potential strategies, including a version of TFT. One is to start out hunting stag, and continue to do so with those who hunt stag with you, but to trap hare when your potential fellow stag hunters switched to hare trapping the last time a stag hunt was undertaken. In general, the conditionally cooperative strategies of stag hunting do far better than invariable hare trapping or strategies that hare trap from time to time or when it appears advantageous. If the stag hunt models the strategic problem facing prehistoric human hunter–gatherers, or perhaps our *Homo erectus* ancestors, then it will be no surprise that social cooperation emerged among them long before the emergence of other forms of life, such as agriculture and the social changes that it produced. And the models show that the emergence of cooperation need not be incompatible with individual fitness maximization. Finally some evolutionary game theorists have also argued that it shows, contrary to Darwin, that we do not need group selection to explain the emergence of other-regarding selflessness of group members. Hunting stag cooperatively is simply better for individual fitness than trapping hare singly.

What the evolutionary game theory models show about dispositions to cooperation, fairness, and equality is that they *could have* arisen by natural selection operating on strategies employed by individual human agents or, for that matter, other organisms (see Skyrms 1996, 2004). But what these models do *not* show is that cooperation, fair dealing, and a preference for equal divisions is, so to speak, *in the genes*! The Darwinian dynamics of removing the less-fit strategies and multiplying the more-fit, which the evolutionary game theorists invoke, can operate over multiple rounds of play in a tournament, just as effectively as it operates over generations of reproduction. It can select for winning strategies and increase their proportions in a population of strategies, on the basis of learning and imitation just as well as differential reproduction. In fact, if we add very simple learning rules to these models, they produce cooperative, fair, and equality-favoring outcomes even more reliably and quickly than pure elimination of less-fit and replication of more-fit strategies at the end of each round. For example, in the ultimatum game, cut the cake, or stag hunt, suppose each player is surrounded by eight neighbors, as on a grid, and we can add to the model the rule: "After each round, switch to the strategy employed by one's most successful neighbor." Under these circumstances, the strategies that adopt short-term altruism almost always do best in terms of long-term self-interest.

One important point to bear in mind is that the Darwinian process of blind variation and selective retention is not restricted to shaping only genetically encoded traits. It is, as we noted in Chapter 3, "substrate neutral." All it needs are replicators and interactors or, equivalently, hereditary variation in fitness. The replicators could just as well be strategies that people (the interactors) hit upon, retain from round to round in iterated interaction (that is "inherit" from themselves, so to speak), discard, and copy from others depending on their success (that is the differential reproduction). We return to this matter in the section on Darwinism without genes below.

There is a second thing to bear in mind about evolutionary game theory, one often raised by skeptics about its explanatory powers and consequently the work it does in reconciling the theory of natural selection with the reality of human cooperation. So far at least, there is little independent evidence that human or infrahuman cooperation arose or is maintained by the operation of mechanisms much like the models developed by evolutionary game theorists. The most powerful arguments so far offered for the explanatory relevance of these models are the computer simulations that theorists have run to explore how robust they are. In particular, human cooperation and the models show similar degrees of sensitivity of cooperative outcomes to variations in the pay-offs, to choice of strategies, and to the number of rounds in a tournament. In other words, the models are evolutionarily plausible. But do they describe the actual evolution of human cooperation? It is not at all clear what sort of evidence could be found that would answer that.

Evolutionary psychology and the argument for innateness

Nevertheless, there is a persistent line of theorizing in social and behavioral science that does attribute the emergence of these dispositions to cooperation, fairness, and equality to genes that have arisen, been transmitted, and been selected for in the same way as other organismic adaptations. These hereditarians reject what they call the "the standard social science model," according to which the mind is—as the British empiricist philosophers supposed—a *tabula rasa*, a "blank slate," meaning that little is "innate," "hardwired," or otherwise genetically preprogrammed. In the standard model, the brain is a kind of general-purpose calculating and learning device.

To the contrary, these "evolutionary psychologists," as they call themselves, argue that the mind and brain are analogous to a "Swiss Army knife," a package of distinct special-purpose instruments, each with its own independent domain of operation, and each the developmental result of a distinct set of genes that were selected for in the environment in which *Homo sapiens* and its immediate ancestors emerged. In other words, on this view, advanced first by Cosmides and Tooby (1992), the brain is composed of functionally specialized *modules*, each of which evolved separately.

The notion of a mental module was introduced by the philosopher Fodor (1983) and has become fashionable among those arguing that many of our behavioral traits are genetically hardwired. As Fodor understood them, a mental module is a kind of biological computer, designed (selected for) to efficiently and quickly solve significant problems in very specific "domains," by processing only a small quantity of the enormous amount of information that may be available to the agent. Modules are required to learn what the environment has to teach us quickly enough for each of us to survive infancy. Accordingly, they will have to be largely hardwired into the brain, will not be consciously implemented or revealed by introspection, and therefore cannot be much influenced by environmental information, conscious or otherwise. In other words, the epistemic powers of mental modules are bounded, or "epistemically encapsulated." One of Fodor's favorite and relatively uncontroversial examples of a module with these features is the part of the brain responsible for visual perception. Given the two-dimensional data available at the retina, this module solves the domain-specific problem of constructing a quite different three-dimensional representation of distances, sizes, and shapes. It does this by processing the retinal image quickly and unconsciously, employing an implicit theory of how the appearance of things is related to how they actually are. The implicit theory is imperfect, of course, so the visual system can be fooled, producing the well-known visual illusions. But, in most circumstances, it works well enough. Now it is uncontroversial that the visual system is the separate and distinct result of selection solving a pressing design problem. The question in dispute between "nativist" evolutionary psychologists and their opponents, the antihereditarians, is how much more of the human mind is composed of such innate modules.

Grounds for nativism include at least one surprising experimental result and one type of general argument. The experimental result is highly relevant to the game-theoretical argument for the emergence of cooperation as an "evolutionarily stable strategy" (ESS) among fitness maximizers. Such a strategy played by members of a group with one another cannot be invaded by an individual playing another strategy that exploits the other player's strategies to its own advantage and their disadvantage. Under many circumstances, "tit for tat" is such a strategy: given a certain set of pay-offs, and a number of iterations of the game, there is no strategy that can do better against it. The strategy is optimal—fittest—in the face of random variations selected for their pay-offs. It is an ESS. Now it is widely recognized that almost all iterated strategic encounters are open to some exploitation by a certain amount of free riding, that is to say defecting, demanding more than a fair share, hare trapping instead of deer hunting, etc. In many reasonable models of these interactions, the cooperative strategy can persist in a stable equilibrium—it will be an ESS—even in the face of a modest amount of cheating, or other short-term selfishness. But under most circumstances, in order to prevent free riding from swamping cooperation over the long run, at least one of three things must be true. Groups of predominant cooperators must send out colonies of predominant cooperators with a frequency sufficient to counteract the rising level of free riding within them, cooperators must find each other and form groups together, or the free riding has to be policed and punished and the free riders shunned in opportunities for cooperative interaction. What this last option requires is a *free-rider-detection device*, and there is some evidence that we have such a device and that it is "hardwired" or genetically encoded (Cosmides and Tooby 1992).

The evidence comes from an experiment called the Wason selection test. In this experiment subjects are asked to solve two problems that are formally the same, i.e. logically identical:

Problem 1 You are a bartender and you must enforce the rule that all beer drinkers are above 18 years of age. There are four persons in the bar: A is possibly underage, B is obviously elderly, C asks for a beer, D asks for a lemonade. Whose identification card should you check to ensure that there is no underage drinking? The answer of course is A and C, and almost every one gets this question right.

Problem 2 There are four cards in front of you, each with a letter on one side and a number on the other. They are marked A, B, 5, and 6. Which cards must you turn over to determine whether the following rule is true: every card with a vowel on one side has an even number on the other? The answer is A and 5, but fewer than 10 percent of subjects get this problem right. Many subjects say that 6 should be turned over to see if it has a vowel or consonant on the back, even though that information does not help determine the truth of the rule. (If it has a consonant on the other side, the rule is not contradicted.) It is the equivalent of carding the person asking for lemonade, who would not be breaking the drinking age rule no matter what age he or she is. And most people miss turning over the 5 card, the equivalent of failing to card the person ordering a beer!

But, logically speaking, the two problems are exactly the same! And yet, even people who have studied logic do no better than others on this problem, on average. What is more, this result is cross-culturally robust. Change the problems in ways that make them familiar across a variety of cultures and groups within them—East/West, developed/less-developed, urban/

rural, educated/uneducated, male/female—and you get the same result. For example, make the rule that if you go to Mecca you must be a Muslim, and Muslims will almost invariably be able to identify who must be checked to enforce such social rules. But across cultures, people cannot similarly solve the logically identical problem in which abstract symbols are substituted for socially significant status markers.

Evolutionary psychologists argue that the universality of this finding suggests that people have an unlearned, hardwired, "domain-specific," cheater detection capacity, one selected for enabling them to monitor social interactions for cooperative rule violations. After all, the only difference between the two problems is the application of reasoning to a problem of cheater detection in a social context that is absent in the other problem. If, cross-culturally, people perform differently on the two problems, then the cause of the performance difference is probably not cultural. Further, the cognitive equipment that solves the cheater detection problem must be different from and independent of general reasoning capacities or whatever we use to solve purely logical problems. Ergo, they reason, there may be an innate, hardwired, genetically encoded, mental module the function of which is to identify in social contexts those people with whom cooperation is profitable and those with whom it is not. And this would enable just the sort of policing capability that would make the evolutionary emergence of a disposition to cooperation, fairness, and equality possible.

The theoretical argument for the claim that our behavior is the result of the operation of cognitive models that are hardwired into our brains by natural selection generalizes one that has been advanced by the linguist Noam Chomsky for the innateness of a language learning module in the human mind. Chomsky's (1980) argument begins by pointing out the "poverty of the stimulus"—that is to say the verbal stimuli that young children use to quickly learn their first language—and the richness of the linguistic competence they acquire in so short a time. Only a year after birth, most children begin to speak their care-giver's language, regardless of their intelligence or the language to which they are exposed, provided that they have been exposed to a minimum amount of that language. (Stunningly, this is true even if the language in the training exposure is highly defective.) Soon thereafter they can encode and decode an indefinitely large number of completely novel and utterly different expressions. More amazingly, they can do this in any of a bewildering variety of alternative grammatical structures, some of which they may have had hardly any exposure to. It was Chomsky's conclusion that this feat was possible only if children came into the world equipped with a hardwired, language-learning device or module, an innately preprogrammed set of rules about language that enable the child very early and quite unconsciously to recognize some of the noise it hears as language. This device further allows the child to frame a series of hypotheses about the grammar of that language, which it then tests against the linguistic and nonlinguistic stimuli of other speakers. In other words, the poverty of the stimulus is made up for by the richness of the child's innate competence. The innateness of a language-learning device is now widely accepted in linguistics and psychology generally.

Chomsky's "poverty of stimulus" argument was so powerful that it spawned arguments for the innateness of a number of other universal human capacities. These arguments claimed that there are parallel "poverties of stimulus" and "richnesses of competence" that would underwrite other attributions of innateness to other human capacities, and thus ground further rejection of the so-called "standard social science model." Evolutionary psychologists have also sought to explain the early and quick emergence of certain phobias about snakes, mushrooms, and other potential threats to health as reflecting the operation of a "folk biology" module. Based on results of infant gaze experiments, they have hypothesized a hardwired "theory of other minds" to explain infants' abilities to attribute motives in human actions. A slightly different argument suggests that there is an innate "folk physics" present in the human mind, and beforehand in the minds of our ancestors. Given the stability of the physical regularities of the world over our evolutionary history, and given how important it has been to learn these regularities and learn them quickly and early in life, it would seem to be more adaptive to have these generalizations hardwired into the brain than for each child in every generation to learn them anew by experience.

In addition to arguments for the innateness of certain cognitive potentials and abilities that shape behavior, there is also an argument for the innateness of certain emotions and other affective psychological phenomena. The universality of certain emotions and the commonality of their expression by humans and other animals was already noticed by Darwin and reported in one of his last books, *The Expression of the Emotions in Man and the Animals* (1872). And the notion that the propensity to feel certain emotions under specific conditions is hardwired and genetically encoded is needed by the evolutionary game theorists to make their models relevant to the emergence of human cooperation. It is easy to see why human beings seldom if ever rely entirely on conscious calculation of long-term advantage to justify their cooperative behaviors. And people rarely free ride or cheat even when they know they can get away with it. Accordingly, conscious calculation of maximum benefit or fitness is by itself insufficient to explain the full extent of actual cooperative behavior. The evolutionary explanations of cooperation therefore need to appeal to selection for a disposition to be emotionally motivated to behave in certain ways that, on average, maximize fitness, an emotional predisposition that is hardwired and modular.

Now, what evolutionary game theory at most shows (provided its assumptions are reasonable) is that if there is anything in the human psychology that causes, or even just encourages cooperative behavior, there will be selection for it, provided that the cooperative behavior is fitness enhancing. Still required is a theory of the innateness of the emotions. The reasoning here is quite similar to the explanation for the near-universality of orgasm among humans. Nature will select for anything that increases reproductive rates, therefore it will select for anything that increases the frequency of sexual relations. Accordingly it will select for those animals that find sex pleasurable, and therefore engage in it with high frequency. Ergo, any physiology that makes orgasm a by-product of sex will be under strong favorable selection and will become nearly universal quite quickly on an evolutionary timescale. The same sort of argument suggests that an invariable linkage between free riding and aversive emotions such as feelings of guilt after free riding or other cheating, or between feelings of sympathy and subsequent acts of sharing, or between the emotions of anger and disdain and the disposition to punish free riding, will be strongly favored by natural selection, owing to the likelihood that they will encourage cooperation. Notice that for such emotions to work effectively to encourage cooperation and discourage selfishness, they will have to be difficult to fake or to suppress even when the agent calculates that it is advantageous to simulate or suppress them. But, the argument goes, only biologically hardwired emotions that are out of conscious control could satisfy this requirement.

Encouraged by these and similar arguments, "innatist" or "nativist" opposition to the so-called standard social science model grew steadily over the last few decades of the twentieth century. The debate between these sociobiologists, evolutionary psychologists, and behavioral biologists on the one hand, and behaviorists, learning theorists, environmental determinists on the other, has become extremely heated and has spilled over from the purely scientific community into the broader academic arena and indeed to a wider public. The reason is pretty clear: "nativism" about socially significant human traits may have profound consequences for public policy, for our choice of strategies for enforcing of social mores and norms, and for people's attitudes and prejudices about others. Nativism explains the distribution of traits as hereditarily fixed, genetically encoded, and adapted by a long process of selection to a local environment. Thus it is easy to infer from such explanations that attempting to eliminate such traits will be harmful or impossible. Accordingly, some nativists argue, society needs to resign itself to their persistence, whether we like them or not.

Among the earliest encouragements to a "nativist" approach to social institutions was the research program aimed at explaining the almost-universal incest taboo. Once Mendelian genetics was combined with Darwin's theory in the early twentieth century, it became apparent that, as a biological practice, incest would be selected against. This is owing to the increased likelihood that the offspring of genetically related individuals will suffer from the expression of recessive fitness-reducing hereditary abnormalities. But this conclusion leaves unanswered the question of how nature implements the avoidance of inbreeding. How do individuals avoid selecting sexual partners when they are such poor detectors of genetic relatedness, indeed when they do not even recognize the connection between sex and procreation, as may be the case in some human groups and undoubtedly in most other species. What is the proximate mechanism for the evolutionarily adaptive pattern of incest avoidance? The most well-confirmed theory of the proximate causes in the human case was proposed by Westermarck (1891), an anthropologist working in the early twentieth century, at the very time Darwin's and Mendel's theories were being harnessed together to explain natural selection against lethal recessive traits. Westermarck's theory suggested that nature solves the problem of incest avoidance by a simple "quick and dirty" solution to the problem of detecting close genetic relatedness. Humans have a hardwired disposition to avoid sex with any person they were reared with during early childhood. By and large in human evolutionary history, co-reared children have been genetically related (community care of unrelated children being a relatively uncommon institution). Thus, Westermarck theorized, simply avoiding sex with any co-reared potential partner is a satisfactory solution to the genetic relatedness problem incest avoidance raises. Evidence for Westermarck's hypothesis has continued to strengthen over the last several decades. For example, when unrelated children are reared together, the frequency of sexual relations among them after puberty is well below normal. For another example, note that the fitness risks of inbreeding for females of polygamous sexual species will in general be greater than for males, since the offspring of any single incestuous union will be a far higher proportion of the female's total number of offspring than of the males. In polygamous species, and perhaps those that have evolved from them (presumably including humans), the Westermarck hypothesis should lead us to expect that females require less co-residence with a potential sexual partner to inhibit sexual relations. And indeed evidence bears this out.

Another case of interest here has to do with the differing reproductive strategies of males and females in many species. In mammals and birds, females typically produce a small number of large ova during their lifetimes, while males produce huge numbers of very small sperm. Thus since typically males can impregnate a large number of females, their fitness-maximizing strategy is to attempt to use all their resources to do so, rather than to mate with just one female and devote resources to their joint offspring. And the universal uncertainty of male paternity adds to the adaptive value of this strategy. By contrast, females have only a limited supply of eggs, so their optimal strategy is to seek mates with "good" genes and in some cases to try to exchange sexual access for the male's long-term commitment to invest resources in her and her offspring. Recent work by ornithologists has also suggested that there is a pay-off to females for undetected "extra pair" copulations with another male who is fitter than the female's partner. According to theory, male birds are already independently under selection for participation in such behavior (as well as to detect or prevent it in other males).

Now consider the inferences that might be drawn for the human case from these fairly robust theoretical claims about these mammals and birds. In humans, the cross-culturally common "double standard" that treats male promiscuity as normal and female faithfulness as the norm has been explained as the evolutionary outcome of differences in egg and sperm number and size. Thus, it is tempting to infer that male marital infidelity is "in the genes," and that it is the result of such a long history of intense selection that there is nothing much that can be done about it. The same goes for the persistence of rape and sexual assault, which are perpetrated almost entirely by males. Further, if these dispositions are in fact firmly entrenched in male psychology by eons of natural selection, then perhaps males who misbehave in these ways should be viewed as victims of their genetic make-up, as not really responsible for their conduct, and therefore to be excused from punishment for it. Thus, the inference from selection for sexual strategies in mammalian males to the explanation of criminal sexual behavior in human males is said by some to encourage complacency about violence against women. Seemingly to some, the only possible conclusion is: "It's inevitable, and all we can expect to do is minimize it. We will never be able to eliminate it."

A similar explanation is advanced for the distribution of gender roles in most societies, in which females typically stay at home and are the primary childcare givers, whereas the males are the out-of-the-house hunters, farmers, craftsmen, traders, etc. These differences are inferred to be the result of natural selection, now fixed by heredity and optimal for men, women, and their children. Gender differences in the norms governing courtship, sex, work, and home, and the distribution of various roles and responsibilities in society between men and women can easily accommodate the adaptive logic that explains sex differences in many other mammalian species. And, again, such explanations are likely to encourage the belief that gender differences in socially significant institutions, norms, and expectations, are genetically determined and have long-term adaptive value. Accordingly, it will be argued by those who take this nativist line, and who approve of conventional gender roles, that attempting to change them may have harmful immediate consequences for the mental and physical health of men, women, and especially children, and perhaps long-term maladaptive consequences in evolution. To antinativists, this makes these arguments controversial.

Of course, it is not just traits deemed adaptive that nativism encourages us to treat as genetic. Alleged differences between groups and genders are also sometimes explained as maladaptations. More than once in the last two generations of social science, it has been argued that (i) intelligence is measured by IQ tests; (ii) racial groups are genetically fairly homogeneous; (iii) mean IQ differences among different racial groups are statistically significant; and therefore, probably, (iv) intelligence is genetically determined and members of some racial groups are on average less intelligent than those of others. The claim is that this is a matter of nature, not nurture. More recently, it has been argued that gender differences in mathematics or spatial reasoning or other cognitive skills are also due to genetically encoded, hardwired differences as a result of selection. Like the two previous arguments, these can also be construed to encourage complacency about inequalities in outcome among men and women or people of various racial groups. If the argument about the genetic basis of intelligence is correct, then even in a society that is truly a color-blind, gender-neutral meritocracy, inequalities will persist and they will reflect real differences in abilities.

Finally, just as there is a tempting Darwinian explanation for reciprocal altruism, and for the psychological predispositions that make it possible, and an argument for the availability of mechanisms for avoiding the suboptimal inbreeding associated with incest, there will be a similar set of considerations that make racism and xenophobia explicable as genetically encoded dispositions. These attitudes may have been selected for in the distant past and, however regrettable, they remain with us now and, adaptive or not, they cannot be quickly or easily eliminated. An adaptive explanation here too is easy to construct. Just as maximizing genetic fitness militates against interbreeding that is too close, there will also be selection against extreme out-breeding, or reproductive relationships far outside of a close kin group. And selection against suboptimal out-breeding will exploit available proximate mechanisms that reduce its likelihood. Among the most obvious such mechanisms will be fear or hatred or other negative emotion toward strangers, and the use of customs, signs, and symbols to identify closely related kin, such as diet, clothing, language, and so on. So positive markers of group membership and negative emotions toward people who are obviously different are to be understood as the result of selection. Further, this process has produced a suite of traits that many might deplore, but to which they may as well resign themselves. Racism, xenophobia, and religious and ethnic prejudices are determined by factors beyond our control, they will always be with us and we should accommodate ourselves to this fact, the argument goes.

This pattern of evolutionary explanations for socially significant traits as individual or group adaptations that fulfill—or once did fulfill—important biological functions is unwelcome to many. In particular, those committed to social change, reform, or revolution to ameliorate the human condition will seek counter-arguments to show such explanations are mistaken. *Mutatis mutandis*, the evolutionary fixity of the status quo is good news—modern reformers argue—only to conservatives eager to defend current social arrangements as optimal or, if not optimal, then at least inevitable.

It is worth noting that there is nothing that logically ties nativism to a politically conservative ideology, nor any logical implication for its repudiation to be found in the denial of nativism. Unwanted traits that are largely genetic in their causal origin can certainly be subject to substantial environmental amelioration, control, or indeed elimination. On the other hand, traits that are largely environmental in their causal origins may prove highly intractable, and their elimination may even turn out to be harmful owing to previously unsuspected side effects. And arguments linking particular nativist theses or their denial with views about public policy will have to be much more sophisticated than those that have dominated the mainstream discussion to date if they are to be sustainable. And they will have to be based on empirical findings that we do not yet have.

Nevertheless, many leading evolutionary biologists have counted themselves among those dissatisfied with the social status quo and eager to ameliorate social problems. And this has motivated them to seek arguments against the general nativist research program—first sociobiology and then its later incarnation, evolutionary psychology. Indeed, the argument of Gould and Lewontin's (1979) influential paper "The spandrels of San Marco and the Panglossian paradigm," which was examined at length in Chapter 3, was motivated as much by a concern to short-circuit nativist arguments as by any other concern. The paper was written in the immediate aftermath of E.O. Wilson's publication of *Sociobiology: the New Synthesis* (1975). Its argument that adaptationist "just so" stories are too easy to construct and even easier to defend against contrary evidence was directed at explanations just like those given in this section. But the "just so" story critique of adaptationism was not the only arrow in the quiver of the opponents of nativism, as we shall now see.

What is wrong with genetic determinism?

The general thesis that some socially significant traits are largely under genetic control and invariant across a range of environmental conditions of development and expression is often called "genetic determinism." As we just noted, it is the consequences of such a thesis for public policy and social attitudes that drives many people to oppose the claim, not just in its individual instances but as a coherent possibility in general. And since the advocacy of genetic determinism often persists even in the absence of evidence for particular cases, it is tempting to accuse its proponents of ideological and political motives. But such accusations will not put an end to the nativist view. And, besides, there are certainly many "nativists" who share the public policy fears of their opponents, and who nonetheless believe that the evidence favors some version of genetic determinism for some traits.

As we saw briefly in Chapter 6, one argument against genetic determinism begins by denying that the concept of a "gene for X" makes any sense, where X is some trait. If the genes play no special role in development, then of course we cannot identify a gene as having a more significant causal responsibility for any trait than any one of several environmental factors also required to bring it into existence. There will be no such thing as the gene or genes for IQ, child rearing, xenophobia, etc. Of course, if the gene does in fact have a special informational role in development of particular traits beyond relatively immediate protein products, then the notion of a "gene for X" might make sense. And if the X refers to socially significant traits such as IQ or child-rearing abilities, then genetic determinism must be taken seriously, with ramifications for ethics and political philosophy, as we discuss in the section on Darwinism and ethics below. One can now see more clearly why the debate over genocentrism has consequences beyond molecular biology.

In any case, the debate about reductionism in genetics suggests that genetic determinism is an improbable thesis anyway. In Chapter 4 we saw the difficulty of individuating genes by reference to their functions, owing first to the need to include a large number of different and disparate nucleic acid sequences in order to actually generate a single specific protein or enzyme, and, second, to the multiple realizability of the same functional gene on a variety of different sequences, and, third, to the fact that the same enzymatic outcome can be the product of a number of different pathways from differing genetic and environmental starting points. In light of the heterogeneity uncovered in molecular genetics, even the notion of the "gene for hemoglobin" or the "gene for sickle-cell anemia" or the "gene for phenylketonuria" (PKU) turns out to be problematic: Where do these genes begin and end? Which regulatory sequences will we consider to be parts of a gene? Are introns parts of genes? What if the introns are required for splicing and regulation?

Consider PKU. As a result of a genetic defect, a child with PKU is unable to produce enough enzyme to metabolize the amino acid phenylalanine and its buildup in the brain leads to mental retardation. This is a clear-cut case of a socially significant developmental defect, but is it genetically determined? It is well known that the syndrome can be avoided by a simple environmental manipulation: keep the child from ingesting phenylalanine. (Notice the label of the next can of diet soft drink that comes into your hands: "Warning to phenylketonurics: contains phenylalanine.") More to the point here, however, the PKU syndrome can be produced by a point mutation in any of a large number of different base-pairs in the genetic material. The syndrome can also result from mutations in genes for the production of any of a variety of enzymes needed to metabolize phenylalanine, and it can result even in what would appear to be a very normal genome if during pregnancy the mother either eats too much phenylalanine or is unable to metabolize it. So, strictly speaking, PKU can have a purely environmental cause and need not be genetically determined at all. And all of these various difficulties for genetic determinism will be vastly multiplied when we move from the relatively simple effects on a known enzymatic product of a gene to the much more complex socially significant traits.

And that is not all. Few of the empirical studies that have claimed to show substantial covariation between a behavioral trait—such as a disposition to violence, or schizophrenia, or alcoholism, or risk taking—and a particular genetic locus have in fact been replicated. As for the IQ studies, suppose we set aside questions about the existence of a single trait properly identified as intelligence (with IQ as a measure of it), or even about a small bundle of more specific cognitive capacities. Even so, the failure of the studies of racial differences adequately to control for systematic environmental differences— e.g. social and familial—between the racial groups from which IQ data is gathered undermines almost all conclusions about genetic determination of intelligence. This point about controlling for environmental variation reveals the importance of another determinant of the phenotype that needs always to be borne in mind when Darwinian theory is applied to social phenomena, the environment. It is universally accepted that all phenotypic traits are the joint product of heredity and the environment—literally all of them. What that means is that there will be no phenotype at all under the various environmental conditions in which the species is not viable. Further, even under a range of environmental conditions that would be considered normal, in which viability is not an issue, the environment can play a considerable role in determining phenotypic outcomes. Many traits are highly "facultative" or environmentally plastic, meaning that the same genotype will result in quite different observed traits under differing environmental conditions. For example, the same species of butterfly will be dark colored if it pupates in winter and light colored if it does so in spring. This means that even if a version of genocentrism can be vindicated that gives content to the notion of a "gene for X," the trait a gene codes for will have to be understood as specified only relative to an environment.

The way in which heritable traits vary in their expression as a function of environmental differences is called "a norm of reaction." For a quantitative trait, such as height, we may graph norms of reaction quite simply. Imagine a graph representing the growth of a plant, perhaps corn. Treat the y-axis as measuring some aspect of phenotype, such as height, and the x-axis as measuring environmental variation, such as annual rainfall, amount of fertilizer used, density of planting, degree of insect infestation, etc. Then the closer to the vertical a norm of reaction is, the more sensitive is the phenotype to environmental variation, and the closer it is to horizontal, the less sensitive is the phenotype. A more nearly horizontal norm of reaction corresponds to what is conventionally thought of as genetically determined. However, for almost any socially significant trait alleged to be genetic in humans, there is almost no evidence about its norm of reaction. And it is obvious why this is so, namely the difficulty, cost, and ethical objections to the experiments that would be required to reliably estimate the norms of reaction for traits such as IQ, schizophrenia, or child rearing. But, without such studies, strong claims that these or other traits are genetic are scientifically irresponsible.

The debate about "genetic determinism" is of course just a modern-dress version of a much older one, the debate about "nature versus nurture." One problem that has long haunted the debate is the lack of clarity and disagreement about the meanings of the key terms "innate" and "acquired" in biology and outside of it. All parties to the dispute about whether any socially significant traits are innate need to accept the fact that phenotypes are the joint products of genes and environment, so that any definition of innateness that could actually apply to any trait will have to accommodate the role of the environment. The same must be said for "acquired." Acquisition of a trait, say by learning, requires some capacities, presumably hardwired, to acquire it. Partly for this reason, and because no single definition for either nature or nurture can be pinned down in ordinary language, and finally because the terms do not appear very frequently in biology (though they certainly do appear in psychology and the social sciences generally), philosophers have considered whether other terms that are to be found in evolutionary biology do the work these terms have been used to do, and whether employing them enables biologists unambiguously to settle questions of nature versus nurture for various traits of interest. However, interestingly, there seems to be no obvious biological alternative to "innate." Simple qualitative identity or similarity from generation to generation—"breeding true," for example—may work for the immediately downstream traits of replicators such as genes but not for a whole organism and its behavior. For one thing, there is the norm-of-reaction issue. When the reaction norm departs much from the horizontal, there will be little similarity of traits despite genetic similarity. If heritability is defined simply in terms of correlation between traits of parent and offspring, instead of their identity, then we will have to treat many traits clearly produced by nurture as "innate." Consider the correlation between a parent's speaking Hausa and his or her children doing so. Surely this is not a matter of hereditary determination. Surely particular languages are not innate. Another possibility is to take the route that population biology offers, defining heritability as a ratio of the amount of variation that is genetic to the total observed phenotypic variation. If the fraction V_g/V_p, genetic variation/phenotypic variation, is close to 1, the phenotypic trait is highly heritable. Of course, even by this definition, heritability can be highly environment dependent. (The ratio can be different in different environments.) Further, as the philosopher André Ariew (1996) has noted, for human populations in which the possession of opposable thumbs is 100 percent, there is no variation, so the denominator is zero. Hence, for most human populations, the heritability of opposable thumbs takes on an undefined value. As such it could hardly do the work that "innate" is supposed to do. Surely opposable thumbs are innate traits among *Homo sapiens*, if ever there were ones.

An alternative approach to understanding innateness has been offered by the philosopher William Wimsatt (1986). His view relies on the fact that our modern understanding of development—of the trajectory an organism follows from embryo to adult—is hierarchical in time. That is to say, capacities, parts, and processes arising later in development are dependent on earlier ones. In humans, for example, the proper development of the brain, a later arising structure, is dependent on the closure of the neural tube early in development. And the development of a particular language late in development (e.g. in late childhood) is dependent on exposure to that language earlier in development (in early childhood). Wimsatt argues that innateness is a matter of degree, and that the degree of innateness of a capacity, part, or process is a function of the degree to which it is "generatively entrenched," in other words, on the extent to which later arising capacities, parts, or processes are dependent on it. Thus, neural tube closure would be more innate than the capacity to speak a particular language, because it is a very early event in development and much of later brain development (including the structures that will later process language) is highly dependent on it. In contrast, capacity to speak a particular language is less innate, in that even in the absence of any language exposure at all, the rest of brain development can proceed fairly normally. Neural tube closure is deeply entrenched in development, and therefore quite innate, whereas acquisition of a particular language is less so.

This approach, Wimsatt argues, gives us most of what we want out of the word innate. Capacities, parts, or processes that are more innate—i.e. more entrenched—will be less variable among individuals, across cultures, and even among species, owing to the fact that the consequences of variation in them are so dire, and therefore variation will have been strongly opposed by selection. Innate capacities will be reliably present, in most individuals, over a broad range of developmental conditions. And less-innate capacities will be more variable, more subject to change, or less reliably present. Accordingly, the failure of neural tube closure is relatively rare, as are other early arising major variations in brain structure, whereas language is quite variable. The great virtue of this approach is that it extracts the issue of innateness from an endless and pointless debate about the relative importance of genes and environment. In Wimsatt's view, crucial inputs early in development would be considered highly innate, regardless of whether their source is genetic or environmental. For neural tube closure, it is known that the risk of closure failure increases as a side effect of certain medications given to a pregnant mother but that there is genetic component to the risk as well. (Interestingly, risk reduction can also be achieved environmentally by adding folic acid to the mother's diet.) But the issue for innateness, in Wimsatt's view, turns on the depth of generative entrenchment and the extent of the downstream consequences of variation, not whether the cause is genetic or environmental. Thus, this approach to innateness acknowledges the complexity introduced by the joint involvement of both genes and environment in the production of every organismal capacity, structure, or process and avoids the difficulties that arise from trying to separate their respective contributions. And it does this while preserving the other most important connotations of the term that make it useful—especially the reduced variability of capacities convention-ally thought of as innate. The drawback, of course, is that it eliminates the definitional connection between innate and genetic, and many will decline to take this approach for that reason.

Recent work by philosophers and biologists (Mameli and Bateson 2006) has canvassed at least two dozen alternative definitions for the terms "innate" and "acquired" to be found in the scientific literature, quite apart from their uses in nonscientific contexts. Given this diversity, it is no surprise therefore that debates about the innateness of traits persist, even when substantial rel-evant evidence has been agreed upon by disputants. The question of whether an agreed-upon set of definitions is possible remains a philosophically open one.

Darwinism without genes

Is the alternative to genetic determinism the repudiation of the relevance of Darwinian natural selection to human affairs? As noted above, the answer is certainly not. Not only do we not need to give up Darwinism if we reject the claim that much human behavior has a genetic basis, in fact we need Darwinism if we are to give any explanation of human behavior at all! Recall that much human behavior and many human institutions show every mark of having functions, sometimes manifest but sometimes only latent. Those social sciences that appeal to functions, especially to latent ones, require some mechanism or other short of final causation to bring about and to maintain those functions. But so far as we know, there is only one such mechanism. If social and behavioral science wants function without genes, then there seems to be no getting around the fact that it needs Darwinism without genes.

One way to see clearly what Darwinism without genes could look like is to consider one worked-out alternative to the evolutionary psychologist's claim that the mind is a set of hardwired modules constructed by the genes. Suppose that the human mind/brain is a single general-purpose learning device that is especially good at learning by imitation, and whose only innate, hardwired modules are the sensory input devices, such as sight, smell, etc., as well as a general learning-by-imitation device of course. In other words, it is not a "Swiss Army knife" style set of domain-specific, epistemically encapsulated modules. So instead of selection for genetically encoded modules, there could have been selection for nongenetically encoded traits, for behavioral predispositions preserved and transmitted outside the brain. The philosopher of biology, Kim Sterelny (2003), has developed a scenario for human evolution in which three factors work together to produce many of the adaptations the evolutionary psychologist is tempted to explain genetically. These are, first of all, the very great developmental plasticity of our brains and its consequent remarkable powers of imitation learning, second, the strong influence on our evolution of cooperation by group selection (reflecting a mechanism of the sort Sober and Wilson [1998] describe, as formalized in the Price equation), and, third—and perhaps most importantly—the construction of relatively long-lasting niches into which subsequent generations are born. These niches will be largely "epistemically engineered" to enable one generation to provide the next generation what Sterelny calls "scaffolded learning," or a learning environment that supports rapid acquisition of the necessary information and skills for survival and reproduction in a social setting. In our own society, this includes parents teaching their children to ride a bicycle, and then providing opportunities to cycle, and so on. It includes teaching them to read, reading to them, providing them with books, giving them opportunities to read, and so on. In the hunter–gatherer environment of human prehistory, scaffolded learning would have employed quite different resources to teach quite different lessons. In effect, scaffolded learning solves the poverty of the stimulus problem for a creature in which a hardwired theory of the world is absent.

Sterelny argues that these three fairly unique factors of human evolution will be mutually reinforcing. As we have seen in our discussion of evolutionary game theory, human cooperation in the long run requires group selection, owing to the subversion problem. This is where the epistemically engineered niche construction—carried on and accumulated over generations—comes into play. For it makes possible the development of learned techniques of free-rider detection and learned enforcement of punishment strategies (policing), along with other strategies that are essential for survival or fitness enhancement. Arguably, scaffolded learning can solve the poverty-of-stimulus problem for all human social competencies except the linguistic one that Chomsky first introduced it to deal with. And group selection plus scaffolded learning also make possible cumulative technological change, specialization of labor, group-strengthening xenophobic traits, and so on, all transmitted culturally and therefore requiring no genetic basis.

Sterelny holds that cultural transmission needs group selection to work. Unless individual teachers receive a fitness pay-off for so doing, there is no fitness benefit to teaching a technological innovation, for example, to non-kin. Teaching to nonkin enhances the fitness of others at one's own expense. In the long run this practice will be selected against, without the guarantee of reciprocation and, Sterelny argues, only group selection can guarantee reciprocity as an evolutionarily stable strategy. So, no cultural evolution without group selection. And the entire process has to get its start from, and continue to be powered by, increasing plasticity in brain development from our primate ancestors through *Homo erectus* and early *Homo sapiens*. For this is what distinguishes us and our primate cousins: at some point in the evolutionary past, we became much more adept at learning by imitation than other primates, and this very general cognitive development, not a suite of separate hardwired modules, may be what made it possible for our ancestors to solve the problems of social living. Indeed, there might be modules, but they are acquired, not inherited.

Thus, on Sterelny's theory, many of the cognitive tasks that evolutionary psychologists believe cried out for a hardwired module, can be accomplished by a genetically unmodularized mind, provided that it is smart enough to quickly assimilate information already generated in previous generations. Testing Sterelny's theory, or for that matter testing the evolutionary psychologist's view, will require some creative experimental studies. And designing them is an important task for both philosophers of biology and biologists. Meanwhile, as noted above, the crucial thing here is that the dispute is a disagreement within Darwinism. Sterelny's view does not deny the theoretical bearing of Darwinism on the elucidation of human capacities and dispositions. The disagreement here is carried on within Darwinism between those who hold that adaptive traits are transmitted genetically, and those who hold that they are transmitted culturally. Both sides agree on the crucial role of blind variation and selective retention in the origin of adaptive cognitive capacities. In this respect, Sterelny's view, despite its reliance on learning, is not just another example of the so-called "standard social science model" that Darwinian nativists repudiate. For it takes sides on the specific mechanism that is responsible for learning and the transmission of learned behaviors, natural selection, in the sense identified by Darwin, but without genes doing the job of transmitting traits across time. In sum, there seemingly must be a Darwinian core in any adequate theory of human psychological traits, not only because humans are after all biological systems, but even more because when it comes to explaining functional psychological traits, there really seems to be no alternative.

Accordingly, biology must be committed not just to a metaphorical application of Darwinian natural selection to the explanation of cultural processes. The applicability of the theory is of course forcefully denied by many social and behavioral scientists who see human affairs, action, and values as standing outside the natural realm, not governed by adaptation through random variation and selective filtration by the environment. This repudiation of the relevance of Darwin's theory, however, will need hard argument, not just wishful thinking. Opponents will have to discover another route for the origin of function. And they will also have to show that the necessary conditions for the operation of natural selection are just not present in culture. One way to do this is to demonstrate that nothing like the replicators and interactors, which make for evolution by natural selection in the wild, are to be found in human culture. If they could do this, there would be no scope for a literal application of the theory.

One obvious objection to a Darwinian account of culture begins by identifying cultural traits that no one would consider adaptive for individuals or groups, that most groups have rightly even considered maladaptive and in fact proscribed, like drug abuse, and that have nevertheless persisted in human society for all of its recorded history and more. Apparently, however, there is a plausible-sounding Darwinian explanation. Consider two dispositions, one with a positive contribution to fitness—such as the disposition to wash hands in hot water before eating—and the other making a negative contribution—such as the disposition to take heroin. The former trait confers an adaptive advantage under most circumstances to people who acquire it, in spite of the costs it imposes (making a fire, collecting the water in a container that can be heated, controlling the heating to prevent the water getting too hot, drying one's hands on clean material, etc.), costs that are certainly something of a barrier to its spread. But if the costs are not too high compared with the benefits, in the long run the frequency of hand washers should increase. If the trait is transmitted quickly and accurately to their offspring (by scaffolded learning), then in the long run the trait should spread in the population because the individuals and their offspring that engage in hand washing will survive and reproduce disproportionately. And presumably the total population size increases as well. Washing hands in hot water is fitness enhancing to those who do it.

By contrast, using heroin is plainly fitness reducing, as it has many unfavorable effects on reproductive success. Yet the trait can spread like wildfire in a population. Once introduced, the practice will be copied, replicated, and spread in spite of the fact that it lowers the reproductive fitness of those who adopt it. Owing to its addictive properties for creatures like us, the practice can be construed as a kind of parasite on *Homo sapiens*. Provided that its virulence is sufficiently moderated, its incidence among potential hosts can increase over time until it becomes fixed in the population, crowding out and interfering with other practices, e.g. hand washing, child care, and often sex for that matter.

So in this view, an evolutionary theory of culture can account for cultural traits by taking into account both their effects on human fitness, and also their effects on their own—the traits'—immediate fitness. But taking this approach creates a graver problem for a Darwinian theory of culture. We have more than once said that the application of the theory to any domain minimally requires that there be heritable variation in the fitness of replicators. Replicators, recall, are units that accurately copy themselves, and build interactors that solve "design problems" well enough to enable their replicators to survive and copy themselves. In biology, genes, at least, play this role. But what plays this role in a Darwinian theory of cultural evolution? If there are no replicators, Darwinian selection is at most a metaphor the application of which to various processes of cultural change may or may not be fruitful and suggestive, but should not be taken seriously as science.

Some exponents of the application of Darwinian theory to explain cultural change have taken this challenge seriously. They have introduced a concept explicitly modeled on the gene to do the work that applying the theory to culture needs: the *meme*, introduced by Dawkins (in his book *The Selfish Gene*, 1976) and defined as "a unit of cultural transmission, or a unit of imitation." This is of course not a very helpful definition. (But then neither was the earliest definition of "gene" as whatever factor or element in the "germ plasm" results in those traits that are distributed in Mendelian ratios.)

Roughly, a meme is something in the brain that causes behaviors, or some feature of behaviors, and that not only recurs in one brain, owing to its behavioral consequences for the agent, but that is contagious and copied in other brains and results in copies of the behavior or its features in others. Dawkins drew examples from animal behavior. Bird songs are copied from generation to generation and are critical to fitness. The song is of course stored in the brain of parent birds and copied by the brains of their offspring. In human culture, a meme might be an advertising jingle that "you can't get out of your head," and that you sing aloud, thereby transmitting it to someone else, who also sings the tune. Or a meme might be an idea about how to dress, which results in others dressing that way and catches on as a fashion, or a way of pronouncing words or making gestures, or, more enduringly, the Arabic system of numerals, or the base ten system of arithmetic, or the rules of addition—in short, anything that can be recorded and stored in the brain, and that increases or decreases in frequency in brains owing to its effects on the people in whose brains it resides. Thus, some memes will be ephemeral, such as "23 skidoo," an expression from the 1920s in the USA, and others long lasting, such as Hamlet's "To be, or not to be" soliloquy. Daniel Dennett, a vigorous exponent of the utility of this concept in the explanation of cultural change, offers *words* generally as an example of memes. In this he follows Darwin, who wrote, "the survival or preservation of certain favored words in the struggle for existence is natural selection" (*Descent of Man*: 343).

It is evident that memes can be ideas, thoughts, beliefs, desires, mental images, formulae, theories, languages and their parts, thoughts about music, art, crafts, farming methods, moral norms, spelling mistakes, board games and field games, swimming strokes, the design of artifacts, dance steps, and all of the adjectival modifications of these and other abstract contents of the mind that result in behaviors of particular sorts. And the neurological structures that realize this heterogeneous set of memes will have to be even more diverse than the diversity of nucleic acid structures that realize genes! But as we saw in Chapter 4, the multiple realizability and supervenience of the genes on diverse sets of contiguous and spatially distributed nucleic acid sequences is very great. So whatever the nature of the structures in the brain that realize memes, they will have to be even more multiply realized and heterogeneous in neural structure, location in the brain, and relation to behavior, that is if there are memes at all! Of course, just as in molecular biology we do not identify genes by their sequences but by their functional roles, mainly by the proteins and RNAs they express, so we should expect to identify memes, if there are any, by their functional roles in producing their selected effects, not by any neural fingerprint. And this taxonomy will also be fearfully heterogeneous!

Though they will be heterogeneous in their neural character, apparently memes will still need to have one thing in common if they are to provide the basis for a Darwinian theory of cultural evolution. They must replicate reasonably accurately. Memes in different heads must be at least fairly accurate copies of the memes in other heads that brought them into existence. The instances or tokens of any one meme will have to be cardinally countable, and there will have to be some basis for distinguishing a token of one meme type from the token of a different type. We will have to be able to count the number of instances of a meme as reflected in the behavior (or perhaps ultimately the brains) of the individuals that the tokens of a given meme type inhabit. For without such criteria of individuation, we will be unable to tell whether a meme has replicated or whether its fitness is increasing or decreasing. We will be unable to distinguish memes from one another in order to discover their competitive and cooperative relations with one another, or dependencies on one another. In short, unless we can be confident about replication and reproduction, memetic evolution by natural selection will be, as we have said, a mere metaphor, not a scientific hypothesis worth taking literally.

So, are there memes? This is obviously a difficult question. We can no more count memes by observing behaviors than we can count genes by observing intergenerational similarities between plants or animals. Even using Mendel's laws to identify genes from the distribution of phenotypic traits depends on the precision and the confirmation of hypotheses about the generation-by-generation distribution of various traits in large populations under a variety of environmental conditions. Presumably, the generalizations of this sort will be much harder to establish in the case of human culture than the case of pea plants! There are several alternatives here. First, it may be the case that within the myriad behaviors that reflect cultural learning to some degree or other, there is a core of memes that are copied accurately enough, that recombine and mutate sufficiently often, to provide the needed substrate for the operation of natural selection to be realized in cultural evolution. And, if so, perhaps we can in fact discover them. This is the most optimistic scenario for the exponent of memetic cultural natural selection. A second, less optimistic scenario for meme theorists is that the operation of natural selection on memes does in fact determine all or a great deal of cultural evolution, but most of the memes are too difficult for us to identify and the process is too complex a matter for us to discern in the blooming, buzzing confusion of cultural change. A third, still less optimistic alternative is the possibility that there are memes, but that their mutation rate is very high, even higher than AIDS virus mutation rates. As such, social evolution will be characterized by a little adaptive improvement and a great deal of mutational drift. This alternative of course will not explain the apparent functional adaptation of so many social processes and institutions. So, even if memes exist, they will not be of much interest to social scientists. Of course if there are some areas of social life in which there is reliable memetic copying and a reasonably moderate rate of evolution, there will be scope for a Darwinian theory. But it will not be a generally accepted account of adaptation everywhere in social phenomena.

Then there is a fourth and even less controversial but also less interesting possibility: the application of natural selection operating on memes to explain culture is a useful and suggestive metaphor at best, but not a general theory of cultural evolution with anything like as much going for it as Darwinism. But this discussion of memes has proceeded on the assumption that the application of Darwinian natural selection to culture really does require a replicator that copies itself accurately in the way that genes do. And not all exponents of the literal application of Darwinism to culture will grant this claim. Some exponents of a literal application of Darwinism to explain cultural evolution consider the entire meme debate to be an irrelevant distraction. They do not think applying Darwinian theory to culture requires the particulate inheritance that memes would provide, and so do not think that their program is hostage to the existence of something in culture that closely parallels the gene. Accordingly to theorists such as Richerson, Boyd, and their collaborators, the units subject to Darwinian natural selection in the evolution of culture need not be much like genes at all. Richerson and Boyd (2005) doubt that what they call "cultural variants" are digital, particulate replicators, largely because they do not think that there is much of anything that is transmitted as intact fair copies from mind to mind. For one thing, there is too much ambiguity and variation in the perception and interpretation behavior to suppose that many different people can extract and internalize exactly the same meme type from observing the behavior of others.

In any case, they argue, Darwinian cultural evolution does not need particulate inheritance. Two alternative possibilities have been explored in mathematical models involving psychological capacities that homogenize or average the continuous—that is nondiscrete—information gleaned from the behavior of others. The models show that given large enough populations, people can share exactly the same trait long enough for it to be selected for or against without anything being accurately copied from any one brain to another! Consider how the social environment helps someone learn a new dance step or fashion by shaping successive attempts positively and negatively until the trait—the step, the look—is identical to its source. These theorists argue that if they are correct, then high-fidelity replicators are not necessary but only sufficient for natural selection, More orthodox Darwinians may call attention to the role in these theories of the psychological machinery that homogenizes disparate cultural variants into classes of behavior similar enough for uniform selection. They may argue that such machinery must be genetic and the product of ordinary natural selection. Such a conclusion bears strong similarities to a nonnativist evolutionary psychology like Sterelny's.

These disputes about memes, cultural variants, whether they are replicators and, if not, whether Darwinian cultural evolution requires replicators have of course made the last half-century's research in the philosophy of biology almost indispensable reading for social scientists.

Darwinism and ethics

As far back as Darwin's time, writers have sought to draw conclusions from his theory for ethics. Most famous of these early writers was Herbert Spencer (1864), who coined the term "survival of the fittest" and argued that Darwin's theory underwrites the thesis that whatever survives in the struggle for existence *should* do so and must be morally superior to whatever does not survive. Furthermore, Spencer's followers argued that failure to recognize this inexorable process results in either morally wrong or at least futile attempts to prevent the inevitable. One ought therefore not to take any altruistic steps to convey resources to the poor or weak, or to cooperate with competitors in the mission of leaving more offspring. This doctrine, which Darwin himself never endorsed, and probably regarded with contempt, should have been called Social Spencerism, for it has no doubt tainted Darwinian science with guilt by association ever since. As we have seen, a great deal of contemporary evolutionary theorizing aims to show that such "dog eat dog" opportunism and refusal to act cooperatively is in fact maladaptive, and loses out ultimately in the "struggle to survive." In this struggle, cooperation can and often does pay, according to Darwin and to latter-day Darwinism.

But there is another question here, one that must first be answered by both the Social Spencerians and the Darwinians. What do concepts such as better and worse, right and wrong, moral and immoral, have to do with evolutionary history? Why is the adaptedness of X relevant to a moral statement, "you ought to do X" or "you ought not do X"? Social Spencerians take for granted that showing self-regard or cooperation to be the result of natural selection, showing them to have been optimal in some sense in the struggle to survive and reproduce, somehow justifies them, somehow adds to the moral authority of these claims. And in fact, there are contexts in which explanations are also justifications, or at least parts of them. But as we can easily see, this is not a general feature of explanations, and when explanations do justify, they do so in virtue of further additional considerations beyond the wholly explanatory or causal. Consider the following case of an explanation that is completely nonjustificatory: some people purchase lottery tickets and believe sincerely that they will win, perhaps because the number they selected is their birthday or phone number. But this explanation does not justify the belief, even if the person wins. On the other hand, sometimes identifying the cause of a belief is justificatory at least to the extent of providing grounds for its truth. I may justify my belief that there is a tree in front of me by giving a causal account of why I came to believe this, an account that includes the way my optical system operates under normal circumstances to cause my visual beliefs, the presence of standard conditions of visual observation that cause perceptions usually to be accurate, along with my perception of a tree before me. All these factors are part of the explanation of my belief as well as part of its justification.

Similarly, a Social Spencerian argues that explaining the origin of moral values in terms of natural selection contributes to the justification of these values (assuming the explanation is correct). The argument is that the judgment that "doing X is right" is likely correct, because it is the product of a causal history in which natural selection favored correct beliefs over incorrect ones, just as it did in the visual system.

But it turns out that this argument, and others like it, have a hidden defect, one that was pointed out by David Hume in the eighteenth century. Evolutionary theory, like any other scientific theory, is a body of factual claims about what *is* the case. Of course, like other factual claims, they may be false, or we may lack good evidence for them, or no one may believe them at all. But their truth or falsity turns on facts about what has happened or will actually happen in the world. They are descriptive statements.

But ethical claims are not descriptive. They are always, explicitly or implicitly, claims about what *ought* to be the case. They are normative or evaluative claims, about what is right, or good, or just, or fair, or virtuous, or valuable in itself. Sometimes, ethical claims are expressed explicitly in the imperative mood: "Thou shalt not commit adultery." Often they are implicitly imperative: "Adultery is wrong." Sometimes they look like descriptive claims: "Pleasure is (intrinsically) good, that is to say good in itself and not just as a means to something else." But the key fact about all normative statements appears to be that the way things turn out in the world has nothing to do with whether we accept them as true or well grounded, justified or correct, as opposed to false or ungrounded, unjustified or incorrect. To see this consider, would adultery still be wrong if no one ever committed it? Would it still be wrong if everyone always committed it? Would it still be wrong if everyone committed it, and their spouses never knew, and there were no unwanted pregnancies that resulted from it, and there were no other consequences? The answer to these questions, for those who accept the Seventh Commandment, for example, is obviously yes, which shows that the way things *do* turn out in the world just does not have anything to do with the way they *should* turn out from the moral point of view. Hume seems to have been the first philosopher to notice this gap between facts and values, between the descriptive and the normative, between the positive and the evaluative. And he noticed that, as such, statements about what ought to be the case, what is right to do, or what is morally, intrinsically good, can never follow from descriptive truths about the world, about the way the facts turn out. He wrote (and we interpolate to make his claim plainer to modern ears):

> In every system of morality, which I have hitherto met with, I have always remark'd [noticed], that the author proceeds for some time in the ordinary way of reasoning, and establishes the being of a God, or makes observations concerning human affairs [statements of alleged facts]; when of a sudden I am surpriz'd to find, that instead of the usual copulations of propositions *is*, and *is not* [statements that something *is* or *is not* the case], I meet with no proposition that is not connected with an *ought*, or an *ought not* [statements that something ought to be the case]. This change is imperceptible; but is, however, of the last consequence. For as this ought, or ought not, expresses some new relation or affirmation [not an assertion of facts], 'tis necessary that it shou'd be observ'd and explain'd; and at the same time that a reason should be given, for what seems altogether inconceivable, how this new relation [a statement of what should be the case] can be a deduction from others [statements of what is the case], which are entirely different from it. But as authors do not commonly use this precaution, I shall presume to recommend it to the readers; and am persuaded, that this small attention wou'd subvert all the vulgar systems of morality.
>
> (Hume 1738: *Treatise* 3.1)

Hume's point has often been described as the condemnation of the "naturalistic fallacy," which is the fallacy of reasoning from some factual claim about nature—human nature or the nature of the world—to some normative conclusion about what ought to be the case. There is a gap, Hume argued, between what "is" and what "ought to be" the case—his famous is–ought gap.

If Hume is correct, then all those who have attempted to erect a normative or moral theory on the foundations of Darwin's purely descriptive theory of how adaptation emerges, are guilty of a fallacy. In particular those who argue that the emergence through natural selection of our cooperative norms, our commitment to justice and fairness and the emotions that enforce them implies that these norms are the right ones, have committed the naturalistic fallacy. One way to see this clearly is to consider how the Darwinian explanation for the emergence of these norms and emotions runs. It tells us that they emerged owing to the advantages in reproductive fitness that they provided. Now, one may well ask, "What's so good about reproductive success?" "Why ought we care about whether we have more grandchildren or fewer grandchildren?" There is nothing intrinsically valuable about having descendants. It may well make a person feel good to have descendants (indeed, we have been selected to feel good about having descendants). It may ensure that we provide care to our descendants in their youth. It may provide an incentive to earn, save, and bequeath wealth to kin. But none of these consequences make maximizing one's descendants the morally right choice! Surely people who decide to have no offspring at all are not making a morally wrong choice.

What about the argument that failure to act cooperatively, justly, and morally may endanger the entire species of *Homo sapiens* along with other species on our planet? Suppose that the theory of natural selection gives grounds to suppose that our own extinction would result from failure to act in accordance with some set of moral rules. Would this underwrite the rules or afford them grounds or justification? Well, as Hume also wrote, " 'Tis not contrary to reason to prefer the destruction of the whole world to the scratching of my finger" (*Treatise* 3.3). Some translation to modern terms is needed here. Clearly by "not contrary to reason" Hume did not mean merely "not unreasonable," in the standard sense of this word today. Obviously, it is much more "reasonable" to prefer the scratching of my finger. He meant something more like "not illogical." There is no violation of logic in preferring the destruction of the world to the scratching of my finger. Thus, given Hume's argument, the theory of natural selection could provide support for rules or practices or institutions that prevent our extinction *only* if we add to them the further premise that the survival of the species in question is morally good, or morally required, or some other such normative premise. Without an added normative premise, we cannot infer a normative conclusion. That is the point of Hume's is–ought argument. And the theory of natural selection has no normative component, hidden or obvious, implicit or explicit.

The influential evolutionary biologist E.O. Wilson (1986) has argued that owing to our evolutionary origins and our shared common ancestry and coevolution with all other species on Earth, humans have an innate unconscious need for the Earth's biota that translates into protective sensitivity to it. Wilson calls this trait of ours, "biophilia." He prizes it and hopes to ground agreement to policies of environmental conservation on this trait. Hume and those who follow his critique of the naturalistic fallacy might well endorse and accept Wilson's values as their own, and even accept a Darwinian explanation for why they embrace biophilia. But they will insist that by itself the adaptive evolutionary history of the value does not demand that we should embrace it, or require that we endorse any policy that encourages such environmental objectives. Doing either of these is moving from "is" to an "ought." And the only way to arrive at some statement couched in the language of moral obligation is to start from such a statement. And there are none in evolutionary biology, or anywhere else in descriptive science.

Indeed, matters may be worse for those who accept the view that Darwinian theory can provide an explanation for why we, *Homo sapiens*, do act morally and why we believe that our morality is well grounded. If Darwinian theory can explain our moral norms, does it not also threaten to explain them away? Recall the Darwinian argument that natural selection helps justify the moral norms of cooperation, fairness, and justice. But we know perfectly well, that many beliefs are highly adaptive for humans without being justified or morally acceptable. Consider some examples. It is said that the prohibition on eating pork among Muslims and Jews was highly adaptive historically in at least two ways. It reduced the incidence of trichinosis among those who obeyed it, and it also tended to protect the grazing lands of the inhabitants of the semi-arid Middle East by reducing the demand for a domestic animal known to harm such environments. But the belief that eating pork is morally wrong is certainly not justified by these ecological facts. Or consider two even clearer cases already discussed in this chapter. The incest taboo is nearly universal, but we now have a good understanding of why belief in the norm was selected for, and we know that it is not really belief in the norm that motivates most persons to act in accordance with it. If Westermarck's hypothesis is correct, even people without any objection to incest will avoid it owing to nature's quick and dirty solution to the problem of inbred recessives. The incest taboo, so far from being underwritten by natural selection, is shown by it to be a mere rationalization for a disposition that we have been selected to have. Or consider the adaptational advantage that xenophobia and racism provide to members of human groups who embrace such unethical norms. Does this adaptive advantage in some environments show such norms to be morally right in those environments?

These cases show how natural selection explains norms such as incest avoidance or racism or dietary restrictions without justifying them. Indeed, it explains them away. It shows that they do not have the sort of grounds, force, or warrant that those who believe in them suppose. But the very same thing may well turn out to be true for those ethical claims that we do endorse, and suppose ourselves to be right in endorsing. If we become convinced that the long-term cause of our acceptance of the moral norms with which we were raised is their pay-off in local adaptation, we will have to conclude that in some actual and possible local environments they will not be adaptive but maladaptive for creatures like us. We will also be able to see that relatively few apparently intractable moral disagreements among people from vastly different cultures living in quite different environments may be easily explained by the adaptive fit of their different moral commitments to the very different design problems faced in these environments.

In all this explanatory work, Darwinian natural selection has no need of the hypothesis that any moral norms are true and justified. And if it does not need this hypothesis, then the hypothesis is one the biologist qua biologist has no reason to believe. Thus, the application of the theory of natural selection to ethics not only fails to justify our morality, it threatens to undermine it, to go a long way towards endorsing moral skepticism or moral relativism, according to which nothing is really *forbidden*.

As moral skepticism is no more popular a doctrine among philosophers than it is among biologists or other people, this line of argument sets a serious problem for the philosopher and the biologist to solve. Some easy solutions are obvious but unsatisfactory. One very popular way of short-circuiting the argument from the Darwinian explanation of ethics to its explaining ethics away is simply to reject Hume's argument against the naturalistic fallacy. But no one has yet offered a nonquestion-begging counter-argument to Hume, though influential philosophers of biology and social theorists have tried.

There is another route to a biologically based morality, one that does not involve evolutionary justification and that Hume himself took. One begins by acknowledging the is–ought gap to be unbridgeable by logic, but arguing that nature simply avoids it, taking an end-run around it, without bridging it. The moral sentiments are, for us, natural facts arising from our evolved feelings. So "X is good," means I prefer X and, if you are a human being with similar evolved feelings, you do also. That preference is simply handed to us, without justification. The moral preferences are for us like the facts of our anatomy and physiology, not the sort of thing that can have any justification, or that needs any for that matter. We do not see the need to justify our having two hands, instead of some other number, for example. We can explain having two hands, in evolutionary terms perhaps, but not justify it in any sense. This route is not without its problems. Our nature demands contradictory things sometimes. We seem to have a natural affinity for notions of equality but also some natural antipathy toward strangers. We favor justice but we are also somewhat xenophobic, and these contradictions can lead to moral dilemmas. Another problem is that the demotion of morality to species-normal preferences might seem to trivialize it. If Hume is right, there are no values out there in the world anywhere, not embedded in the mind of God, nor in nature, nor in reason. Values are emotional responses to the world, and therefore entirely in our heads. Worse, they are entirely local to a given species at a given time in its evolutionary history. A different species would have different moral emotions. And at other times in our own evolutionary history, our moral preferences could have been different. And then, of course, there is the problem of the variability of the emotions within a species. Some see the moral sentiments as quite variable among cultures, and even within cultures over time, denying in effect that there is anything like a species-normal human moral nature. The argument at this point enters the domain of moral philosophy, taking it beyond the scope of this book. Here the point is just that the is–ought gap does not preclude a biologically based morality, even if it forbids an evolutionary justification for one.

Summary

It is hard to deny that most of the phenomena that social and behavioral science deals with are adaptations or functions. As such they require causal, nonpurposive, nonteleological explanations. Some human institutions, such as the United Nations or a joint stock company, that are the result of conscious, intentional design may not need such explanations, but these artificial constructions are the exception in human affairs, not the rule. If Darwin's theory of natural selection is "the only game in town," the only explanation available for the appearance of conscious design, without the reality of it, then it must play an important role in the social and behavioral sciences.

In this chapter we have explored the problems that its playing such a role raises for the theory of natural selection, and the way in which those social scientists who employ it have attempted to deal with these problems. By and large, social scientists are "nurturists." They hold that most of our socially significant traits are learned, derived from experience, in other words, that they are not innate. This, in the view of many, already severely limits the scope for evolutionary theory in human affairs. Some exponents of the relevance of natural selection to human behavior reject this implication, and also environmentalism, and they offer strongly nativist accounts of important human traits, beginning with language. Others try to build theories of cultural evolution free from any commitment to the genetic determinism or fixity of important human traits. This stratagem has obvious attractions in light of the need for a causal theory of unconscious or latent adaptations in social structures, institutions, and human behavior, and has led to some novel explorations of the foundations of the theory of natural selection. Finally, in this chapter we identified the features of moral philosophy and Darwinism that make for a fatal attraction between them, and considered whether there are alternative ways to construct a biological ethics.

Suggestions for further reading

The classic argument for functional social science is Durkheim's *The Rules of Sociological Method*. Jon Elster's *Nuts and Bolts for the Social Sciences* is an excellent introduction that makes clear the need such theories have for a Darwinian mechanism.

The combination of Darwinian biology and game theory in explaining human cooperation begins with Robert Axelrod's *The Evolution of*

Cooperation. Some of the most philosophically interesting modeling of the evolution of social norms and institutions is to be found in two books of Brian Skyrms, *The Evolution of the Social Contact* and *The Stag Hunt and the Evolution of Social Structure.*

Sociobiology began with a big book by that name by Edward O. Wilson, and it was subject to withering criticism by Philip Kitcher, much of it motivated by moral outrage, owing to anxiety about the prospects for genetic determinism it is feared that Wilson's views may encourage. The two names most closely connected with arguments for evolutionary psychology are Leda Cosmides and John Tooby, whose latest work is available online at *www.psych.ucsb.edu/research/cep/primer.html.* Their critics are legion but often intemperate. A reliable place to begin for criticisms is Fiona Cowie's *What's Within? Nativism Reconsidered.* Kim Sterelny's prize-winning alternative is *Thought in a Hostile World.*

Among the most important recent works in the application of the theory of natural selection to explain cultural evolution, the place to start is Peter J. Richerson and Robert Boyd's *Not By Genes Alone.* There are a number of useful introductions to this theory and others similar to it, including Kevin Laland and Gillian Brown's *Sense and Nonsense: Evolutionary Perspectives on Human Behavior.*

Paul Thompson's *Issues in Evolutionary Ethics* reprints many of the most important papers on Darwinism and moral philosophy. Richard Joyce's *The Evolution of Morality* is a contemporary defense of moral skepticism advanced from a Darwinian point of view. The last three chapters of Dennett's *Darwin's Dangerous Idea* argue that natural selection leaves ethics pretty much alone. And see Robert McShea's *Morality and Human Nature* for an updated version of Hume's moral argument.

Bibliography

Agar, Nicholas, 2001. *Life's Intrinsic Value*. New York: Columbia University Press.

Allen, C., M. Bekoff, and A. Lauder (eds) 1998. *Nature's Purposes: Analyses of Function and Design in Biology*. Cambridge, MA: MIT Press.

Amundsen, Ron and George Lauder, 1994. Functions without purpose: the uses of causal role function in evolutionary biology, *Biology and Philosophy* 9: 443–469.

Ariew, André, 1996, Innateness and canalization, *PSA 1996*: 19–27.

Ariew, André, Robert Cummins, and Mark Perlman (eds) 2002. *Functions: New Essays in the Philosophy of Psychology and Biology*. Oxford, Oxford University Press.

Axelrod, Robert, 1984. *The Evolution of Cooperation*. New York: Basic Books.

Ayala, F.J., 1974. The concept of biological progress, in F.J. Ayala, T. Dobzhansky (eds) *Studies in the Philosophy of Biology*, 19. New York: Macmillan, pp. 339–55.

Behe, M.J., 1996. *Darwin's Black Box*. New York: The Free Press.

Carroll, L., 1960. *The Annotated Alice*. New York: Bramhall House. [1872]

Barkow, Jerome, Leda Cosmides, and John Tooby, 1992. *The Adapted Mind*. New York: Oxford University Press.

Beatty, John, 1984. Chance and natural selection, *Philosophy of Science* 51: 183–211.

Bouchard, F. and A. Rosenberg, 2004. Fitness, probability and the principles of natural selection, *British Journal for the Philosophy of Science* 55: 693–712.

Brandon, Robert N., 1990. *Adaptation and Environment*. Princeton, NJ: Princeton University Press.

Brandon, Robert N., 2006. The principle of drift: biology's first law, *The Journal of Philosophy* 102: 319–335.

Buss, L., 1987. *The Evolution of Individuality*. Princeton, NJ: Princeton University Press.

Campbell, D.T., 1974. Evolutionary epistemology, in P.A. Schilpp (ed.) *The Philosophy of Karl Popper*. La Salle, IL: Open Court Publishing, pp. 413–463.

Campbell, Richmond and Jason Robert, 2005. The structure of evolution by natural selection, *Biology and Philosophy* 20: 673–696.

Cartwright, Nancy, 1983. *How the Laws of Physics Lie*. Oxford: Oxford University Press.

Cartwright, Nancy, 1999. *The Dappled World: A Study of the Boundaries of Science*. Cambridge, Cambridge University Press.

Chomsky, N., 1980. *Rules and Representations*. Oxford, Basil Blackwell.

Cosmides, Leda and John Tooby, 1992. The psychological foundations of culture, in Jerome Barkow, Leda Cosmides, and John Tooby (eds) *The Adapted Mind:*

Evolutionary Psychology and the Generation of Culture. New York: Oxford University Press.

Cowie, Fiona, 1998. *What's Within? Nativism Reconsidered.* Oxford: Oxford University Press.

Crick, Francis H.C., 1958. The biological replication of macromolecules, *Symposia of the Society of Experimental Biology* 12: 138–163.

Cummins, Robert, 1975. Functional analysis, *Journal of Philosophy* 72: 741–64.

Darwin, Charles, 1859. *On the Origin of Species.* John Murray, London [1964 facsimile edition, Cambridge, MA: Harvard University Press].

Darwin, Charles, 1871. *The Descent of Man*, London: John Murray.

Darwin, Charles, 1872. *The Expression of the Emotions in Man and the Animals.* London: John Murray.

Dawkins, Richard, 1976. *The Selfish Gene.* Oxford: Oxford University Press.

Dawkins, Richard, 1982. Replicators and vehicles, in King's College Sociobiology Group (ed.) *Current Problems in Sociobiology.* Cambridge: Cambridge University Press, pp. 45–64.

Dawkins, Richard, 1986. *The Blind Watchmaker.* New York: Norton.

Dawkins, Richard, 1994. Burying the vehicle, *Behavioral and Brain Science*, 17: 616–617.

Dawkins, Richard, 1995. *River out of Eden.* New York: Basic Books.

Dawkins, Richard, 1999. *The Extended Phenotype.* New York: Oxford University Press.

Dennett, Daniel, 1969. *Content and Consciousness.* London: Routledge & Kegan Paul.

Dennett, Daniel, 1995. *Darwin's Dangerous Idea: Evolution and the Meanings of Life.* Harmondsworth: Penguin.

Dretske, Fred I., 1988. *Explaining Behavior.* Cambridge, MA: MIT Press.

Dupré, John, 1987. *The Latest on the Best: Essays on Evolution and Optimality.* Cambridge, MA: MIT Press.

Durkheim, Emile, 1897 [1956]. *Suicide.* Glencoe, IL: Free Press.

Durkheim, Emile, [1962]. *The Rules of Sociological Method*, 8th edition, transl. Sarah A. Solovay and John H. Mueller, ed. George E.G. Catlin. New York: Free Press of Glencoe.

Eldredge, Niles and Stephen J. Gould, 1972. Punctuated equilibria, in T.M. Schopf (ed.) *Models in Paleobiology.* San Francisco, CA: Freeman, Cooper & Co.

Elster, Jon, 1989. *Nuts and Bolts for the Social Sciences.* Cambridge: Cambridge University Press.

Fisher, D.C., 1986. Progress in organismal design, in D.M. Raup and D. Jablonski (eds) *Patterns and Processes in the History of Life.* Berlin: Springer-Verlag, pp. 99–117.

Fodor, Jerry A., 1974. Special science, or the disunity of science as a working hypothesis. *Synthese* 28: 97–115; reprinted in Ned Block (ed.) 1980. *Readings in the Philosophy of Psychology*, Vol I. Cambridge, MA: Harvard University Press.

Fodor, Jerry A., 1983, *The Modularity of Mind.* Cambridge, MA: MIT Press.

Fodor, Jerry A., 1990. *A Theory of Content and Other Essays.* Cambridge, MA: MIT Press.

Ghiselin, Michael T., 1969. *The Triumph of the Darwinian Method.* Berkeley, CA: University of California Press

Ghiselin, Michael, T., 1974. A radical solution to the species problem, *Systematic Zoology* 23: 536–544.

Goodwin, B.C., 1996. *How the Leopard Changed Its Spots*. New York: Simon & Schuster.

Goudge, T., 1956. *The Ascent of Life*. Toronto: University of Toronto Press.

Gould, Stephen J., 1977. *Ever Since Darwin*. New York: Norton.

Gould, Stephen J., 1988. On replacing the idea of progress with an operational notion of directionality, in M.H. Nitecki (ed.) *Evolutionary Progress*. Chicago: University of Chicago Press, pp. 319–338.

Gould, Stephen J., 1989. *Wonderful Life*. New York: Norton [2nd edition, 2000, London: Vintage].

Gould, Stephen J., 1980. *The Panda's Thumb: More Reflections in Natural History*. New York: Norton.

Gould, Stephen J., 1996. *Full House*. New York: Harmony Books.

Gould, Stephen J., 2002. *The Structure of Evolutionary Theory*. Cambridge, MA: Harvard University Press.

Gould, Stephen J. and Richard Lewontin, 1979. The spandrels of San Marco and the Panglossian paradigm: a critique of the adaptationist programme, *Proceedings of the Royal Society of London B* 205: 581–598.

Gould, Stephen J. and Elizabeth S. Vrba, 1982. Exaptation: a missing term in the science of form, *Paleobiology* 8: 4–15.

Griffiths, Paul, 2001. What is innateness? *The Monist* 85: 70–85.

Griffiths, Paul and Russell Gray, 1994. Developmental systems and evolutionary explanation, *Journal of Philosophy* 91: 277–304.

Griffiths, Paul and Eva M. Neumann-Held, 1999. The many faces of the gene. *BioScience* 49: 656–662.

Hamilton, William D., 1964. The genetical evolution of social behaviour, I and II, *Journal of Theoretical Biology* 7: 1–16 and 17–52.

Hamilton, William D., 1996. *The Narrow Roads of Gene Land*. New York: Oxford University Press.

Hodge, J. and G. Raddick, 2003. *The Cambridge Companion to Darwin*. Cambridge: Cambridge University Press [2nd edition, 2007].

Hull, David L., 1978. A matter of individuality, *Philosophy of Science* 45: 335–360; reprinted in Sober, Elliottt (ed.) 1994. *Conceptual Issues in Evolutionary Biology*, 2nd edition. Cambridge, MA: MIT Press.

Hull, David L., 1988. *Science as a Process*, Chicago: University of Chicago Press.

Hull, David L. and Michael Ruse (eds) 1998. *The Philosophy of Biology*. Oxford: Oxford University Press.

Hume, David, 1738 [1939–40]. *A Treatise of Human Nature* [2nd edition, 1978, revised by P.H. Nidditch, Oxford: Oxford University Press].

Huxley, J., 1942. *Evolution, the Modern Synthesis*. London: G. Allen & Unwin.

Jablonski, D., 2005. Mass extinctions and macroevolution. *Paleobiology* 31:192–210.

Joyce, Richard, 2006. *The Evolution of Morality*. Cambridge, MA: MIT Press.

Kant, I., 1790 [2005]. *The Critique of Judgment*, Cambridge: Cambridge University Press.

Kauffman, Stuart A., 1993. *The Origins of Order: Self-organization and Selection in Evolution*. New York: Oxford University Press.

Kauffman, Stuart A., 1995. *At Home in the Universe: The Search for the Laws of Self-organization and Complexity*. New York, Oxford University Press.

Kim, Jaegwon, 1993. *Supervenience and Mind*. Cambridge: Cambridge University Press.

Kim, Jaegwon, 1999. *Mind in a Physical World*. Cambridge MA: MIT Press.

Kitcher, Philip, 1984. 1953 and all that: a tale of two sciences, *Philosophical Review* 93: 335–373.

Kitcher, Philip, 1995. *The Advancement of Science*. New York, Oxford University Press.

Kitcher, Philip., 1999. The hegemony of molecular biology. *Biology and Philosophy* 14: 195–210.

Laland, Kevin N. and Gillian R. Brown, 2002. *Sense and Nonsense: Evolutionary Perspectives on Human Behavior*. Oxford: Oxford University Press.

Lamarck, J.B.P.A.M., 1809. *Zoological Philosophy*. [1963 translation, New York: Hafner Publishing].

Lange, Marc, 2007. *Natural Laws in Scientific Practice*. New York: Oxford University Press.

Levins, R., 1993. A response to Orzack and Sober: formal analysis and the fluidity of science, *Quarterly Review of Biology* 68: 547–555.

Levins, R., 1966, The strategy of model building in population biology, *American Scientist* 54: 420–431.

Levi-Strauss, C., 1949 [1971]. *The Elementary Structures of Kinship*, Boston, MA: Beacon Press.

Lewens, Walsh and André Ariew, 2002. The trials of life: natural selection and random drift, *Philosophy of Science* 69: 429–446.

Lewontin, R., 1970. The units of selection, *Annual Review of Ecology and Systematics* 1: 1–18.

Lewontin, R., 1978. Adaptation, *Scientific American* 239: 212–228.

Lovejoy, O., 1936. *The Great Chain of Being*. Cambridge, MA: Harvard University Press.

McLaurin, James, 2002. The resurrection of innateness, *The Monist* 85: 105–130.

McShea, Daniel W., 2001. The hierarchical structure of organisms: a scale and documentation of a trend in the maximum. *Paleobiology* 27: 405–423.

McShea, Robert, 1990. *Morality and Human Nature*. Philadelphia: Temple University Press.

Mameli, M. and Bateson, P., 2006. Innateness and the sciences, *Biology and Philosophy* 21: 155–188.

Maynard Smith, John, 1970. Time in the evolutionary process, *Studium Generale* 23: 266–272.

Maynard Smith, John and Eörs Szathmáry, 1995. *The Major Transitions in Evolution*. Oxford: W.H. Freeman.

Maynard Smith, John and Eörs Szathmáry, 1999. *The Origins of Life*. Oxford: Oxford University Press.

Mayr, E., 1982. *Growth of Biological Thought*. Cambridge, MA: Harvard University Press.

Miller, K., 2004. The flagellum unspun, in W. Dembski and M. Ruse (eds) *Debating Design*. New York: Cambridge University Press.

Millikan, Ruth, 1984. *Language, Thought and Other Biological Categories*. Cambridge, MA: MIT Press.

Nitecki, Matthew H., 1988. *Evolutionary Progress*. Chicago: University of Chicago Press.

Okasha, Samir, 2001. Why won't the group selection controversy go away? *British Journal for the Philosophy of Science* 52: 25–30.

Okasha, Samir, 2006. *Evolution and the Levels of Selection*. Oxford: Clarendon Press.

Orzack, Steven and Elliott Sober (eds) 2001. *Adaptationism and Optimality*. Cambridge: Cambridge University Press.

Paley, William, 1809. *Natural Theology or Evidences of the Existence and Attributes of the Deity*, 12th edition. London: J. Faulder.

Plutynski, Anya, 2005. Parsimony and the Fisher–Wright debate, *Biology and Philosophy* 20: 697–713.

Price, G.R., 1971 [1995]. The nature of selection, *Journal of Theoretical Biology* 175: 389–396.

Richerson, Peter J. and Robert Boyd, 2005. *Not by Genes Alone*. Chicago: University of Chicago Press

Rosenberg, Alex, 2007. *Darwinian Reductionism or How to Stop Worrying and Love Molecular Biology*. Chicago: University of Chicago Press.

Rosenberg, Alex and Yuri Balashov, 2002. *Philosophy of Science: Contemporary Readings*. London: Routledge

Ruse, Michael, 1979. *The Darwinian Revolution*. Chicago: University of Chicago Press.

Ruse, Michael, 1996. *Monad to Man: The Concept of Progress in Evolutionary Biology*. Cambridge, MA: Harvard University Press.

Samson, Roger, 2003. Constraining the adaptationism debate, *Biology and Philosophy* 18: 493–512.

Sarkar, Sahotra, 1998. *Genetics and Reductionism*. Cambridge: Cambridge University Press.

Schaffner, Kenneth, 1993. *Discovery and Explanation in Biology and Medicine*. Chicago: University of Chicago Press.

Simpson, George G., 1967. *The Meaning of Evolution*. New Haven, CT: Yale University Press.

Skyrms, B., 1996. *The Evolution of the Social Contract*, Cambridge: Cambridge University Press

Skyrms, B., 2004. *The Stag Hunt and the Evolution of Social Structure*. Cambridge: Cambridge University Press.

Smart, J.J.C., 1963. *Philosophy and Scientific Realism*. London: Routledge.

Sober, Elliott, 1984. *The Nature of Selection*. Cambridge, MA: MIT Press.

Sober, Elliott, 1993. *The Philosophy of Biology*, Boulder, CO: Westview.

Sober, Elliott (ed.), 1994. *Conceptual Issues in Evolutionary Biology*, 2nd edition. Cambridge, MA: MIT Press.

Sober, Elliott, 1999. The multiple realizability argument against reductionism. *Philosophy of Science* 66: 542–564.

Sober, Elliott and Richard Lewontin, 1982. Artifact, cause, and genic selection, *Philosophy of Science* 47: 157–180.

Sober, Elliott and Steven Orzack, 1993. A critical assessment of Levins' 'The strategy of model building (1966).' *Quarterly Review of Biology* 68: 534–546.

Sober, Elliott and David Sloan Wilson, 1998. *Unto Others*. Cambridge, MA: Harvard University Press.

Spencer, Herbert, 1864. *Principles of Biology*. London: Williams and Norgate.

Stamos, David, 2004. *The Species Problem*. New York: Lexington Books.

Stebbins, G.L., 1969. *The Basis of Progressive Evolution*. Chapel Hill, NC: University of North Carolina Press.

Sterelny, Kim, 2001. *Dawkins vs. Gould: Survival of the Fittest*. Cambridge: Icon Books.

Sterelny, Kim, 2003. *Thought in a Hostile World*, Oxford: Blackwell Publishing.

Sterelny, Kim and Philip Kitcher, 1988. The return of the gene, *Journal of Philosophy* 85: 339–361.

Thompson, Paul (ed.), 1995. *Issues in Evolutionary Ethics*. Albany, NY: State University of New York Press.

Trivers, Robert L., 2002. *Natural Selection and Social Theory*. New York: Oxford University Press.

Twain, Mark, 1962. *Letters from the Earth*. New York: Harper & Row.

Valentine, J.W., A.G. Collins and C P. Meyer, 1994. Morphological complexity increase in metazoans, *Paleobiology* 20: 131–142.

Van Valen, L., 1973. A new evolutionary law, *Evolutionary Theory* 1: 1–30.

Van Valen, L., 1984. A resetting of Phanerozoic community evolution, *Nature* 307: 50–52.

Van Valen, L., 1989. Three paradigms of evolution, *Evolutionary Theory* 9: 1–17.

Vermeij, G., 1987. *Evolution and Escalation*. Princeton, NJ: Princeton University Press.

Waters, C. Kenneth, 1990. Why the anti-reductionist consensus won't survive: The case of classical Mendelian genetics. *PSA 1990*: 125–139.

Westermarck, Edvard, 1891. *The History of Human Marriage*. London: Macmillan.

Williams, George, 1966. *Adaptation and Natural Selection*. Princeton, NJ: Princeton University Press.

Wilson, Edward O., 1975. *Sociobiology: The New Synthesis*. Harvard: Belknap.

Wilson, Edward O., 1986. *Biophilia*. Cambridge, MA: Harvard University Press.

Wilson, Edward O., 1998. *Consilience*. New York: Knopf.

Wimsatt, W.C., 1986. Developmental constraints, generative entrenchment, and the innate-acquired distinction, in W. Bechtel (ed.) *Integrating Scientific Disciplines*. Dordrecht: Martinus Nijhoff, pp. 185–208.

Wright, Larry, 1972. Explanation and teleology, *Philosophy of Science* 39: 204–218.

Wright, Larry, 1973. Functions, *Philosophical Review* 82: 139–168.

Zimmerman, Michael J., 2001. *The Nature of Intrinsic Value*. Lanham, MD: Rowman & Littlefield.

Index